MULTIPLE INTELLIGENCES

MULTIPLE INTELLIGENCES

The Theory in Practice

HOWARD GARDNER

BASIC
BOOKS

A Member of the Perseus Books Group

Library of Congress Cataloging-in-Publication Data
Gardner, Howard.
    Multiple intelligences : the theory in practice / Howard Gardner.
        p. cm.
    Includes bibliographical references and index.
    ISBN 0-465-01822-x
        1. Learning.   2. Intellect.   3. Education—Philosophy.   I. Title.
    LB1060.G357   1993
    370.15'23—dc20   92–53241
                                                                                          CIP

Designed by Ellen Levine

        01 CC/HC 30 29 28

*To my colleagues at Harvard Project Zero,
who have extended the theory of multiple intelligences
in significant ways;*

*To the practitioners,
who have demonstrated the usefulness of the
theory in diverse settings;*

*To the funders, who have generously made
our work possible.*

Contents

Contents

PART III

ASSESSMENT AND BEYOND:
THE COMPONENTS OF AN
MI EDUCATION

PART IV

THE FUTURE OF WORK ON
MULTIPLE INTELLIGENCES

Contents

APPENDICES

Introduction

In 1979 a small team of researchers at the Harvard Graduate School of Education was asked by the Bernard Van Leer Foundation of the Hague to undertake an inquiry on a grand topic: The Nature and Realization of Human Potential. As a junior member of that research group, one trained primarily in developmental psychology, I undertook a daunting but beguiling assignment. My task was no less than the authoring of a monograph on what had been established in the human sciences about the nature of human cognition.

When I began the study that culminated in the 1983 publication of *Frames of mind*, I viewed the enterprise as an opportunity to synthesize my own research efforts with children and brain-damaged adults, as well as some other intriguing lines of investigation of which I was aware. My goal was to come up with a view of human thought that was broader and more comprehensive than that which was then accepted in cognitive studies. My particular "targets" were the influential theories of Jean Piaget, who viewed all of human thought as striving toward the ideal of scientific thinking; and the prevalent conception of intelligence that tied it to the ability to provide succinct answers in speedy fashion to problems entailing linguistic and logical skills.

Had I simply noted that human beings possess different talents, this claim would have been uncontroversial—and my book would have gone unnoticed. But I made a deliberate decision to write about "multiple intelligences": "multiple" to stress an unknown number of separate human capacities, ranging from musical intelligence to the intelligence involved in understanding oneself; "intelligences" to underscore that these capacities were as fundamental as those historically captured within the IQ test. Mostly because of the funder's interest, I concluded the book with some pages that discussed possible educational implications of the theory.

Theories do not always betray their origins, nor do they always anticipate their fates. As a developmental psychologist who had already written several works within that discipline, I believed that my work would be of interest chiefly to those trained in my discipline, and particularly those who studied intelligence from a Piagetian perspective, or from the perspective of test construction and measurement. I was wrong. *Frames* did not arouse much interest within the discipline; as one not unsympathetic critic wrote, "Trying to change psychology's definition of intelligence is like trying to move gravestones in a grave yard." A few psychologists liked the theory; a somewhat larger number did not like it; most ignored it.

Frames did, however, attract a considerable amount of attention. Artist Andy Warhol once commented whimsically that, in the future, everyone will be famous for fifteen minutes. I suppose that I had my allotted fling with celebrity in the year following the publication of *Frames.* For the only time in my life, I received from the press and from the broadcast media a steady stream of requests to discuss the nature of my claims. Some television programs created special video segments to embody the different intelligences; many newspaper writers contrived handy procedures by which readers could test their own or their children's intelligences; I "debated" the theory—soon abbreviated to "MI theory"—with colleagues on the platform and on television. The red, white, orange, and black book jacket, with its single eye peering unflinchingly at the viewer, was displayed in many store windows and I signed many copies of the book. A paperback was published eighteen months later, editions were issued in several foreign languages, and the book has continued to sell here and abroad during the ensuing decade.

Some months after the publication of *Frames,* I was invited to address the annual meeting of the National Association of Independent Schools, the umbrella organization for American private or "independent" schools. I expected the typical audience of fifty to seventy-five persons, a customary talk of fifty minutes followed by a small number of easily anticipated questions. Instead, arriving at the auditorium a few minutes early, I encountered a new experience: a much larger hall, entirely filled with people, and humming with excitement. It was almost as if I had walked by mistake into a talk given by someone who was famous. But the audience had in fact come to hear me: it listened attentively, and grew steadily in size until it spilled out into the hallways on both sides of the room. The talk was very well received, thought-provoking questions poured forth, and, after the session had concluded, I was ringed by interested headmasters, teachers, trustees, and journalists who wanted to hear more and were reluctant to allow me to slip back into anonymity. Again, this was an unprecedented experience for me, but—violating Andy Warhol's principle—it was one with which I was to become increasingly familiar in subsequent years.

Before this moment, I had concluded that my book was not of much interest to my fellow psychologists but that it was of interest to that amorphous community called "the general public." The talk to the NAIS audience announced to me something that I had not hitherto anticipated. There was another audience with a genuine interest in my ideas—the audience of professional educators. This audience includes, though it is not limited to, teachers, administrators, supervisors, school board members, legislators, and journalists whose "beat" is education. It spills over into the worlds of college professors, parents, and educated laypersons. As concerns about the quality of education have magnified both in the United States and abroad, this audience has increased significantly in size and it shows every indication of continuing to mushroom in the years ahead.

I could, I suppose, have closed the *Frames* chapter of my life by returning to the research laboratory and continuing my experimental studies with children and brain-damaged patients. Alternatively, I could have taken a more frankly entrepreneurial angle, preparing "tests" of the multiple intelligences, setting up an organization to promote multiple intelligences, joining the lecture circuit that is populated by educators presenting their wares to a public all too eager for the latest nostrums. I could have addressed the particular concerns of the various special interest groups that were attracted to MI theory: teachers of the gifted and talented, advocates for exceptional populations, those concerned with multicultural or multilingual issues. Indeed, there are now several educators in the land who give regular workshops on "MI theory," as well as a number of organizations that highlight an "MI perspective." There are dozens of graphic renditions of the MI array, dozens of popular articles about the theory, a growing shelf of books, and even a regular magazine, *Provoking Thoughts*, dedicated to the solution of MI puzzles. I have assembled a list of these endeavors in a set of appendices to this volume. While I maintain cordial relations with these individuals, organizations, and publications, I do not in any sense endorse (nor do I dissociate myself from) their efforts.

But, as Fate has it, my post-*Frames* life has taken a different turn. Working with a large number of colleagues at Harvard Project Zero, the research group where I have spent the last twenty-five years, and alongside many colleagues associated with other research-and-development organizations, I have devoted the bulk of my energies since 1983 to an exploration of the educational implications of the theory of multiple intelligences. This exploration has taken a number of forms, ranging from a consideration of how to enhance intelligences, to an attempt to devise new kinds of assessment instruments, to collaborations with schools, school systems, and cultural institutions that have elected to adopt an "MI" perspective. Less formally, I have corresponded with well over a thousand individuals in the United States and abroad, answering targeted queries about the theory, absorbing experiences and anecdotes offered by these correspondents, participating in a kind of invisible network of individuals who rarely know of one another's existence but who are linked by their interest in the remarkable flowering of and interaction among different human cognitive faculties.

As I have carried out formal research-and-development projects in the schools, and forged associations with numerous private citizens interested in MI theory, I have been faced with a large and ever-growing number of inquiries about the educational implications of MI theory. Most often, I answer these inquiries myself; sometimes I pass them on to colleagues; sometimes I recommend writings by myself or by others immersed in the theory; on more than a few occasions, I am not sure just what to do. But one thing has become increasingly clear to me over the years: it would be advantageous to have between two covers a distillation of work on the education of the frames of mind, as it were, "from the horse's mouth." This "MI reader," along with a tenth-anniversary edition of *Frames of mind*, represent the distillation called for by those interested in "Educating Frames of Mind."

Insofar as possible, I attempt in these pages to present a single, coherent, and self-contained story. Whether or not one has already read *Frames of mind*, it is possible to read the present volume from beginning to end. However, for those with a specific interest in one or another angle of MI theory, it is also possible to use the volume as a reference source and to read individual sections or chapters in virtually any order.

Each of these parts has its own introduction, and, consistent with my aim of presenting a coherent story, I have added explanatory and linking materials whenever appropriate.

In part I, I present a capsule version of the original theory, along with responses to the most frequently raised questions. I provide the background to the theory, define an "intelligence," describe my research methods, and introduce each of the seven intelligences in turn. This introductory part concludes with a view of the cognitive landscape, in which I relate intelligence to creativity, genius, prodigiousness, expertise, and other desirable mental achievements.

Serious consideration of a wide range of human intelligences leads to a new view of education that I have termed "individual-centered education." In part II, I first delineate the general configuration of an educational system based upon a multiple intelligences perspective; this perspective draws as much on the traditional apprenticeship and on the contemporary children's museum as it draws on schooling as customarily conducted in the twentieth century. I then review a set of ongoing projects, based on "MI thinking," that run the gamut from preschool through high school. Among the projects reviewed are Project Spectrum, the Key School in Indianapolis, and Arts PROPEL.

While our educational work has ranged from curriculum development to teacher education, our primary point of leverage has been the creation of new forms of assessment. This work on assessment constitutes the focus of part III. These forms of assessment, dramatically different from standardized paper-and-pencil tests, allow individuals to demonstrate their strengths and their understandings in ways that are comfortable for them yet subject to public accountability. These assessments are "intelligence-fair": they allow one to look directly at the functioning of intelligences, rather than forcing the individual to reveal his or her intelligences through the customary lens of a linguistic-logical instrument. The assessments also promote self-assessment, an essential step if the individual is to continue learning once he or she leaves a formal school setting.

In the final section of the book, and in the Epilogue, I turn my attention to the new directions that I expect will be taken by the MI community. Some of this enterprise extends the work in new conceptual directions. As an example, I introduce the notions of "contextualization of intelligences" and "distributed intelligences"; these are both efforts to extend intelligence beyond the skin of the individual, and to show the ways in which our intellectual capacities are inextricably bound with the contexts in which we live and the human and artifactual resources at our disposal. Other portions of the enterprise extend the work to new kinds of settings, such as museums and workplaces, and to more challenging pedagogical goals, such as the enhancement of deep understanding within and across the disciplines. I conclude this Reader with a glimpse ahead to a possible "MI World" twenty years from now.

Most of the chapters and sections in this book have been published in some form before. Information about the original form of the publication, including acknowledgments and references, is presented in appendix A. I have tried to respect the spirit of these original formulations and the forums in which they were presented. I have also permitted a certain amount of presentation of similar materials, when these appeared to consolidate points introduced earlier or to allow sections to be self-standing. At the same time, I have not hesitated to eliminate sections when they were redundant or erroneous; nor have I refrained from adding sections when they seemed to be indicated. This book is a state-of-the-art document of 1993, not a thinly disguised historical record of the previous decade.

For their help in bringing this collection of writings to publication, I should like to thank Karen Donner, Phoebe Hoss, Martin Kessler, Emma Laskin, Jo Ann Miller, Akiko Takano, Gwynne Wiatrowski, and Michael Wilde.

While it is understandable and appropriate that this introductory essay be in the first person, nearly all of my work since the publication of *Frames* has been collaborative. Indeed, close to half of the essays in this book were coauthored and, as often as not, I was the junior author. I owe a great debt to those who have worked with me, both in Cambridge and elsewhere, on the exploration and expansion of the notion of multiple intelligences. My debt to dozens of wonderful collaborators at Harvard Project Zero can never be repaid. Not least, I am grateful to my coauthors who have allowed me not only to reprint their words but also to revise them whenever necessary. It is only appropriate that this book be dedicated to them, to their sometimes anonymous partners who share an interest in the nurturance of multiple intelligences, and to the funders who made our collaborations possible.

Part I

THE THEORY OF MULTIPLE INTELLIGENCES

Introductory Note

After the publication of *Frames of mind*, I was often asked to summarize the main points of the theory. Of the various versions that I concocted, a brief "unbuttoned" talk given in 1986 at the 350th anniversary of the founding of Harvard University has proved the most popular; it appears here as chapter 1. Around the same time my colleague Joseph Walters and I also prepared a number of more formal summaries of the theory; I have reworked one of these papers to form chapter 2. Taken together, these two essays serve as a comfortable introduction to the major claims and arguments that constitute the theory of multiple intelligences.

Once the theory became known, many thoughtful individuals raised questions about its principal claims, as well as its educational implications. Walters and I responded to some of the most common questions in one piece, and, at other times, I answered questions put to me by Helen Weinreich-Haste, and by several other interviewers (see appendix C). In chapter 3, I present a collection of these recurring "issues and answers," grouped under the following topics: terminology; the theoretical status of MI theory; the fine structure of each intelligence; the relationships among the various intelligences; the relationship between intelligence and critical thinking; the relationship between intelligence and artistry; the possibility of additional intelligences; the possible existence of different intellectual profiles in different groups; and sundry educational considerations.

While it is possible to build a theory of cognition around the concept of intelligence—and some have accused me of precisely that move—intelligence is best apprehended as one among a family of related concepts concerning the human mind. In chapter 4, I discuss the relationships that obtain among the concept of intelligence, as I have redefined it, and such other common coins of the intellectual realm as giftedness, prodigiousness, creativity, expertise, and genius.

Chapter 1

In a Nutshell

llow me to transport all of us to the Paris of 1900—La Belle
Epoque—when the city fathers of Paris approached a psychologist named Alfred Binet with an unusual request: Could he
devise some kind of a measure that would predict which youngsters
would succeed and which would fail in the primary grades of Paris
schools? As everybody knows, Binet succeeded. In short order, his
discovery came to be called the "intelligence test"; his measure, the
"IQ." Like other Parisian fashions, the IQ soon made its way to the
United States, where it enjoyed a modest success until World War I.
Then, it was used to test over one million American recruits, and it had
truly arrived. From that day on, the IQ test has looked like psychology's
biggest success—a genuinely useful scientific tool.

What is the vision that led to the excitement about IQ? At least in
the West, people had always relied on intuitive assessments of how
smart other people were. Now intelligence seemed to be quantifiable.
You could measure someone's actual or potential height, and now, it
seemed, you could also measure someone's actual or potential intelligence. We had one dimension of mental ability along which we could
array everyone.

The search for the perfect measure of intelligence has proceeded
apace. Here, for example, are some quotations from an ad for a widely
used test:

5

Need an individual test which quickly provides a stable and reliable estimate of intelligence in four or five minutes per form? Has three forms? Does not depend on verbal production or subjective scoring? Can be used with the severely physically handicapped (even paralyzed) if they can signal yes or no? Handles two-year-olds and superior adults with the same short series of items and the same format? Only $16.00 complete.

Now, that's quite a claim. The American psychologist Arthur Jensen suggests that we could look at reaction time to assess intelligence: a set of lights go on; how quickly can the subject react? The British psychologist Hans Eysenck suggests that investigators of intelligence should look directly at brain waves.

There are also, of course, more sophisticated versions of the IQ test. One of them is called the Scholastic Aptitude Test (SAT). It purports to be a similar kind of measure, and if you add up a person's verbal and math scores, as is often done, you can rate him or her along a single intellectual dimension. Programs for the gifted, for example, often use that kind of measure; if your IQ is in excess of 130, you're admitted to the program.

I want to suggest that along with this one-dimensional view of how to assess people's minds comes a corresponding view of school, which I will call the "uniform view." In the uniform school, there is a core curriculum, a set of facts that everybody should know, and very few electives. The better students, perhaps those with higher IQs, are allowed to take courses that call upon critical reading, calculation, and thinking skills. In the "uniform school," there are regular assessments, using paper and pencil instruments, of the IQ or SAT variety. They yield reliable rankings of people; the best and the brightest get into the better colleges, and perhaps—but only perhaps—they will also get better rankings in life. There is no question but that this approach works well for certain people—schools such as Harvard are eloquent testimony to that. Since this measurement and selection system is clearly meritocratic in certain respects, it has something to recommend it.

But there is an alternative vision that I would like to present—one based on a radically different view of the mind, and one that yields a very different view of school. It is a pluralistic view of mind, recognizing many different and discrete facets of cognition, acknowledging that people have different cognitive strengths and contrasting cognitive styles. I would also like to introduce the concept of an individual-centered school that takes this multifaceted view of intelligence seriously. This model for a school is based in part on findings from sciences that did not even exist in Binet's time: cognitive science (the study of the mind), and neuroscience (the study of the brain). One such approach I have called my "theory of multiple intelligences." Let me tell you something about its sources, its claims, and its educational implications for a possible school of the future.

Dissatisfaction with the concept of IQ and with unitary views of intelligence is fairly widespread—one thinks, for instance, of the work of L. L. Thurstone, J. P. Guilford, and other critics. From my point of view, however, these criticisms do not suffice. The whole concept has to be challenged; in fact, it has to be replaced.

I believe that we should get away altogether from tests and correlations among tests, and look instead at more naturalistic sources of information about how peoples around the world develop skills important to their way of life. Think, for example, of sailors in the South Seas, who find their way around hundreds, or even thousands, of islands by looking at the constellations of stars in the sky, feeling the way a boat passes over the water, and noticing a few scattered landmarks. A word for intelligence in a society of these sailors would probably refer to that kind of navigational ability. Think of surgeons and engineers, hunters and fishermen, dancers and choreographers, athletes and athletic coaches, tribal chiefs and sorcerers. All of these different roles need to be taken into account if we accept the way I define intelligence—that is, as the ability to solve problems, or to fashion products, that are valued in one or more cultural or community settings. For the moment I am saying nothing about whether there is one dimension, or more than one dimension, of intelligence; nothing about whether intelligence is inborn or developed. Instead I emphasize the ability to solve problems and to fashion products. In my work I seek the building blocks of the intelligences used by the aforementioned sailors and surgeons and sorcerers.

The science in this enterprise, to the extent that it exists, involves trying to discover the *right* description of the intelligences. What is an intelligence? To try to answer this question, I have, with my colleagues, surveyed a wide set of sources which, to my knowledge, have never been considered together before. One source is what we already know concerning the development of different kinds of skills in normal children. Another source, and a very important one, is information on the ways that these abilities break down under conditions of brain damage. When one suffers a stroke or some other kind of brain damage, various abilities can be destroyed, or spared, in isolation from other abilities. This research with brain-damaged patients yields a very powerful kind of evidence, because it seems to reflect the way the nervous system has evolved over the millennia to yield certain discrete kinds of intelligence.

My research group looks at other special populations as well: prodigies, idiot savants, autistic children, children with learning disabilities, all of whom exhibit very jagged cognitive profiles—profiles that are extremely difficult to explain in terms of a unitary view of intelligence. We examine cognition in diverse animal species and in dramatically different cultures. Finally, we consider two kinds of psychological evidence: correlations among psychological tests of the sort yielded by a careful statistical analysis of a test battery; and the results of efforts of skill training. When you train a person in skill A, for example, does that training transfer to skill B? So, for example, does training in mathematics enhance one's musical abilities, or vice versa?

Obviously, through looking at all these sources—information on development, on breakdowns, on special populations, and the like—we end up with a cornucopia of information. Optimally, we would perform a statistical factor analysis, feeding all the data into a computer and noting the kinds of factors or intelligences that are extracted. Alas, the kind of material with which I was working didn't exist in a form that is susceptible to computation, and so we had to perform a more subjective factor analysis. In truth, we simply studied the results as best we could, and tried to organize them in a way that made sense to us, and hopefully, to critical readers as well. My resulting list of seven intelligences is a preliminary attempt to organize this mass of information.

I want now to mention briefly the seven intelligences we have located, and to cite one or two examples of each intelligence. Linguistic intelligence is the kind of ability exhibited in its fullest form, perhaps, by poets. Logical-mathematical intelligence, as the name implies, is logical and mathematical ability, as well as scientific ability. Jean Piaget, the great developmental psychologist, thought he was studying *all* intelligence, but I believe he was studying the development of logical-mathematical intelligence. Although I name the linguistic and logical-mathematical intelligences first, it is not because I think they are the most important—in fact, I am convinced that all seven of the intelligences have equal claim to priority. In our society, however, we have put linguistic and logical-mathematical intelligences, figuratively speaking, on a pedestal. Much of our testing is based on this high valuation of verbal and mathematical skills. If you do well in language and logic, you should do well in IQ tests and SATs, and you may well get into a prestigious college, but whether you do well once you leave is probably going to depend as much on the extent to which you possess and use the other intelligences, and it is to those that I want to give equal attention.

Spatial intelligence is the ability to form a mental model of a spatial world and to be able to maneuver and operate using that model. Sailors, engineers, surgeons, sculptors, and painters, to name just a few examples, all have highly developed spatial intelligence. Musical intelligence is the fourth category of ability we have identified: Leonard Bernstein had lots of it; Mozart, presumably, had even more. Bodily-kinesthetic intelligence is the ability to solve problems or to fashion products using one's whole body, or parts of the body. Dancers, athletes, surgeons, and craftspeople all exhibit highly developed bodily-kinesthetic intelligence.

Finally, I propose two forms of personal intelligence—not well understood, elusive to study, but immensely important. Interpersonal intelligence is the ability to understand other people: what motivates them, how they work, how to work cooperatively with them. Successful salespeople, politicians, teachers, clinicians, and religious leaders are all likely to be individuals with high degrees of interpersonal intelligence. Intrapersonal intelligence, a seventh kind of intelligence, is a correlative ability, turned inward. It is a capacity to form an accurate, veridical model of oneself and to be able to use that model to operate effectively in life.

These, then, are the seven intelligences that we have uncovered and described in our research. This is a preliminary list, as I have said; obviously, each form of intelligence can be subdivided, or the list can be rearranged. The real point here is to make the case for the plurality of intellect. Also, we believe that individuals may differ in the particular intelligence profiles with which they are born, and that certainly they differ in the profiles they end up with. I think of the intelligences as raw, biological potentials, which can be seen in pure form only in individuals who are, in the technical sense, freaks. In almost everybody else the intelligences work together to solve problems, to yield various kinds of cultural endstates—vocations, avocations, and the like.

This is my theory of multiple intelligence in capsule form. In my view, the purpose of school should be to develop intelligences and to help people reach vocational and avocational goals that are appropriate to their particular spectrum of intelligences. People who are helped to do so, I believe, feel more engaged and competent, and therefore more inclined to serve the society in a constructive way.

These thoughts, and the critique of a universalistic view of mind with which I began, lead to the notion of an individual-centered school, one geared to optimal understanding and development of each student's cognitive profile. This vision stands in direct contrast to that of the uniform school that I described earlier.

The design of my ideal school of the future is based upon two assumptions. The first is that not all people have the same interests and abilities; not all of us learn in the same way. (And we now have the tools to begin to address these individual differences in school.) The second assumption is one that hurts: it is the assumption that nowadays no one person can learn everything there is to learn. We would all like, as Renaissance men and women, to know everything, or at least to believe in the potential of knowing everything, but that ideal clearly is not possible anymore. Choice is therefore inevitable, and one of the things that I want to argue is that the choices that we make for ourselves, and for the people who are under our charge, might as well be informed choices. An individual-centered school would be rich in assessment of individual abilities and proclivities. It would seek to match individuals not only to curricular areas, but also to particular ways of teaching those subjects. And after the first few grades, the school would also seek to match individuals with the various kinds of life and work options that are available in their culture.

I want to propose a new set of roles for educators that might make this vision a reality. First of all, we might have what I will call "assessment specialists." The job of these people would be to try to understand as sensitively and comprehensively as possible the abilities and interests of the students in a school. It would be very important, however, that the assessment specialists use "intelligence-fair" instruments. We want to be able to look specifically and directly at spatial abilities, at personal abilities, and the like, and not through the usual lenses of the linguistic and logical-mathematical intelligences. Up until now nearly all assessment has depended indirectly on measurement of those abilities; if students are not strong in those two areas, their abilities in other areas may be obscured. Once we begin to try to assess other kinds of intelligences directly, I am confident that particular students will reveal strengths in quite different areas, and the notion of general brightness will disappear or become greatly attenuated.

In addition to the assessment specialist, the school of the future might have the "student-curriculum broker." It would be his or her job to help match students' profiles, goals, and interests to particular curricula and to particular styles of learning. Incidentally, I think that the new interactive technologies offer considerable promise in this area: it will probably be much easier in the future for "brokers" to match individual students to ways of learning that prove comfortable for them.

10

There should also be, I think, a "school-community broker," who would match students to learning opportunities in the wider community. It would be this person's job to find situations in the community, particularly options not available in the school, for children who exhibit unusual cognitive profiles. I have in mind apprenticeships, mentorships, internships in organizations, "big brothers," "big sisters"—individuals and organizations with whom these students might work to secure a feeling for different kinds of vocational and avocational roles in the society. I am not worried about those occasional youngsters who are good in everything. They're going to do just fine. I'm concerned about those who don't shine in the standardized tests, and who, therefore, tend to be written off as not having gifts of any kind. It seems to me that the school-community broker could spot these youngsters and find placements in the community that provide chances for them to shine.

There is ample room in this vision for teachers, as well, and also for master teachers. In my view, teachers would be freed to do what they are supposed to do, which is to teach their subject matter, in their preferred style of teaching. The job of master teacher would be very demanding. It would involve, first of all, supervising the novice teachers and guiding them; but the master teacher would also seek to ensure that the complex student-assessment-curriculum-community equation is balanced appropriately. If the equation is seriously imbalanced, master teachers would intervene and suggest ways to make things better.

Clearly, what I am describing is a tall order; it might even be called utopian. And there is a major risk to this program, of which I am well aware. That is the risk of premature billeting—of saying, "Well, Johnny is four, he seems to be musical, so we are going to send him to Juilliard and drop everything else." There is, however, nothing inherent in the approach that I have described that demands this early overdetermination—quite the contrary. It seems to me that early identification of strengths can be very helpful in indicating what kinds of experiences children might profit from; but early identification of weaknesses can be equally important. If a weakness is identified early, there is a chance to attend to it before it is too late, and to come up with alternative ways of teaching or of covering an important skill area.

We now have the technological and the human resources to implement such an individual-centered school. Achieving it is a question of will, including the will to withstand the current enormous pressures toward uniformity and unidimensional assessments. There are strong pressures now, which you read about every day in the newspapers, to compare students, to compare teachers, states, even entire countries, using one dimension or criterion, a kind of a crypto-IQ assessment. Clearly, everything I have described today stands in direct opposition to that particular view of the world. Indeed that is my intent—to provide a ringing indictment of such one-track thinking.

I believe that in our society we suffer from three biases, which I have nicknamed "Westist," "Testist," and "Bestist." "Westist" involves putting certain Western cultural values, which date back to Socrates, on a pedestal. Logical thinking, for example, is important; rationality is important; but they are not the only virtues. "Testist" suggests a bias towards focusing upon those human abilities or approaches that are readily testable. If it can't be tested, it sometimes seems, it is not worth paying attention to. My feeling is that assessment can be much broader, much more humane than it is now, and that psychologists should spend less time ranking people and more time trying to help them.

"Bestist" is a not very veiled reference to a book by David Halberstam called *The best and the brightest.* Halberstam referred ironically to figures such as Harvard faculty members who were brought to Washington to help President John F. Kennedy and in the process launched the Vietnam War. I think that any belief that all the answers to a given problem lie in one certain approach, such as logical-mathematical thinking, can be very dangerous. Current views of intellect need to be leavened with other more comprehensive points of view.

It is of the utmost importance that we recognize and nurture all of the varied human intelligences, and all of the combinations of intelligences. We are all so different largely because we all have different combinations of intelligences. If we recognize this, I think we will have at least a better chance of dealing appropriately with the many problems that we face in the world. If we can mobilize the spectrum of human abilities, not only will people feel better about themselves and more competent; it is even possible that they will also feel more engaged and better able to join the rest of the world community in working for the broader good. Perhaps if we can mobilize the full range of human intelligences and ally them to an ethical sense, we can help to increase the likelihood of our survival on this planet, and perhaps even contribute to our thriving.

Chapter 2

A Rounded Version

Coauthored by Joseph Walters

T wo eleven-year-old children are taking a test of "intelligence."
They sit at their desks laboring over the meanings of different
words, the interpretation of graphs, and the solutions to arithmetic problems. They record their answers by filling in small circles on a
single piece of paper. Later these completed answer sheets are scored
objectively: the number of right answers is converted into a standardized score that compares the individual child with a population of
children of similar age.

The teachers of these children review the different scores. They notice
that one of the children has performed at a superior level; on all sections
of the test, she answered more questions correctly than did her peers.
In fact, her score is similar to that of children three to four years older.
The other child's performance is average—his scores reflect those of
other children his age.

A subtle change in expectations surrounds the review of these test
scores. Teachers begin to expect the first child to do quite well during
her formal schooling, whereas the second should have only moderate
success. Indeed these predictions come true. In other words, the test
taken by the eleven-year-olds serves as a reliable predictor of their later
performance in school.

How does this happen? One explanation involves our free use of the word "intelligence": the child with the greater "intelligence" has the ability to solve problems, to find the answers to specific questions, and to learn new material quickly and efficiently. These skills in turn play a central role in school success. In this view, "intelligence" is a singular faculty that is brought to bear in any problem-solving situation. Since schooling deals largely with solving problems of various sorts, predicting this capacity in young children predicts their future success in school.

"Intelligence," from this point of view, is a general ability that is found in varying degrees in all individuals. It is the key to success in solving problems. This ability can be measured reliably with standardized pencil-and-paper tests that, in turn, predict future success in school.

What happens after school is completed? Consider the two individuals in the example. Looking further down the road, we find that the "average" student has become a highly successful mechanical engineer who has risen to a position of prominence in both the professional community of engineers as well as in civic groups in his community. His success is no fluke—he is considered by all to be a talented individual. The "superior" student, on the other hand, has had little success in her chosen career as a writer; after repeated rejections by publishers, she has taken up a middle management position in a bank. While certainly not a "failure," she is considered by her peers to be quite "ordinary" in her adult accomplishments. So what happened?

This fabricated example is based on the facts of intelligence testing. IQ tests predict school performance with considerable accuracy, but they are only an indifferent predictor of performance in a profession after formal schooling (Jencks, 1972). Furthermore, even as IQ tests measure only logical or logical-linguistic capacities, in this society we are nearly "brain-washed" to restrict the notion of intelligence to the capacities used in solving logical and linguistic problems.

To introduce an alternative point of view, undertake the following "thought experiment." Suspend the usual judgment of what constitutes intelligence and let your thoughts run freely over the capabilities of humans—perhaps those that would be picked out by the proverbial Martian visitor. In this exercise, you are drawn to the brilliant chess player, the world-class violinist, and the champion athlete; such outstanding performers deserve special consideration. Under this experiment, a quite different view of *intelligence* emerges. Are the chess player, violinist, and athlete "intelligent" in these pursuits? If they are, then why do our tests of "intelligence" fail to identify them? If they are not "intelligent," what allows them to achieve such astounding feats? In general, why does the contemporary construct "intelligence" fail to explain large areas of human endeavor?

In this chapter we approach these problems through the theory of multiple intelligences (MI). As the name indicates, we believe that human cognitive competence is better described in terms of a set of abilities, talents, or mental skills, which we call "intelligences." All normal individuals possess each of these skills to some extent; individuals differ in the degree of skill and in the nature of their combination. We believe this theory of intelligence may be more humane and more veridical than alternative views of intelligence and that it more adequately reflects the data of human "intelligent" behavior. Such a theory has important educational implications, including ones for curriculum development.

What Constitutes an Intelligence?

The question of the optimal definition of intelligence looms large in our inquiry. Indeed, it is at the level of this definition that the theory of multiple intelligences diverges from traditional points of view. In a traditional view, intelligence is defined operationally as the ability to answer items on tests of intelligence. The inference from the test scores to some underlying ability is supported by statistical techniques that compare responses of subjects at different ages; the apparent correlation of these test scores across ages and across different tests corroborates the notion that the general faculty of intelligence, g, does not change much with age or with training or experience. It is an inborn attribute or faculty of the individual.

Multiple intelligences theory, on the other hand, pluralizes the traditional concept. An intelligence entails the ability to solve problems or fashion products that are of consequence in a particular cultural setting or community. The problem-solving skill allows one to approach a situation in which a goal is to be obtained and to locate the appropriate route to that goal. The creation of a *cultural* product is crucial to such functions as capturing and transmitting knowledge or expressing one's views or feelings. The problems to be solved range from creating an end for a story to anticipating a mating move in chess to repairing a quilt. Products range from scientific theories to musical compositions to successful political campaigns.

MI theory is framed in light of the biological origins of each problem-solving skill. Only those skills that are universal to the human species

15

are treated. Even so, the biological proclivity to participate in a particular form of problem solving must also be coupled with the cultural nurturing of that domain. For example, language, a universal skill, may manifest itself particularly as writing in one culture, as oratory in another culture, and as the secret language of anagrams in a third.

Given the desire of selecting intelligences that are rooted in biology, and that are valued in one or more cultural settings, how does one actually identify an "intelligence"? In coming up with our list, we consulted evidence from several different sources: knowledge about normal development and development in gifted individuals; information about the breakdown of cognitive skills under conditions of brain damage; studies of exceptional populations, including prodigies, idiots savants, and autistic children; data about the evolution of cognition over the millenia; cross-cultural accounts of cognition; psychometric studies, including examinations of correlations among tests; and psychological training studies, particularly measures of transfer and generalization across tasks. Only those candidate intelligences that satisfied all or a majority of the criteria were selected as bona fide intelligences. A more complete discussion of each of these criteria for an "intelligence" and the seven intelligences that have been proposed so far, is found in *Frames of mind* (1983). This book also considers how the theory might be disproven and compares it to competing theories of intelligence.

In addition to satisfying the aforementioned criteria, each intelligence must have an identifiable core operation or set of operations. As a neurally based computational system, each intelligence is activated or "triggered" by certain kinds of internally or externally presented information. For example, one core of musical intelligence is the sensitivity to pitch relations, whereas one core of linguistic intelligence is the sensitivity to phonological features.

An intelligence must also be susceptible to encoding in a symbol system—a culturally contrived system of meaning, which captures and conveys important forms of information. Language, picturing, and mathematics are but three nearly worldwide symbol systems that are necessary for human survival and productivity. The relationship of a candidate intelligence to a human symbol system is no accident. In fact, the existence of a core computational capacity anticipates the existence of a symbol system that exploits that capacity. While it may be possible for an intelligence to proceed without an accompanying symbol system, a primary characteristic of human intelligence may well be its gravitation toward such an embodiment.

The Seven Intelligences

Having sketched the characteristics and criteria of an intelligence, we turn now to a brief consideration of each of the seven intelligences. We begin each sketch with a thumbnail biography of a person who demonstrates an unusual facility with that intelligence. These biographies illustrate some of the abilities that are central to the fluent operation of a given intelligence. Although each biography illustrates a particular intelligence, we do not wish to imply that in adulthood intelligences operate in isolation. Indeed, except for abnormal individuals, intelligences always work in concert, and any sophisticated adult role will involve a melding of several of them. Following each biography we survey the various sources of data that support each candidate as an "intelligence."

MUSICAL INTELLIGENCE

When he was three years old, Yehudi Menuhin was smuggled into the San Francisco Orchestra concerts by his parents. The sound of Louis Persinger's violin so entranced the youngster that he insisted on a violin for his birthday and Louis Persinger as his teacher. He got both. By the time he was ten years old, Menuhin was an international performer (Menuhin, 1977).

Violinist Yehudi Menuhin's musical intelligence manifested itself even before he had touched a violin or received any musical training. His powerful reaction to that particular sound and his rapid progress on the instrument suggest that he was biologically prepared in some way for that endeavor. In this way evidence from child prodigies supports our claim that there is a biological link to a particular intelligence. Other special populations, such as autistic children who can play a musical instrument beautifully but who cannot speak, underscore the independence of musical intelligence.

A brief consideration of the evidence suggests that musical skill passes the other tests for an intelligence. For example, certain parts of the brain play important roles in perception and production of music. These areas are characteristically located in the right hemisphere, although musical skill is not as clearly "localized," or located in a specifia-

17

ble area, as language. Although the particular susceptibility of musical ability to brain damage depends on the degree of training and other individual differences, there is clear evidence for "amusia" or loss of musical ability.

Music apparently played an important unifying role in Stone Age (Paleolithic) societies. Birdsong provides a link to other species. Evidence from various cultures supports the notion that music is a universal faculty. Studies of infant development suggest that there is a "raw" computational ability in early childhood. Finally, musical notation provides an accessible and lucid symbol system.

In short, evidence to support the interpretation of musical ability as an "intelligence" comes from many different sources. Even though musical skill is not typically considered an intellectual skill like mathematics, it qualifies under our criteria. By definition it deserves consideration; and in view of the data, its inclusion is empirically justified.

BODILY-KINESTHETIC INTELLIGENCE

> Fifteen-year-old Babe Ruth played third base. During one game his team's pitcher was doing very poorly and Babe loudly criticized him from third base. Brother Mathias, the coach, called out, "Ruth, if you know so much about it, YOU pitch!" Babe was surprised and embarrassed because he had never pitched before, but Brother Mathias insisted. Ruth said later that at the very moment he took the pitcher's mound, he KNEW he was supposed to be a pitcher and that it was "natural" for him to strike people out. Indeed, he went on to become a great major league pitcher (and, of course, attained legendary status as a hitter) (Connor, 1982).

Like Menuhin, Babe Ruth was a child prodigy who recognized his "instrument" immediately upon his first exposure to it. This recognition occurred in advance of formal training.

Control of bodily movement is, of course, localized in the motor cortex, with each hemisphere dominant or controlling bodily movements on the contra-lateral side. In right-handers, the dominance for such movement is ordinarily found in the left hemisphere. The ability to perform movements when directed to do so can be impaired even in individuals who can perform the same movements reflexively or on a nonvoluntary basis. The existence of specific *apraxia* constitutes one line of evidence for a bodily-kinesthetic intelligence.

The evolution of specialized body movements is of obvious advantage to the species, and in humans this adaptation is extended through the use of tools. Body movement undergoes a clearly defined developmental schedule in children. And there is little question of its universality across cultures. Thus it appears that bodily-kinesthetic "knowledge" satisfies many of the criteria for an intelligence.

The consideration of bodily-kinesthetic knowledge as "problem solving" may be less intuitive. Certainly carrying out a mime sequence or hitting a tennis ball is not solving a mathematical equation. And yet, the ability to use one's body to express an emotion (as in a dance), to play a game (as in a sport), or to create a new product (as in devising an invention) is evidence of the cognitive features of body usage. The specific computations required to solve a particular bodily-kinesthetic *problem*, hitting a tennis ball, are summarized by Tim Gallwey:

> At the moment the ball leaves the server's racket, the brain calculates approximately where it will land and where the racket will intercept it. This calculation includes the initial velocity of the ball, combined with an input for the progressive decrease in velocity and the effect of wind and after the bounce of the ball. Simultaneously, muscle orders are given: not just once, but constantly with refined and updated information. The muscles must cooperate. A movement of the feet occurs, the racket is taken back, the face of the racket kept at a constant angle. Contact is made at a precise point that depends on whether the order was given to hit down the line or cross-court, an order not given until after a split-second analysis of the movement and balance of the opponent.
>
> To return an average serve, you have about one second to do this. To hit the ball at all is remarkable and yet not uncommon. The truth is that everyone who inhabits a human body possesses a remarkable creation (Gallwey, 1976).

LOGICAL-MATHEMATICAL INTELLIGENCE

In 1983 Barbara McClintock won the Nobel Prize in medicine or physiology for her work in microbiology. Her intellectual powers of deduction and observation illustrate one form of logical-mathematical intelligence that is often labeled "scientific thinking." One incident is particularly illuminating. While a researcher at Cornell in the 1920s McClintock was faced one day with a problem: while *theory* predicted 50 percent pollen sterility in corn, her research assistant (in the "field") was finding plants that were only 25 to 30 percent sterile. Disturbed by this discrepancy, McClintock left the cornfield and returned to her office where she sat for half an hour, thinking:

> Suddenly I jumped up and ran back to the (corn) field. At the top of the field (the others were still at the bottom) I shouted "Eureka, I have it! I know what the 30% sterility is!" ... They asked me to prove it. I sat down with a paper bag and a pencil and I started from scratch, which I had not done at all in my laboratory. It had all been done so fast; the answer came and I ran. Now I worked it out step by step—it was an intricate series of steps—and I came out with [the same result]. [They] looked at the material and it was exactly as I'd said it was; it worked out exactly as I had diagrammed it. Now, why did I know, without having done it on paper? Why was I so sure? (Keller, 1983, p. 104).

This anecdote illustrates two essential facts of the logical-mathematical intelligence. First, in the gifted individual, the process of problem solving is often remarkably rapid—the successful scientist copes with many variables at once and creates numerous hypotheses that are each evaluated and then accepted or rejected in turn.

The anecdote also underscores the *nonverbal* nature of the intelligence. A solution to a problem can be constructed *before* it is articulated. In fact, the solution process may be totally invisible, even to the problem solver. This need not imply, however, that discoveries of this sort—the familiar "Aha!" phenomenon—are mysterious, intuitive, or unpredictable. The fact that it happens more frequently to some people (perhaps Nobel Prize winners) suggests the opposite. We interpret this as the work of the logical-mathematical intelligence.

Along with the companion skill of language, logical-mathematical reasoning provides the principal basis for IQ tests. This form of intelligence has been heavily investigated by traditional psychologists, and it is the archetype of "raw intelligence" or the problem-solving faculty that purportedly cuts across domains. It is perhaps ironic, then, that the actual mechanism by which one arrives at a solution to a logical-mathematical problem is not as yet properly understood.

This intelligence is supported by our empirical criteria as well. Certain areas of the brain are more prominent in mathematical calculation than others. There are idiots savants who perform great feats of calculation even though they remain tragically deficient in most other areas. Child prodigies in mathematics abound. The development of this intelligence in children has been carefully documented by Jean Piaget and other psychologists.

LINGUISTIC INTELLIGENCE

At the age of ten, T. S. Eliot created a magazine called "Fireside" to which he was the sole contributor. In a three-day period during his winter vacation, he created eight complete issues. Each one included poems, adventure stories, a gossip column, and humor. Some of this material survives and it displays the talent of the poet (see Soldo, 1982).

As with the logical intelligence, calling linguistic skill an "intelligence" is consistent with the stance of traditional psychology. Linguistic intelligence also passes our empirical tests. For instance, a specific area of the brain, called "Broca's Area," is responsible for the production of grammatical sentences. A person with damage to this area can understand words and sentences quite well but has difficulty putting words together in anything other than the simplest of sentences. At the same time, other thought processes may be entirely unaffected.

The gift of language is universal, and its development in children is strikingly constant across cultures. Even in deaf populations where a manual sign language is not explicitly taught, children will often "invent" their own manual language and use it surreptitiously! We thus see how an intelligence may operate independently of a specific input modality or output channel.

SPATIAL INTELLIGENCE

Navigation around the Caroline Islands in the South Seas is accomplished without instruments. The position of the stars, as viewed from various islands, the weather patterns, and water color are the only sign posts. Each journey is broken into a series of segments; and the navigator learns the position of the stars within each of these segments. During the actual trip the navigator must envision mentally a reference island as it passes under a particular star and from that he computes the number of segments completed, the proportion of the trip remaining, and any corrections in heading that are required. The navigator cannot *see* the islands as he sails along; instead he maps their locations in his mental "picture" of the journey (Gardner, 1983).

Spatial problem solving is required for navigation and in the use of the notational system of maps. Other kinds of spatial problem solving are brought to bear in visualizing an object seen from a different angle and in playing chess. The visual arts also employ this intelligence in the use of space.

Evidence from brain research is clear and persuasive. Just as the left hemisphere has, over the course of evolution, been selected as the site of linguistic processing in right-handed persons, the right hemisphere proves to be the site most crucial for spatial processing. Damage to the right posterior regions causes impairment of the ability to find one's way around a site, to recognize faces or scenes, or to notice fine details.

Patients with damage specific to regions of the right hemisphere will attempt to compensate for their spacial deficits with linguistic strategies. They will try to reason aloud, to challenge the task, or even make up answers. But such nonspatial strategies are rarely successful.

Blind populations provide an illustration of the distinction between the spatial intelligence and visual perception. A blind person can recognize shapes by an indirect method: running a hand along the object translates into length of time of movement, which in turn is translated into the size of the object. For the blind person, the perceptual system of the tactile modality parallels the visual modality in the seeing person. The analogy between the spatial reasoning of the blind and the linguistic reasoning of the deaf is notable.

There are few child prodigies among visual artists, but there are idiots savants such as Nadia (Selfe, 1977). Despite a condition of severe autism, this preschool child made drawings of the most remarkable representational accuracy and finesse.

INTERPERSONAL INTELLIGENCE

With little formal training in special education and nearly blind herself, Anne Sullivan began the intimidating task of instructing a blind and deaf seven-year-old Helen Keller. Sullivan's efforts at communication were complicated by the child's emotional struggle with the world around her. At their first meal together, this scene occurred:

> Annie did not allow Helen to put her hand into Annie's plate and take what she wanted, as she had been accustomed to do with her family. It became a test of wills—hand thrust into plate, hand firmly put aside. The family, much upset, left the dining room. Annie locked the door and proceeded to eat her breakfast while Helen lay on the floor kicking and screaming, pushing and pulling at Annie's chair. [After half an hour] Helen went around the table looking for her family. She discovered no one else

was there and that bewildered her. Finally, she sat down and began to eat her breakfast, but with her hands. Annie gave her a spoon. Down on the floor it clattered, and the contest of wills began anew (Lash, 1980, p. 52).

Anne Sullivan sensitively responded to the child's behavior. She wrote home: "The greatest problem I shall have to solve is how to discipline and control her without breaking her spirit. I shall go rather slowly at first and try to win her love."

In fact, the first "miracle" occurred two weeks later, well before the famous incident at the pumphouse. Annie had taken Helen to a small cottage near the family's house, where they could live alone. After seven days together, Helen's personality suddenly underwent a profound change—the therapy had worked:

> My heart is singing with joy this morning. A miracle has happened! The wild little creature of two weeks ago has been transformed into a gentle child (p. 54).

It was just two weeks after this that the first breakthrough in Helen's grasp of language occurred; and from that point on, she progressed with incredible speed. The key to the miracle of language was Anne Sullivan's insight into the *person* of Helen Keller.

Interpersonal intelligence builds on a core capacity to notice distinctions among others; in particular, contrasts in their moods, temperaments, motivations, and intentions. In more advanced forms, this intelligence permits a skilled adult to read the intentions and desires of others, even when these have been hidden. This skill appears in a highly sophisticated form in religious or political leaders, teachers, therapists, and parents. The Helen Keller–Anne Sullivan story suggests that this interpersonal intelligence does not depend on language.

All indices in brain research suggest that the frontal lobes play a prominent role in interpersonal knowledge. Damage in this area can cause profound personality changes while leaving other forms of problem solving unharmed—a person is often "not the same person" after such an injury.

Alzheimer's disease, a form of presenile dementia, appears to attack posterior brain zones with a special ferocity, leaving spatial, logical, and linguistic computations severly impaired. Yet, Alzheimer's patients will often remain well groomed, socially proper, and continually apologetic for their errors. In contrast, Pick's disease, another variety of presenile dementia that is more frontally oriented, entails a rapid loss of social graces.

Biological evidence for interpersonal intelligence encompasses two additional factors often cited as unique to humans. One factor is the prolonged childhood of primates, including the close attachment to the mother. In those cases where the mother is removed from early development, normal interpersonal development is in serious jeopardy. The second factor is the relative importance in humans of social interaction. Skills such as hunting, tracking, and killing in prehistoric societies required participation and cooperation of large numbers of people. The need for group cohesion, leadership, organization, and solidarity follows naturally from this.

INTRAPERSONAL INTELLIGENCE

In an essay called "A Sketch of the Past," written almost as a diary entry, Virginia Woolf discusses the "cotton wool of existence"—the various mundane events of life. She contrasts this "cotton wool" with three specific and poignant memories from her childhood: a fight with her brother, seeing a particular flower in the garden, and hearing of the suicide of a past visitor:

> These are three instances of exceptional moments. I often tell them over, or rather they come to the surface unexpectedly. But now for the first time I have written them down, and I realize something that I have never realized before. Two of these moments ended in a state of despair. The other ended, on the contrary, in a state of satisfaction.
>
> The sense of horror (in hearing of the suicide) held me powerless. But in the case of the flower, I found a reason; and was thus able to deal with the sensation. I was not powerless.
>
> Though I still have the peculiarity that I receive these sudden shocks, they are now always welcome; after the first surprise, I always feel instantly that they are particularly valuable. And so I go on to suppose that the shock-receiving capacity is what makes me a writer. I hazard the explanation that a shock is at once in my case followed by the desire to explain it. I feel that I have had a blow; but it is not, as I thought as a child, simply a blow from an enemy hidden behind the cotton wool of daily life; it is or will become a revelation of some order; it is a token of some real thing behind appearances; and I make it real by putting it into words (Woolf, 1976, pp. 69–70).

This quotation vividly illustrates the intrapersonal intelligence—knowledge of the internal aspects of a person: access to one's own feeling life, one's range of emotions, the capacity to effect discriminations among these emotions and eventually to label them and to draw upon them as a means of understanding and guiding one's own behavior. A person with good intrapersonal intelligence has a viable and effective model of himself or herself. Since this intelligence is the most private, it requires evidence from language, music, or some other more expressive form of intelligence if the observer is to detect it at work. In the above quotation, for example, linguistic intelligence is drawn upon to convey intrapersonal knowledge; it embodies the interaction of intelligences, a common phenomenon to which we will return later.

We see the familiar criteria at work in the intrapersonal intelligence. As with the interpersonal intelligence, the frontal lobes play a central role in personality change. Injury to the lower area of the frontal lobes is likely to produce irritability or euphoria; while injury to the higher regions is more likely to produce indifference, listlessness, slowness, and apathy—a kind of depressive personality. In such "frontal-lobe" individuals, the other cognitive functions often remain preserved. In contrast, among aphasics who have recovered sufficiently to describe their experiences, we find consistent testimony: while there may have been a diminution of general alertness and considerable depression about the condition, the individual in no way felt himself to be a different person. He recognized his own needs, wants, and desires and tried as best he could to achieve them.

The autistic child is a prototypical example of an individual with impaired intrapersonal intelligence; indeed, the child may not even be able to refer to himself. At the same time, such children often exhibit remarkable abilities in the musical, computational, spatial, or mechanical realms.

Evolutionary evidence for an intrapersonal faculty is more difficult to come by, but we might speculate that the capacity to transcend the satisfaction of instinctual drives is relevant. This becomes increasingly important in a species not perennially involved in the struggle for survival.

In sum, then, both interpersonal and intrapersonal faculties pass the tests of an intelligence. They both feature problem-solving endeavors with significance for the individual and the species. Interpersonal intelligence allows one to understand and work with others; intrapersonal intelligence allows one to understand and work with oneself. In the individual's sense of self, one encounters a melding of inter- and intrapersonal components. Indeed, the sense of self emerges as one of the most marvelous of human inventions—a symbol that represents all kinds of information about a person and that is at the same time an invention that all individuals construct for themselves.

Summary: The Unique Contributions of the Theory

As human beings, we all have a repertoire of skills for solving different kinds of problems. Our investigation has begun, therefore, with a consideration of these problems, the contexts they are found in, and the culturally significant products that are the outcome. We have not approached "intelligence" as a reified human faculty that is brought to bear in literally any problem setting; rather, we have begun with the problems that humans *solve* and worked back to the "intelligences" that must be responsible.

Evidence from brain research, human development, evolution, and cross-cultural comparisons was brought to bear in our search for the relevant human intelligences: a candidate was included only if reasonable evidence to support its membership was found across these diverse fields. Again, this tack differs from the traditional one: since no candidate faculty is *necessarily* an intelligence, we could choose on a motivated basis. In the traditional approach to "intelligence," there is no opportunity for this type of empirical decision.

We have also determined that these multiple human faculties, the intelligences, are to a significant extent *independent*. For example, research with brain-damaged adults repeatedly demonstrates that particular faculties can be lost while others are spared. This independence of intelligences implies that a particularly high level of ability in one intelligence, say mathematics, does not require a similarly high level in another intelligence, like language or music. This independence of intelligences contrasts sharply with traditional measures of IQ that find high correlations among test scores. We speculate that the usual correlations among subtests of IQ tests come about because all of these tasks in fact measure the ability to respond rapidly to items of a logical-mathematical or linguistic sort; we believe that these correlations would be substantially reduced if one were to survey in a contextually appropriate way the full range of human problem-solving skills.

Until now, we have supported the fiction that adult roles depend largely on the flowering of a single intelligence. In fact, however, nearly every cultural role of any degree of sophistication requires a combination of intelligences. Thus, even an apparently straightforward role, like playing the violin, transcends a reliance on simple musical intelligence. To become a successful violinist requires bodily-kinesthetic dexterity and the interpersonal skills of relating to an audience and, in a different way, choosing a manager; quite possibly it involves an intrapersonal intelligence as well. Dance requires skills in bodily-kinesthetic, musical, interpersonal, and spatial intelligences in varying degrees. Politics requires an interpersonal skill, a linguistic facility, and perhaps some logical aptitude. Inasmuch as nearly every cultural role requires several intelligences, it becomes important to consider individuals as a collection of aptitudes rather than as having a singular problem-solving faculty that can be measured directly through pencil-and-paper tests. Even given a relatively small number of such intelligences, the diversity of human ability is created through the differences in these profiles. In fact, it may well be that the "total is greater than the sum of the parts." An individual may not be particularly gifted in any intelligence; and yet, because of a particular combination or blend of skills, he or she may be able to fill some niche uniquely well. Thus it is of paramount importance to assess the particular combination of skills that may earmark an individual for a certain vocational or avocational niche.

Implications for Education

The theory of multiple intelligences was developed as an account of human cognition that can be subjected to empirical tests. In addition, the theory seems to harbor a number of educational implications that are worth consideration. In the following discussion we will begin by outlining what appears to be the natural developmental trajectory of an intelligence. Turning then to aspects of education, we will comment on the role of nurturing and explicit instruction in this development. From this analysis we find that assessment of intelligences can play a crucial role in curriculum development.

THE NATURAL GROWTH OF AN INTELLIGENCE: A DEVELOPMENTAL TRAJECTORY

Since all intelligences are part of the human genetic heritage, at some basic level each intelligence is manifested universally, independent of education and cultural support. Exceptional populations aside for the moment, *all* humans possess certain core abilities in each of the intelligences.

The natural trajectory of development in each intelligence begins with *raw patterning ability*, for example, the ability to make tonal differentiations in musical intelligence or to appreciate three-dimensional arrangements in spatial intelligence. These abilities appear universally; they may also appear at a heightened level in that part of the population that is "at promise" in that domain. The "raw" intelligence predominates during the first year of life.

Intelligences are glimpsed through different lenses at subsequent points in development. In the subsequent stage, the intelligence is encountered through a *symbol system:* language is encountered through sentences and stories, music through songs, spatial understanding through drawings, bodily-kinesthetic through gesture or dance, and so on. At this point children demonstrate their abilities in the various intelligences through their grasp of various symbol systems. Yehudi Menuhin's response to the sound of the violin illustrates the musical intelligence of a gifted individual coming in contact with a particular aspect of the symbol system.

As development progresses, each intelligence together with its accompanying symbol system is represented in a *notational system.* Mathematics, mapping, reading, music notation, and so on, are second-order symbol systems in which the marks on paper come to stand for symbols. In our culture, these notational systems are typically mastered in a formal educational setting.

Finally, during adolescence and adulthood, the intelligences are expressed through the range of *vocational and avocational pursuits.* For example, the logical-mathematical intelligence, which began as sheer pattern ability in infancy and developed through symbolic mastery of early childhood and the notations of the school years, achieves mature expression in such roles as mathematician, accountant, scientist, cashier. Similarly, the spatial intelligence passes from the mental maps of the infant, to the symbolic operations required in drawings and the notational systems of maps, to the adult roles of navigator, chess player, and topologist.

Although all humans partake of each intelligence to some degree, certain individuals are said to be "at promise." They are highly endowed with the core abilities and skills of that intelligence. This fact becomes important for the culture as a whole, since, in general, these exceptionally gifted individuals will make notable advances in the cultural manifestations of that intelligence. It is not important that *all* members of the

Puluwat tribe demonstrate precocious spatial abilities needed for navigation by the stars, nor is it necessary for all Westerners to master mathematics to the degree necessary to make a significant contribution to theoretical physics. So long as the individuals "at promise" in particular domains are located efficiently, the overall knowledge of the group will be advanced in all domains.

While some individuals are "at promise" in an intelligence, others are "at risk." In the absence of special aids, those at risk in an intelligence will be most likely to fail tasks involving that intelligence. Conversely, those at promise will be most likely to succeed. It may be that intensive intervention at an early age can bring a larger number of children to an "at promise" level.

The special developmental trajectory of an individual at promise varies with intelligence. Thus, mathematics and music are characterized by the early appearance of gifted children who perform relatively early at or near an adult level. In contrast, the personal intelligences appear to arise much more gradually; prodigies are rare. Moreover, mature performance in one area does not imply mature performance in another area, just as gifted achievement in one does not imply gifted achievement in another.

IMPLICATIONS OF THE DEVELOPMENTAL TRAJECTORY FOR EDUCATION

Because the intelligences are manifested in different ways at different developmental levels, both assessment and nurturing need to occur in apposite ways. What nurtures in infancy would be inappropriate at later stages, and vice versa. In the preschool and early elementary years, instruction should emphasize opportunity. It is during these years that children can discover something of their own peculiar interests and abilities.

In the case of very talented children, such discoveries often happen by themselves through spontaneous "crystallizing experiences" (Walters & Gardner, 1986). When such experiences occur, often in early childhood, an individual reacts overtly to some attractive quality or feature of a domain. Immediately the individual undergoes a strong affective reaction; he or she feels a special affinity to that domain, as did Menuhin when he first heard the violin at an orchestral concert. Thereafter, in many cases, the individual persists working in the domain, and, by drawing on a powerful set of appropriate intelligences, goes on to achieve high skill in that domain in relatively quick compass.

In the case of the most powerful talents, such crystallizing experiences seem difficult to prevent; and they may be especially likely to emerge in the domains of music and mathematics. However, specifically designed encounters with materials, equipment, or other people can help a youngster discover his or her own métier.

During the school-age years, some mastery of notational systems is essential in our society. The self-discovery environment of early schooling cannot provide the structure needed for the mastery of specific notational systems like the sonata form or algebra. In fact, during this period some tutelage is needed by virtually all children. One problem is to find the right form, since group tutelage can be helpful in some instances and harmful in others. Another problem is to orchestrate the connection between practical knowledge and the knowledge embodied in symbolic systems and notational systems.

Finally, in adolescence, most students must be assisted in their choice of careers. This task is made more complex by the manner in which intelligences interact in many cultural roles. For instance, being a doctor certainly requires logical-mathematical intelligence; but while the general practitioner should have strong interpersonal skills, the surgeon needs bodily-kinesthetic dexterity. Internships, apprenticeships, and involvement with the actual materials of the cultural role become critical at this point in development.

Several implications for explicit instruction can be drawn from this analysis. First, the role of instruction in relation to the manifestation of an intelligence changes across the developmental trajectory. The enriched environment appropriate for the younger years is less crucial for adolescents. Conversely, explicit instruction in the notational system, appropriate for older children, is largely inappropriate for younger ones.

Explicit instruction must be evaluated in light of the developmental trajectories of the intelligences. Students benefit from explicit instruction only if the information or training fits into their specific place on the developmental progression. A particular kind of instruction can be either too early at one point or too late at another. For example, Suzuki training in music pays little attention to the notational system, while providing a great deal of support or scaffolding for learning the fine points of instrumental technique. While this emphasis may be very powerful for training preschool children, it can produce stunted musical development when imposed at a late point on the developmental trajectory. Such a highly structured instructional environment can accelerate progress and produce a larger number of children "at promise," but in the end it may ultimately limit choices and inhibit self-expression.

An exclusive focus on linguistic and logical skills in formal schooling can shortchange individuals with skills in other intelligences. It is evident from inspection of adult roles, even in language-dominated Western society, that spatial, interpersonal, or bodily-kinesthetic skills often play key roles. Yet linguistic and logical skills form the core of most diagnostic tests of "intelligence" and are placed on a pedagogical pedestal in our schools.

THE LARGE NEED: ASSESSMENT

The general pedagogical program described here presupposes accurate understanding of the profile of intelligences of the individual learner. Such a careful assessment procedure allows informed choices about careers and avocations. It also permits a more enlightened search for remedies for difficulties. Assessment of deficiencies can predict difficulties the learner will have; moreover, it can suggest alternative routes to an educational goal (learning mathematics via spatial relations; learning music through linguistic techniques).

Assessment, then, becomes a central feature of an educational system. We believe that it is essential to depart from standardized testing. We also believe that standard pencil-and-paper short-answer tests sample only a small proportion of intellectual abilities and often reward a certain kind of decontextualized facility. The means of assessment we favor should ultimately search for genuine problem-solving or product-fashioning skills in individuals across a range of materials.

An assessment of a particular intelligence (or set of intelligences) should highlight problems that can be solved *in the materials of that intelligence.* That is, mathematical assessment should present problems in mathematical settings. For younger children, these could consist of Piagetian-style problems in which talk is kept to a minimum. For older children, derivation of proofs in a novel numerical system might suffice. In music, on the other hand, the problems would be embedded in a musical system. Younger children could be asked to assemble tunes from individual musical segments. Older children could be shown how to compose a rondo or fugue from simple motifs.

An important aspect of assessing intelligences must include the individual's ability to solve problems or create products using the materials of the intellectual medium. Equally important, however, is the determination of which intelligence is favored when an individual has a choice. One technique for getting at this proclivity is to expose the individual

31

to a sufficiently complex situation that can stimulate several intelligences; or to provide a set of materials drawn from different intelligences and determine toward which one an individual gravitates and how deeply he or she explores it.

As an example, consider what happens when a child sees a complex film in which several intelligences figure prominently: music, people interacting, a maze to be solved, or a particular bodily skill, may all compete for attention. Subsequent "debriefing" with the child should reveal the features to which the child paid attention; these will be related to the profile of intelligences in that child. Or consider a situation in which children are taken into a room with several different kinds of equipment and games. Simple measures of the regions in which children spend time and the kinds of activities they engage in should yield insights into the individual child's profile of intelligence.

Tests of this sort differ in two important ways from the traditional measures of "intelligence." First, they rely on materials, equipment, interviews, and so on to generate the problems to be solved; this contrasts with the traditional pencil-and-paper measures used in intelligence testing. Second, results are reported as part of an individual profile of intellectual propensities, rather than as a single index of intelligence or rank within the population. In contrasting strengths and weaknesses, they can suggest options for future learning.

Scores are not enough. This assessment procedure should suggest to parents, teachers, and, eventually, to children themselves, the sorts of activities that are available at home, in school, or in the wider community. Drawing on this information, children can bolster their own particular sets of intellectual weaknesses or combine their intellectual strengths in a way that is satisfying vocationally and avocationally.

COPING WITH THE PLURALITY OF INTELLIGENCES

Under the multiple intelligences theory, an intelligence can serve both as the *content* of instruction and the *means* or medium for communicating that content. This state of affairs has important ramifications for instruction. For example, suppose that a child is learning some mathematical principle but is not skilled in logical-mathematical intelligence. That child will probably experience some difficulty during the learning process. The reason for the difficulty is straightforward: the mathematical principle to be learned (the content) exists only in the logical-mathematical world and it ought to be communicated through mathematics (the medium). That is, the mathematical principle cannot be translated *entirely* into words (a linguistic medium) or spatial models (a spatial medium). At some point in the learning process, the mathematics of the principle must "speak for itself." In our present case, it is at just this level that the learner experiences difficulty—the learner (who is not especially "mathematical") and the problem (which is very much "mathematical") are not in accord. Mathematics, as a *medium*, has failed.

Although this situation is a necessary conundrum in light of multiple intelligences theory, we can propose various solutions. In the present example, the teacher must attempt to find an alternative route to the mathematical content—a metaphor in another medium. Language is perhaps the most obvious alternative, but spatial modeling and even a bodily-kinesthetic metaphor may prove appropriate in some cases. In this way, the student is given a *secondary* route to the solution to the problem, perhaps through the medium of an intelligence that is relatively strong for that individual.

Two features of this hypothetical scenario must be stressed. First, in such cases, the secondary route—the language, spatial model, or whatever—is at best a metaphor or translation. It is not mathematics itself. And at some point, the learner must translate back into the domain of mathematics. Without this translation, what is learned tends to remain at a relatively superficial level; cookbook-style mathematical performance results from following instructions (linguistic translation) without understanding why (mathematics retranslation).

Second, the alternative route is not guaranteed. There is no *necessary* reason why a problem in one domain *must be translatable* into a metaphorical problem in another domain. Successful teachers find these translations with relative frequency; but as learning becomes more complex, the likelihood of a successful translation may diminish.

While multiple intelligences theory is consistent with much empirical evidence, it has not been subjected to strong experimental tests within psychology. Within the area of education, the applications of the theory are currently being examined in many projects. Our hunches will have to be revised many times in light of actual classroom experience. Still there are important reasons for considering the theory of multiple intelligences and its implications for education. First of all, it is clear that many talents, if not intelligences, are overlooked nowadays; individuals with these talents are the chief casualties of the single-minded, single-funneled approach to the mind. There are many unfilled or poorly filled niches in our society and it would be opportune to guide individuals with the right set of abilities to these billets. Finally, our world is beset with problems; to have any chance of solving them, we must make the very best use of the intelligences we possess. Perhaps recognizing the plurality of intelligences and the manifold ways in which human individuals may exhibit them is an important first step.

Chapter 3

Questions and Answers About Multiple Intelligences Theory

Coauthored by Joseph Walters

O nce the theory of multiple intelligences had been introduced, numerous questions were raised by friendly (and, at times, by not-so-friendly) critics. In this chapter, parts of which were originally coauthored by Joseph Walters, I answer the more common questions, grouping them as appropriate. In the next chapter, I take a more comprehensive look at the relations among the concept of "intelligence" and other efforts to describe significant human achievement.

The Term "Intelligence"

Your "intelligences"—musical, bodily-kinesthetic, and so on—are what others call talents or gifts. Why confuse the issue by using the word "intelligence" to describe them?

There is nothing magical about the word "intelligence." I have purposely chosen it to join issue with those psychologists who consider logical reasoning or linguistic competence to be on a different plane than musical problem-solving or bodily-kinesthetic aptitude. Placing logic and language on a pedestal reflects the values of our Western culture and the great premium placed on the familiar tests of intelligence. A more Olympian view sees all seven as equally valid. To call some "talent" and some "intelligence" displays this bias. Call them all "talents" if you wish; or call them all "intelligences."

Isn't it odd to speak of skill in gym class as intelligence? And wouldn't such usage convert bodily defects into forms of mental retardation?

I don't find it odd to speak of the bodily skill used by, say, an athlete, a dancer, or a surgeon as embodying intelligence. Recall that MI theory begins with the identification of products, problems, and solutions that matter within a given cultural context. Very often, performances in sports or dance are very important within a society, and innovations in these areas are honored. It is sensible to speak of intelligent use and control over one's body for the performance of highly subtle and technical moves; this facility is just what coaches attempt to enhance.

As for the issue of retardation, it is true that the loss of a certain physical capacity could cause an individual to have problems in the bodily-kinesthetic area, just as loss of hearing or sight could cause problems, respectively, with linguistic or with spatial capacities. And, as in those cases, therapists are challenged to substitute other systems, be they other bodily areas or certain kinds of prosthetics, including ones involving computers or other technologies.

In our culture we use the term *retardation* primarily with respect to linguistic or logical problems. It is salutary to envision a culture in which people are primarily evaluated for their musical or painting skills. Tone-deaf or color-blind people would be retarded in those settings.

Just as societies change, so do evaluations of skills. Who would now value the massive feats of rote linguistic memory so prized before books were widely available? Perhaps, if computers assume (or consume) an increasing proportion of the domain in which linguistic and mathematical skills are exercised, our own society may evolve into one where artistic skills *are* the most highly valued because computers handle everything else!

I am confused by usage. Is intelligence a product, a process, a content, a style, or all of the above?

Unfortunately, this is not as simple a matter as I'd like it to be. Consumers of the theory have used the term "intelligence" in a variety of ways and I myself have probably added to the confusion.

Fundamentally, I think of an intelligence as a *biopsychological potential.* That is, all members of the species have the potential to exercise a set of intellectual faculties of which the species is capable. When I speak of an individual's linguistic or interpersonal intelligence, then, this is a shorthand way of saying that the individual has developed the potential to deal with specific contents in her environment—such as the linguistic signals that she hears or produces, or the social/emotional information that she gleans from interacting with other persons. Persons deemed "at promise" simply exhibit a high degree of intelligence with relatively little need for formal tutelage.

If one bears this initial conception in mind, it is possible to extend the use of the term "intelligence" in various ways. I presume that each of the intelligences has its attendant psychological processes, and so it is perfectly proper to speak about linguistic or interpersonal processing. It is also permissible to speak about certain kinds of contents in the environment that presumably draw on particular intelligences: thus, books customarily evoke linguistic intelligence, while mathematical problems customarily evoke logical-mathematical intelligence.

Can one say, then, that a musician must exhibit a high degree of musical intelligence?

Again, this is a point that is more complex than it appears, and one for which I definitely bear some of the burden for confusing the issue.

When I wrote *Frames of mind*, I was too promiscuous in the use of the term intelligence, and I applied it in areas where it would have been preferable to deploy other terminology. I have been helped to see the complexity of the issue by my colleagues David Feldman and Mihaly Csikszentmihalyi. Thanks to collaborative work with them, I now make a distinction between *intelligence* as a biopsychological potential; *domain* as the discipline or craft that is practiced in a society; and *field*, the set of institutions and judges that determine which products within a domain are of merit.

How do these distinctions help? It is no doubt the case that the domain of music, as practiced in our society, requires a significant amount of musical intelligence. However, depending on which aspect of music is at issue, other intelligences are clearly at a premium as well. A violinist must have bodily-kinesthetic intelligence; a conductor requires considerable interpersonal intelligence; the director of an opera requires spatial, personal, and linguistic as well as musical intelligences. Just as a domain may require more than one intelligence, so, too, an intelligence can be deployed in many domains. Finally, it is the field that renders the ultimate decision about the construction of the domain and the kinds of intelligences that are valued. For example, in the case of physics, spatial thinking used to be at a premium, but in the modern era, logical-mathematical abilities seem to be much more important.

The Theoretical Status of Multiple Intelligences Theory

Is multiple intelligences really a "theory?" It selects certain data in support of its hypotheses while ignoring others. Furthermore, it is not confirmed by experiment. Therefore, the theory cannot be disproved as it stands, nor can it be contrasted with competing theories. And since the possibility of contradiction is a prerequisite for any nontrivial theory, MI fails the test.

MI theory does not consider all data since such consideration would not be possible. Instead it surveys a wide variety of independent research traditions: neurology, special populations, development, psychometrics, anthropology, evolution, and so on. The theory is a product of the synthesis of this survey. That the various research traditions point to and support a single theory does not confirm the theory but does support the contention that this theory is on the right track.

To be sure, the theory at best only explains existing research findings; it can be confirmed only through experiments and other kinds of empirical investigations. Still, the contention that MI is not a theory until the experiments are performed is unwarranted.

Controlled experiments could either confirm or disconfirm MI. Several come to mind: a test of the independence of intelligences, for example; a test of the universality of intelligences across cultures; or a test of the developmental stability of an intelligence. There is another way that the theory can be disconfirmed, however, even before such experiments are performed. My original program, presented in *Frames of mind*, might be described as a "subjective factor analysis," which aimed to discover a reasonably small set of human faculties that formed "natural kinds" and that had biological validity and educational utility. If other researchers, looking at the same empirical data or at new empirical data, were to come up with a list of faculties that were better supported, the current version of MI theory would be called into question. If there turned out to be a significant correlation among these faculties, as measured by appropriate assessments, the supposed independence of the faculties would be invalidated.

Moreover, the theory could be partially discomfirmed on any number of finer points. Perhaps one or more of the candidate intelligences will be found to be inadequately justified based on further review. Perhaps there are candidates that I have not considered. Or perhaps the intelligences are not nearly as independent as claimed. Each of these alternatives can be empirically verified and can provide means for disconfirming or reformulating the theory, although in the case of certain revisions, there might still be some utility to the theory itself.

There is a great deal of evidence in the psychometric literature that suggests that humans differ from one another in general intelligence. This trait, labeled g, can be measured quite reliably through statistical analysis of test scores. There is no place for g in MI theory, so how can this large body of data be explained?

I do not deny that *g* exists; instead, I question its explanatory importance outside the relatively narrow environment of formal schooling. For example, evidence for *g* is provided almost entirely by tests of linguistic or logical intelligence. Since these tests measure skills that are valuable in the performance of school-related tasks, they provide reliable prediction of success or failure in school. So, for that matter, do last year's grades. The tests are not nearly as reliable in predicting success outside of school tasks.

Second, these tests almost always rely on short answers. Again, a particular test-taking skill, relevant to school success but not much else, contributes to the measured individual differences and the correlations that result. If reliable tests could be constructed for different intelligences, and these tests did not rely solely on short answers, often through pencil-and-paper presentations, but instead used the materials of the domain being measured, I believe that the correlations that yield *g* would greatly diminish. Tests of musical intelligence would examine the individual's ability to analyze a work of music or to create one, not simply to compare two single tones on the basis of relative pitch. We need tests of spatial ability that involve finding one's way around, not merely giving multiple choice responses to depictions of a geometric form as rendered from different visual angles.

For example, tasks that require the memorization of letters versus digits often return correlated results, even though these tasks appear to require different intelligences. I am dubious of the ecological significance of these measures. But, putting that aside, according to my analysis, the memorization of both numbers and letters involves linguistic memory and thus both tasks tap the same underlying facility. As an alternative, one might ask subjects to memorize a poem on the one hand and a mathematical proof on the other. I predict that results from tasks of this type would show relatively low correlations. Finally, it is worth noting that students trained to memorize long strings of digits (up to 80 to 100) show no transfer when they are asked to memorize other putatively meaningless strings of information (Ericsson, 1984).

Even if g is a valid concept for describing the capacities of certain individuals, it seems to pass by many others who have striking individual talents. Consequently, from a societal point of view, a focus on g is biased and often unproductive.

Is a rapprochement between MI and competing theories of intelligence possible?

Certainly. For example, there are many intriguing points of contact between MI and the triarchic theory articulated by Sternberg (1984). Sternberg's theory distinguishes three different forms of cognition that might be mapped into different intelligences. Expansion of the connections between, say, Sternberg's "practical intelligence" and my "interpersonal intelligence" might provide some grounds for rapprochement (see chapter 8).

Whatever the future holds, it is desirable, when a new theory is introduced, to accentuate its unique properties so that it can be more readily contrasted with its competitors. Consequently, I resist the attempt to combine MI with other theories at this point. Better a forceful and monistic theory than an all-encompassing but innocuous first attempt (see Sternberg, 1983).

Why is it worth attending to a subjective factor analysis, when objective factor analyses exist?

In using the term subjective, I am poking gentle fun at my primitive methodology. However, it is important to look seriously at the data on which the so-called objective measures are based. In the "test approach," what have been correlated with one another are the short answer, switch-from-one-context-to-another-as-quickly-as-you-can,do-it-in-half-an-hour instruments that ETS and other testing agencies have developed to a high degree. Competence in performance on such tests may, of course, justify their use in a factor analysis. But I will not be convinced that a factor analysis can really uncover intelligence unless it is based on considerations of culturally valued expertise.

The problem with any factor analysis is the quality of the input—the "garbage in, garbage out" peril clearly applies. Thus, I see myself as trying to improve the quality of the input and not holding too many preconceived ideas about what the output might be. My goal is to perform "objective" factor analyses only when the psychologists and the experts in the relevant domains have satisfied themselves that they have really identified capacities that are important and valued in society. Only someone with a jaundiced view could make that claim with respect to most standardized tests.

The Fine Structure of Each of the Intelligences and Their Combination

*T*ests *rely on tasks developed from a careful and complete articulation of the mechanisms underlying each intelligence. How can these tasks be constructed when MI has yet to provide an explanation of "how" each particular intelligence works?*

It is true that the focus of MI theory thus far has been on identification and description of the faculties rather than on the fine structuring and functioning of the intelligences. In principle, there is certainly no reason why information-processing accounts could not be given for each of these intelligences and their manner of interaction; indeed, this would be a worthwhile project. Certainly careful articulation of each intelligence is required in the diagnostic process. I believe that operational definitions of each intelligence along with diagnostic procedures can be constructed, and my colleagues and I are engaged in efforts that address that objective (see part II). I realize that it may be difficult to come up with precise definitions and assessment procedures for the personal intelligences and that considerable ingenuity will be required in creating formulations that are faithful to the scope of these intelligences and yet lend themselves to some kind of objective assessment. But the difficulty of this undertaking certainly does not excuse our ignoring these forms of knowing, a practice that has been the rule in mainstream psychology in the last several decades.

Need the intelligences be entirely independent?

The theory is simpler, both conceptually and biologically, if the various intelligences are totally independent. However, there is no theoretical

41

reason why two or more intelligences could not overlap or correlate with one another more highly than with the others.

The independence of intelligences makes a good working hypothesis. It can only be tested by using appropriate measures in different cultures. Otherwise, one might prematurely jump to the conclusion that two candidate intelligences are correlated, only to find that the results are artifactual or culture bound.

What about the often noted connection between mathematical and musical intelligences?

People who are mathematically talented often show considerable interest in music; perhaps this is because music presents itself as an extremely fertile field for the mathematical mind, which is fascinated by patterns of any sort. But musicians to whom I have spoken maintain that a mathematician's interest in music does not necessarily amount to genuine musicality—for example, knowing how to perform a piece of music to bring out its deeper structures or its contrasting moods. One must be cautious, then, about confusing interest with expertise; it may just be an *interest* in music that is correlated with mathematical intelligence. Note, too, that musicians are not particularly associated with an interest in mathematics (any more than, say, with dance or with foreign languages); rather, it is the mathematicians (and other scientists) who seem to be attracted to music.

What about capacities that cut across the different intelligences, such as memory?

I am skeptical about the claim that memory operates in a way that is blind to content. There is considerable neuropsychological evidence for the separation of linguistic memory from spatial, facial, bodily, or musical memory (Gardner, 1975). It is instructive to realize that, normally, when we say a person has a good memory, we mean that he or she is good at using memory for certain kinds of linguistic assignments. We tend not to think of a good memory for a piece of music or the steps of a dance or the route to a shopping mall, though each of these is certainly a mnemonic process and, quite possibly, one that operates by distinctive mechanisms.

The theory of multiple intelligences outlines several independent faculties but fails to provide any discussion of how these are orchestrated into the symphony of human behavior. How can diverse and independent intelligences function effectively without a leader, an executive?

A theory that does not posit an executive function has certain advantages over one that does. For one thing, such a theory is simpler; it also avoids many of the temptations of infinite regression involved in the explanation of such a function. Moreover, an executive is not a necessary attribute of such a theory. Committees, for example, can be effective without a leader. The composer Richard Rodgers and lyricist Oscar Hammerstein were able to collaborate brilliantly with neither serving as the executive.

At the same time, however, it does appear on the basis of daily experience that many people can evaluate their intelligences and plan to use them together in certain putatively effective ways. Perhaps this is a component of the sense of self that I view as an outgrowth of the intrapersonal intelligence, leavened by the other intelligences, like language and logic. In our "particle" society, individuals themselves do the planning and negotiating. But that role can be played by someone else; for example, the mother often plays the role with the prodigy, and the rest of society plays the role in many other so-called "field" societies. The phenomenal experience of an executive sense of self may make sense in our society, but it does not appear to be an imperative of successful human functioning.

It is also possible to have what Jerry Fodor (1983) and others have termed a "dumb executive," a mechanism that simply makes sure that wires don't get crossed, and arranges a stacked order among various mental functions, but does not make strategic decisions that one associates with an empowered executive. Such a mechanism poses no problem for MI theory.

But surely there must be a general capacity called "critical thinking," which we seek to develop in schools and which is at a particular premium in a modern industrial society?

As is the case with the central executive, it is tempting to agree with colleagues about the existence and the desirability of critical thinking. And, indeed, I do value individuals who can analyze world events or literature critically, or who are able to reflect usefully on their own work or on that of colleagues. Indeed, I hope that my own children and students will exhibit these capacities.

Yet, while the term "critical thinking" is useful in lay discourse, one must be careful not to assume that it is a particular, dissociable variety of human cognition. My analysis suggests that, as with the case of memory and other apparently "across-the-board" faculties, a closer analysis calls their existence into question. Instead, particular domains of human competence seem to require their own brand of critical thinking. Musicians, historians, taxonomic biologists, choreographers, computer programmers, and literary critics all value critical thinking. But the kind of thinking required to analyze a fugue is simply different from that involved in observing and categorizing different animal species, or scrutinizing a poem, or debugging a program, or choreographing and analyzing a new dance. There is little reason to think that training of critical thinking in one of these domains provides significant "savings" when one enters another domain. Rather, one needs to develop the forms of critical thinking that are relevant to that particular domain: on closer analysis each domain exhibits its own particular *logic of implications.*

It is possible that certain habits of thought, such as taking one's time, considering alternatives, sharing one's work with another colleague, assuming the perspective of other persons, may well prove useful across domains. Certainly, I believe that such habits of mind ought to be cultivated early and widely. However, the crucial point to stress is that *each of these forms of critical thinking must be practiced explicitly in every domain where it might be appropriate.* It is unrealistic to expect individuals to know how to transfer even these rather generic schemes across domains. For this reason, it makes little sense to have "stand-alone" courses in critical thinking, or to teach critical thinking in history class, on the assumption that it will magically reappear as appropriate in a music or mathematics course. On the contrary, I believe that only if the lessons of critical thinking are deliberately revisited in each of the relevant classes or exercises is there any possibility that a more general virtue like "reflectiveness" or "taking the perspective of the other" has any chance of emerging.

Are intelligences the same thing as "learning styles" or "working styles"?

Without doubt, some of the distinctions made in the theory of multiple intelligences resemble those made by educators who speak of different learning or working styles. Many of them speak of spatial or linguistic styles, for example. But MI theory begins from a different point and ends up at a different place from most schemes that emphasize stylistic approaches.

In MI theory I begin with a human organism that responds (or fails to respond) to different kinds of *contents* in the world, such as language, number, and other human beings. I assume that faculties like perception or memory may well differ in strength or mode of operation across intelligences, with memory for spatial information being better or worse than memory for musical information in a particular individual. Those who speak of learning styles are searching for approaches that ought to characterize *all* contents: a person who is deliberate with respect to music as well as to mathematics, a person who sees the "big picture" whether he is doing physics or painting.

Work in Project Spectrum (see chapter 6) casts doubt on the notion that such styles are generic. A more complex picture has emerged. Children may well exhibit one style with one kind of information (such as being impulsive in the musical realm) while exhibiting a contrasting style with other information (such as being reflective when working on a jigsaw puzzle). The most comprehensive analysis of individual differences may need to chart *both* the styles and the contents, in order to determine which styles seem yoked to specific contents and which may operate across the board, at least in the case of a particular individual.

The Existence of Further Intelligences

What prevents the ambitious theoretician from constructing a new "intelligence" for every skill found in human behavior? In that case, instead of seven intelligences, there might be 700!

A list of 700 intelligences would be forbidding to the theoretician and useless to the practitioner. Therefore MI theory attempts to articulate only a manageable number of intelligences that appear to form natural kinds. There is every reason to expect that each natural kind will have several (or more) subcomponents. For example, linguistic intelligence clearly entails several dissociable elements, such as the capacities to conduct syntactic analyses, to acquire literacy, and to learn languages by ear. However, it is also likely that, in most normal human behaviors, the several subcomponents of an intelligence should cluster together, while they should show little inclination to correlate with subcomponents of other intelligences. This claim could and should be tested empirically.

As indicated in *Frames of mind*, the decision to search for a small number of intelligences or faculties is a deliberate one. Without question, one might want to have a larger set of intelligences if one were pursuing other theoretical or practical ends. In this sense, the decision is a meta-theoretical one.

Why is moral or spiritual intelligence not considered?

Moral or spiritual intelligence serves as a reasonable candidate for an eighth intelligence, although there is equally good reason to consider it as an amalgam of interpersonal intelligence and intrapersonal intelligence with a value component added. What is moral or spiritual depends greatly on cultural values; in describing intelligences we are dealing with abilities that can be mobilized by the values of a culture rather than the behaviors that are themselves valued in one way or another.

Is there an artistic intelligence?

Many individuals have spoken informally of the artistic intelligence or the artistic intelligences, and I see nothing wrong with this manner of speaking—it can serve as a shorthand for musical intelligence, or for aspects of spatial or linguistic intelligence.

Technically, however, no intelligence is inherently artistic or nonartistic. Rather, intelligences function artistically (or nonartistically) to the extent that they exploit certain properties of a symbol system. Should an individual use language in an ordinary, expository way, as I do here, he or she is not using the linguistic intelligence in an aesthetic manner. If, on the other hand, language is used metaphorically, expressively, or in such a way as to call attention to sound or structural properties, then it is being used artistically. By the same token, the same "spatial" intelligence may be exploited aesthetically by a sculptor, nonartistically by a geometer or surgeon. Even a musical signal can function nonartistically, as do bugle calls in the armed forces, while many patterns derived for mathematical purposes have ended up on display in art galleries.

Whether an intelligence is used artistically is a decision made by the individual and/or by the culture. An individual can decide whether to deploy linguistic intelligence as a writer, a lawyer, a salesperson, a poet, or an orator. However, cultures highlight or thwart the possibility of artistic uses of intelligence. In some cultures, almost everyone develops some poetic capacities; but Plato sought to eliminate poetry from his Republic. Clearly, then, the exercise of a particular intelligence in an artistic fashion involves a judgment of value.

Group Differences

*A*re intelligences the same in quantity or quality across groups? For instance, do men exhibit profiles of intelligence that differ from those exhibited by women? And how about different ethnic or racial groups?

This is a potentially explosive question. I suspect that, if the appropriate studies were done in an intelligence-fair way, they might suggest differences across groups. Even if these differences were found, however, the reasons for them would remain obscure. Thus, women might perform worse than men on spatial tasks in the West; but if there existed an environment where spatial orientation were as important for survival for women as for men, those differences might well disappear or even be reversed. Apparently this erasure of group differences happens among the Eskimo.

I have avoided looking at this question quite deliberately. In the still recent past, apparent group differences on psychological instruments have been exploited for politically dubious ends. I prefer not to provide additional ammunition for such efforts. In any event, should any investigator demonstrate differences among groups, I would regard those differences as the starting point for remediation efforts, rather than as any kind of proof of inherent limitations within a group.

Educational Considerations

*A*re the intelligences modifiable?

Possibly genetic factors set some kind of upper bound on the extent to which an intelligence may be realized or modified in the course of a human life. As a practical matter, however, it is likely to be the case that this biological limit is rarely if ever approached. Given enough exposure to the materials of an intelligence, nearly anyone who is not brain damaged can achieve quite significant results in that intellectual realm. (This is the lesson of the Suzuki musical method and other "hot house" techniques.) By the same token, no one—whatever his or her biological potential—is likely to develop an intelligence without at least some opportunities for exploration of the materials that elicit a particular intellectual strength (Walters & Gardner, 1986). In sum, the surrounding culture plays a prepotent role in determining the extent to which an individual's intellectual potential is realized.

It is important to challenge the notion that all individuals come equipped with exactly equivalent predispositions in each area. Based on his work with people who are outstanding in various domains, Benjamin Bloom (1985) makes the kind of claim that I reject—namely, that the all-important determination of ability is training. And Samuel Johnson epitomized the view I challenge when he said "True genius is a mind of large general powers, accidentally determined to some particular direction." I do not deny the existence of the occasional figure of Johnsonian breadth, but such persons represent a minuscule minority. It is no accident that an individual develops strengths in one area as opposed to another; counter to what the behaviorists believed, parents cannot just arbitrarily decide what to bring their children up to do or to be.

How can one train a specific intelligence?

I am impressed with the method of training developed by the Japanese master Shinichi Suzuki for teaching music to young children (Gardner, 1983, chapter 14). The method works because Suzuki has identified the factors that matter in developing musical skill in early life—such as the finger arrangements possible on the violin, the kinds of patterns that can be readily recognized and sung by young children, the capacity to imitate mothers, the tendency to identify with slightly older peers, and so on.

What Suzuki did for musical performance can, I think, be accomplished for every other intelligence, and indeed each intelligence may require its own specific educational theory. One cannot simply assume that the techniques that work at different ages in specific domains will prove applicable "across the board."

Chapter 4

The Relation of Intelligence to Other Valued Human Capacities

During the celebrations commemorating the 200th anniversary of the death of Wolfgang Amadeus Mozart, this master musician was put to many different uses. Such exploitation is not surprising, because the work of Mozart has spoken *to* so many individuals over so many years in so many powerful ways. Mozart has also been spoken *of* in many ways: as a genius, a prodigy, an expert, an individual who is talented, creative, intelligent, and gifted. I hope it will be seen as a token of respect, rather than as a mark of further exploitation, if I draw on the case of Mozart for yet two further purposes: (1) to clarify the nature of the terminology that we use in talking about exceptional individuals; and (2) to introduce a particular perspective that I have brought to bear in the area of human talents or gifts.

Mozart evokes a plethora of positive characterizations. He is our prototype of a prodigy, as precocious as Pablo Picasso or John Stuart Mill, as preternaturally talented as his fellow musicians Felix Mendelssohn or Camille Saint-Saëns. He is seen as infinitely creative, as unmistakably individualistic as Igor Stravinsky or Richard Wagner, though exhibiting an ingenuity that is evolutionary rather than revolutionary in character. He is as productive as his prolific contemporaries, Antonio Salieri or Karl Ditters von Dittersdorf. And he is granted a deep intelligence, an insight into the human condition that is as profound as that associated with Samuel Johnson or Goethe, with Velázquez or Rembrandt.

Students of Mozart, and, for that matter, students of psychology might well leave this situation just as is. Terminology has a tendency to proliferate; and ordinarily, little harm is done by a cornucopia of terms. Yet at times it can be valuable to step back and consider how one might extend and apply this termnology in a consistent way. And if such application is based upon a coherent theoretical framework, it can sometimes aid in discussion, research, and understanding. Hence, in what follows I introduce a general framework for the consideration of what I shall term the *giftedness matrix*, in the process presenting a set of distinctions that I hope will prove useful.

A Framework for Analysis

Every cognitive act involves an agent who carries out an action or a set of actions in some task or domain. Even when the agent is operating in a solitary fashion, his or her acts can potentially be evaluated by someone competent in that particular task or domain space (Csikszentmihalyi, 1988; Feldman with Goldsmith, 1986; Gardner, 1988a). Whether one is dealing with the most remarkable acts of genius, or the meanest accomplishment of the average citizen, this analytic perspective proves applicable. In the social sciences, this analytic framework has been decomposed as follows (Gardner, 1988b).

The *biopsychological* perspective examines the agent and his or her capacities, inclinations, values, and goals. Included are a consideration of the genetic and neurological substrates of behavior, as well as the analysis of an individual in terms of cognitive powers, traits, and temperamental disposition.

A perspective from the point of view of *domains* or *tasks* examines a task or activity as it has been realized within a societal domain or discipline. Traditionally, tasks have been analyzed by philosophers or by individuals expert in a domain; since the advent of computer science, experts in the field of artificial intelligence have brought forth analyses of the structural and processual properties of a task.

Finally, evaluations or judgments of actions (or works) performed in a domain are put forth by individuals knowledgeable in that domain— by members of the *field*, in Csikszentmihalyi's term (1988). Absent a judgment by individuals or groups who are knowledgeable, it is simply not possible to tell whether a task has been executed satisfactorily or in an exemplary fashion. It is not the case that in the absence of such judgment, a task or work is necessarily inadequate; rather, one simply is unable to render a judgment one way or another. Disciplines that can clarify the operation of the field are sociology and social psychology.

The Framework and the Words

Using this analytic framework as a point of departure, I now return to the lexical members of the giftedness matrix and offer some provisional definitions.

Intelligence is a biopsychological potential. Whether and in what respects an individual may be deemed intelligent is a product in the first instance of his genetic heritage and his psychological properties, ranging from his cognitive powers to his personality dispositions. Recent advances in cognitive studies suggest how best to conceptualize intelligence.

Giftedness is a sign of precocious biopsychological potential in whichever domains exist in a culture. An individual who advances quickly, who is "at promise" in an available task area or domain, earns the epithet "gifted." Individuals can be gifted in any area that is recognized as involving intelligence.

Prodigiousness is an extreme form of giftedness in a domain. Mozart qualified as prodigious because of his extraordinary gifts in the musical sphere. By and large, prodigiousness occurs in a domain: the giftedness of the youthful mathematician Carl Gauss is quite different from the precociousness of the English painter John Everett Millais or the prodigiousness of the chess player Samuel Reshevsky. Similarly, Mozart differed from other gifted youngsters, including his sister Nannerl. On occasion, however, there may be universal or omnibus prodigies.

The terms *expertise* and *expert* are appropriately invoked only after an individual has worked for a decade or so within a domain. By this time, the individual will have mastered the skills and lore that are requisite to performance at the highest levels of the domain. However, there is no implication of originality, dedication, or passion in such a performance; expertise is better conceived as a kind of technical excellence. Colleagues of Mozart (long since forgotten) who could produce on demand a set of concerti or symphonies may have attained expertise without evincing originality.

Creativity is a characterization reserved to those products that are initially seen to be novel within a domain but that are ultimately recognized as acceptable within an appropriate community. Judgments of originality or creativity can be made only by knowledgeable members of the field, though that field can be ancient or newly constituted. There is a tension between creativity and expertise: certainly one may be expert without being creative; and, possibly, some creativity can be manifest prior to a determination that someone has attained the level of a master.

It is with some trepidation that I introduce a final term into the discussion: that of *genius*. I reserve this honorific label for those persons or works that are not only expert and creative but that also assume a universal, or quasi-universal significance. Within the scientific arena, it is individuals of genius, such as Isaac Newton or Charles Darwin, who make discoveries of principles of universal significance. And within the artistic arena, it is individuals of genius who create works which speak to individuals from diverse cultures and eras. We are comfortable in applying the epithet genius to Shakespeare, Goethe, Rembrandt, and Mozart, because their works have transcended their own era. Presumably individuals from other cultures and eras also merit the term *genius*, but that determination can only be made when these individuals have passed the test of various relevant fields.

Traditional Psychological Approaches to the Giftedness Matrix

In most traditional approaches, the focus has fallen sharply on the individual agent. As a result of this bias, there has been too little consideration of the specific tasks or domains in question: the assumption has obtained that abilities will emerge irrespective of the particular domains that happen to be available in one's culture. Also, as a result of this bias, there has been little consideration of the processes by which judgments of quality are made: at least among psychologists, the field has been as little visible as the domain.

The most influential approach to the giftedness matrix has been a direct descendant of work in the area of intelligence and intelligence testing. In the Binet-Spearman tradition, intelligence is the trait of the isolated individual, who can be assessed alone; there is typically the additional assumption that individuals are born with a certain amount of intelligence, which can be measured early in life, and which proves relatively insensitive to environment or training. Even when there have been efforts to pluralize intelligence, as in the work of Thurstone, intelligence is still seen as a relatively fixed trait, one that is readily elicited through the administration of paper and pencil–style instruments (see Gardner, 1983, 1991).

Given this view of intelligence, an ensemble of moves can be made with respect to the giftedness matrix. The "gifted" are those with high IQs; the "precocious" are those with even higher IQs, as ascertainable at an even younger age. "Genius" can be applied to either a youngster or an adult, so long as his or her IQ is high enough—perhaps over the level of 150. On some definitions, creativity and intelligence are viewed as related, while other investigators have stressed the relative independence of intelligence and creativity. Recently an informal consensus has emerged that above IQ levels of 120 creativity is not connected to psychometric intelligence. Yet from my point of view, the measures of creativity growing out of the psychometric tradition are even more impoverished than the measures of intelligence. Such measures focus almost exclusively on the most mundane instances of creativity, the type associated with clever repartee at cocktail parties, rather than with human accomplishments of scope and depth. Finally, the word *expert* seems somewhat anomalous in the context of intelligence testing, because it makes contact with specific areas of competence, while intelligence is styled as the most general property of an individual. Certainly many members of Mensa are expert in nothing—except in taking tests of intelligence.

A Contemporary View of Intelligence and Related Matters

Countering the notion of a single intelligence has been the view, which has recurred from time to time, that intellect is better conceived of as pluralistic in nature. Typically, as noted earlier, this conclusion has been reached as the result of factor analytic studies of test scores; and, as such, it is limited by the nature of the instruments used to assess various competences.

In my own work, I have approached issues of intelligence from a quite different perspective. The problem that I set myself some years ago was this: Given the wide range of competences, of "end states" that are valued around the world, what is the nature of the mind that can give rise to a plethora of possibilities? Posing the question in this way was heterodox: it made no use of standardized tests; it focused on meaningful roles in a society rather than on abstract competences; and it harbored a culturally relative perspective. So long as a capacity is valued in a culture, it can count as an intelligence; but in the absence of such a cultural or "field" endorsement, a capacity would not be considered an intelligence. It was from this perspective that I developed my theory of multiple intelligences (see chapters 1 and 2).

Building upon this concept of intelligence, it proves possible to come up with a new and consistent way of speaking about the giftedness matrix. An individual is "gifted" if he or she is "at promise" in any domain where intelligences figure; and the term *prodigy* would be applied to an individual of unusual precocity. An *expert* is a person who rapidly achieves a high level of competence within a domain, irrespective of whether any of his or her approaches are novel or experimental in any way. Conversely, an individual is considered "creative" if he or she regularly solves problems or fashions products in a domain in a way that is initially seen as novel but that ultimately is recognized as appropriate for a domain. No definition of genius flows directly from this work. But I would propose that an individual merits the term *genius* to the extent that his or her creative work in a domain exerts a material effect on the definition and delineation of the domain—so that in the future, individuals who work in that domain will have to wrestle with the contributions made by the creative genius. The more universal the contribution, the more it travels across cultures and eras, the greater the genius. That is why young writers traditionally shudder when confronted with the example of Shakespeare or Goethe; these titanic individuals have cast a formidable shadow over the future dimensions of the domain.

In the preceding discussion, I introduced an innovative way of conceiving intelligence; I then went on to suggest how the remainder of the giftedness matrix can be conceptualized with reference to this view of intelligence. The effectiveness of such an analysis can be determined in part on the basis of its internal coherence; but for a behavioral scientist, a more important test is the extent to which the analysis is consistent with what is known about human behavior, and the extent to which the analysis can lead to increased understanding.

Accordingly, in what follows, I carry out a developmental analysis. I examine four different points in the developmental trajectory of individuals, with special reference to the issues of intelligence, giftedness, and creativity being treated here. Major notions are recorded in the accompanying table 4.1. Then, in conclusion I touch on a few educational implications of this perspective.

TABLE 4.1.
The Giftedness Matrix at a Glance

Term	Sphere	Age Focus	Domain/Field Status	Relevant Issues
Intelligence	biopsychological	all	—	crystallizing experience
Giftedness	biopsychological	young/growing	predomain/prefield	wide resources
Prodigiousness	biopsychological	growing	current domain/field	cumulative knowledge/skills
Expertise	current domain/field	postadolescence	accept domain/field	fruitful asychrony
Creativity	future domain/field	postadolescence	clash with domain/field	link to childhood
Genius	broad domain/wide field	mature person	universal	

The Five-Year-Old: Indifferent to Domain and Field

In the first years of life, young children the world over develop powerful theories and conceptions of how the world works—the physical world and the world of other people. They also develop at least a first-draft level of competence with the basic human symbol systems—language, number, music, two-dimensional depiction, and the like. What is striking about these acquisitions is that they do not depend on explicit tutelage. Children develop these symbolic skills and these theoretical conceptions largely by dint of their own spontaneous interactions with the world in which they live. This is not to deny that specific cultures exert specific effects, but rather to make the assertion that the kinds of capacities that evolve would be difficult to thwart, given any reasonably rich and supportive environment.

With respect to most youngsters, then, one can speak of early development as being "predomain" and "prefield." That is, youngsters develop with only dim alertness to the domains that exist in their culture and with even less sensitivity to the existence of fields that judge. At young ages, children are sometimes attracted to specific domains—what I have elsewhere termed crystallizing experiences (Walters & Gardner, 1986). However, for the most part, those who are attracted are more interested than they are proficient.

There are exceptions: Mozart was certainly one. There is the occasional prodigy who early on discovers an affinity to a culturally approved domain, and who begins an early mastery of that domain. In such instances, the child has a jump start on the attainment of expertise, and, perhaps, creativity.

The issue of childhood creativity is a vexing one. In many ways, I have argued, all young children partake of the elixir of creativity. They are willing to transcend boundaries of which they are at least peripherally aware; they throw themselves into their play and work with great passion; they create products that often strike "the field" as more impressive than those of much older youngsters. And yet, I think it is fair to say that such creativity occurs outside of the field. Even though the field may be impressed by works of young children—and legitimately so—the young child proceeds in sublime indifference to the operations of the field.

The Ten-Year-Old: Mastering the Rules of the Domain

Shortly after the age at which school begins, youngsters begin to assume a quite different stance toward the opportunities in their culture. Whether or not this trend is abetted by school, it seems evident that youngsters want to know the rules of domains and the conventions of culture, and that they seek to master these as rapidly, as expeditiously as possible. In the arts we encounter a period of literalness—students averting metaphor, students striving to produce works of art that are representationally as accurate as possible. But the same trends occur in every domain—the students want to know the rules of the game.

And so one might say that the existence of the domain, and a sensitivity to the field, arise with a vengeance. To the extent that students choose (or are chosen) to work in a specific domain, they attempt to gain expertise as quickly as possible. And even with reference to the wider society, the student attempts to become acculturated in as fully a manner as possible.

This period then functions as an apprenticeship—an apprenticeship en route to expertise in specific domains, an apprenticeship en route to expertise in the ways of one culture. Those who advance most rapidly may be seen as gifted or prodigious, but reference to creativity or genius seems inappropriate here. The free-ranging explorations of the young child have ceased, while the kind of informed exploration of the boundaries of the domain cannot yet be undertaken.

If creative work is not yet forthcoming, the conditions for a creative (or noncreative) life may already be falling into place, for creativity depends heavily on dispositional and personality traits, and on the accidents of demography (Gardner, in press; Perkins, 1981; Sternberg, 1988). Those youngsters who are marginal within their culture, those who are ambitious and stubborn, those who can ignore criticism and stick to their guns, are "at risk" for a creative life; while those who feel comfortably a part of the group, and who advance in their domain with little feeling of pressure or asynchrony, are probably headed for (or consigned to) the life of the expert.

The Adolescent: At the Crossroads

The period between the ages of fifteen and twenty-five represents a moment of truth in the development of the giftedness matrix. The possibility for prodigiousness is already at an end—and genius lurks in the distant future. The crucial issue surrounds expertise. Individuals who devote themselves for a decade to a domain are likely to attain the level of the expert and have the option of continuing to make at least modest contributions to the domain for the foreseeable future. They may also become members "in good standing" of the dominant field. Their intelligences are being deployed in the service of the normal, productive functioning of their current society. Here they work comfortably within the tastes of the current field.

But at least some individuals do not remain simply at the level of expertise. At some point they make a decisive turn—a turn toward greater risk-taking, increased testing of orthodoxy, determined iconoclasm. No longer do they wish simply to follow in the steps of their mentors; instead, they address challenges and seek to go beyond what has come before. This heightened tension may result in a so-called mid-life crisis, and, indeed, some adolescents cease their creativity altogether, either temporarily or permanently (Bamberger, 1982; Csikszentmihalyi, in press). Others directly challenge the field, with unpredictable and varying degrees of success. In any event, if this period of crisis is successfully navigated, then the opportunities for sustained creative achievement remain alive.

The Mature Practitioner: Ensconced
Somewhere on the Matrix of Giftedness

Speed forward another decade or so, to the age of thirty to thirty-five, and one encounters an individual whose ultimate location on the giftedness matrix is likely to have been determined. On an actuarial basis, most individuals committed to a domain will either be contented experts, discontented experts, or individuals who sought to transcend expertise but who failed.

Of special interest, however, is the individual who, for whatever reason, transcends "mere" intelligence, giftedness, or expertise, and seeks an existence of creativity. We have long known some of the characteristics of such individuals: ambitious, self-confident, mildly neurotic, adventurous (Albert & Runco, 1986; Barron, 1969; MacKinnon, 1961). My own studies confirm that creative individuals, whatever their domain differences, have quite consistent personalities, and that they are typically demanding, self-centered individuals, with whom it is difficult to remain on good terms.

But I have also sought to understand what it is like to be operating on the edge of current knowledge and expertise (Gardner, in press). It is a bracing but frightening prospect to consider ideas and practices that have never, to one's knowledge, been attempted before. Such individuals, no matter how solitary, seem to need both cognitive and affective support at such times. And in a way that approaches the uncanny, they are reminiscent of the mother who is teaching a first language and introducing an initial culture to her child. To confirm that he is not mad, the creator needs to be able to convince at least one other person that he has invented a language, a way of seeing things, that makes sense. Absent an unusual set of intellectual, social, affective, and personality traits, such dedication to the enterprise of creativity is difficult to fathom.

My studies have suggested a certain pattern to the enterprise of the highly creative individual. After the first decade of expertise, the individual goes on to make a quite radical statement, one that shakes up the domain and field in which the person is working. A more synthetic statement is likely to emerge a decade later. In some domains, such as mathematics, physical science, or lyric poetry, the prospect of continuing breakthroughs is quite modest. But in others, it is possible to continue to make breakthroughs for several more decades. This is why artists such as Pablo Picasso, Igor Stravinsky, and Martha Graham could continue to lead highly creative lives; and why some scientists, such as Sigmund Freud and Charles Darwin, could locate a lode that they could tap for the remainder of their active lives.

Understanding creativity is difficult enough; to shed light on genius borders on the impossible. Let me simply propose that the genius is a creative individual who is able to arrive at insights that are novel and yet strike a deeply responsive chord across the world's diverse cultures. It is difficult enough to make an advance within one's domain; but to make an advance that can reverberate loudly within human society borders on the miraculous. Perhaps it is not fanciful to consider Mozart or Confucius or Shakespeare as miraculous—the incredible coinciding of a human being with the secrets of the universe.

With the genius, the developmental path comes full circle. The young child creates without respect to the domain and the field. The expert accepts the domain and the field, while the would-be creator challenges that domain and the field. It is the special province of the genius to challenge the domain and the field and yet to arrive at a product or a solution that once again constitutes a new, more comprehensive domain—revealing an insight of broad human significance.

In speaking of genius, one moves rather far from the province of behavioral science—invoking a term that smacks more of the literary or artistic pages than of the volumes of a scientific journal. Yet, even if we cannot explain genius, we are wrong to pretend that it does not exist. Whether or not he can inspire social scientific progress, Mozart is at least a perennial reminder of the heights to which a human being can occasionally rise.

Educational Implications

A developmental scheme designed to describe giftedness and its corollaries leads naturally to the question, What can be done to foster or educate giftedness? It has sometimes been quipped, more in sorrow than in joy, that it is easier to thwart gifted and creative youngsters than it is to encourage their flowering. And, indeed, precisely because we know so little about these precious phenomena, it is most important that parents and teachers "do no harm."

Nonetheless, I believe that the foregoing discussion yields at least a few modest implications. To begin with, the very delineation of the varying forms that constitute giftedness, expertise, creativity, and the like can be of aid to educators in that it raises the question, What kind of extraordinary performances or achievements are wanted? To seek to develop an individual who is creative is a far different challenge than to nurture an individual who is to be prodigious, or to train an individual who will become an expert. What is deemed a gift in China may seem a frill or even a burden in Chicago—or vice versa. Disaggregating these "end states" and deciding which are desired and which are not desirable seems a useful step for any educator.

A second implication is entailed in the adoption of a developmental approach. Once one recognizes that children of different ages or stages have different needs, attend to different forms of cultural information, and assimilate content to different motivational and cognitive structures, then the kinds of educational regimens that we design ought to take into account these developmental factors. It is as inappropriate to subject a five-year-old to the critique of the field as it is to withhold such critique from an aspiring master.

A third point concerns the kinds of educational models that are provided to children. Quite different messages are gleaned by the child, depending upon whether the adults or masters with whom she comes into contact embody expertise, creativity, or even some form of genius; and which sorts of early intimations of these end states they encourage or discourage. The simple decision about which teachers or mentors to include in a "giftedness" program carries powerful signals about the direction that children should ultimately pursue.

Overlaying the decision about specific individuals is the broader question of the messages about giftedness that are conveyed in the wider society. As I have shown in a study of arts education in China and the United States (Gardner 1989), two societies can convey contrasting messages about the uses to which talents can be put and the ways in which they can be developed within a culture. Within our own society, as well, there can be contrasting and even contradictory models of what counts as a gift—and what *should* count in the future.

Perhaps inevitably, discussions of giftedness and education within our present cultural context highlight the importance of the individual child. Yet, if the above discussion has validity, it reminds us that gifts of all sorts can never be properly conceptualized as existing solely within the head or the body of individuals. By calling attention to the domain and field characteristics that surround any kind of activity—and, in particular, any kind of extraordinary activity—I hope to remind educators that they too should keep in mind the extra-personal factors that play a vast role in the development (or thwarting) of talent.

A discussion of values seems out of place in a contribution that purports to be scientific. Yet, if there is any societal realm in which issues of value are prominent, it is the terrain that must wrestle with the questions of what constitutes gifts, how they should be identified, fostered, and mobilized within a community. For example, equity and excellence need not be in direct conflict, but there is undeniably a tension between them, and particularly so in times of limited resources. Those of us who elect to devote our energies to the exploration of such fascinating topics have a special obligation to keep these issues of value in mind and, when possible, help make the value considerations and choices clear to colleagues, educators, and the wider public.

Part II

EDUCATING THE INTELLIGENCES

Introductory Note

I began this volume by noting the considerable interest shown by educators in the theory of multiple intelligences. No doubt this interest arose from a variety of sources, ranging from curiosity about recent findings in neuropsychology to a search for programs that might prove effective with students who exhibit learning difficulties. Indeed, so varied are the sources of interest in the theory, that I have sometimes thought it a kind of Rorschach test, in which every observer "projects" upon an amorphous inkblot the ideas with which he or she was already burdened before encountering that ambiguous form.

But if I had to offer one reason above others, it would be the following. Anyone who has spent a significant amount of time with children, whether as teacher, counselor, therapist, or family member, will have been struck by the vast differences among children, including ones reared in the same family. This fact is captured in an old saying related by developmental psychologists: "When a developmentalist has one child, all children are seen as alike. When the developmentalist has two children, the universe is seen as dichotomized (extroverts vs. introverts; masculine vs. feminine). When the developmentalist has three children, all children are acknowledged to be different."

By mid-century the strand of folk wisdom that recognizes "different kinds of minds" had become obscured in scientific psychology, and most especially, in that branch of psychology concerned with the measurement of intellect. As if by edict, all of these differences had mysteriously been ruled out of court, and all children were assessed and arrayed along a single, rather narrow dimension called "intelligence." In my view, the intuition that there was something fundamentally askew about such an approach, and that there was a need for a counterview that categorized and celebrated the astonishing range of the human mind, strongly fueled the excitement about MI theory.

Many readers accepted the idea of multiple intelligences, perhaps even too uncritically. Like me, they were more concerned with breaking out of the hegemony of a single intelligence, and recognizing the inherent plurality of faculties of the mind, than they were obsessed with defining the precise number and detailed nature of each of the candidate intelligences. But soon, perhaps inevitably, the questions arose: How do we educate the multiple intelligences? What would an MI school be like? And how do we get from here to there?

The brief answer—and still the correct one—is that there is no recipe for a multiple intelligences education. MI theory was developed in an effort to describe the evolution and the topography of the human mind and not as a program for developing a certain kind of mind or nurturing a certain kind of human being. Indeed an ensemble of scholastic visions—including ones that stand in apparent contradiction with one another—could be teased out, or constructed from, the general passages at the end of *Frames of mind*.

Yet, in time, I began to evolve some notions about an education framed in the "spirit" of multiple intelligences. These sets of notions took two primary tacks. The first was to sketch out some of the general features that one might expect to encounter in a school community imbued with the spirit of multiple intelligences. A portrait of such a school, as well as a brief road map on how one might bring it into existence, is found in chapter 5.

The second tack entailed the development, in collaboration with numerous valued colleagues, of certain model programs that drew in appropriate ways on MI theory. These programs generally had their origin in a specific issue—for example, how to assess intelligences in preschool children or how to improve arts education at the high school level—but they naturally evolved into more comprehensive "approaches" to education.

The last four chapters of part II introduce four such model programs, ordered for the sake of convenience in terms of the age group that was targeted. In chapter 6, I describe Project Spectrum, a long-term collaboration with David Feldman and Mara Krechevsky, which focuses on the identification and fostering of multiple intelligences in young children. In chapter 7, I describe work on student projects in the elementary grades, as carried out in many schools, among them the Key School in Indianapolis. In chapter 8, I describe the PIFS (Practical Intelligences for School) Project, a collaboration with Robert Sternberg and several other researchers, in which an attempt has been made to prepare students to master the challenging environments of middle and high schools. And in chapter 9, I describe Arts PROPEL, a collaboration among many teachers and researchers in Pittsburgh, the Educational Testing Service, and Harvard Project Zero. Begun originally as an attempt to assess student intelligences in a more "intelligence-fair" way, it has evolved into a curricular approach that can be used not only in the arts but across the spectrum of disciplines.

Chapter 5

A School of the Future

Coauthored by Tina Blythe

As if it were the weather, everyone is talking these days about the desperate need for educational reform in the United States. The reasons for this heightened concern are not difficult to identify. To begin with, there is the perceived economic challenge from Japan and other Pacific rim countries; no longer are we the undisputed industrial and scientific leader of the world. Added to this is the clear decline in literacy and common cultural knowledge as evidenced by a number of statistical indices, official "white papers," and the best-selling works of Allan Bloom and E. D. Hirsch. Finally, there is the virtual compulsion of Americans to reexamine the quality and mission of their schools at least once each generation. These and other pressures combine to make the current concern with education nearly inevitable. And yet, again like the weather, there is the considerable chance that the talk will remain mere talk, that each interested party will look to "others" to institute reform, and that, in the end, changes wrought in the educational system will be modest.

As I see it, American education is at a turning point. There are considerable pressures to move very sharply in the direction of "uniform schooling"; there is also the possibility that our educational system can embrace "individual-centered schooling." A struggle is underway at this moment about the probable direction in which the schools will veer. My own analysis of the scientific evidence indicates that we should as a polity move in the direction of individual-centered schooling. In what follows I indicate why and how such an education might be achieved.

At present the most vocal contributors to the debate are calling for "uniform" schools. Stripped to its essentials, their argument goes as follows. There is a basic set of competences, and a core body of knowledge, which every individual in our society should master. Some individuals are more able than others, and can be expected to master this knowledge more rapidly. Schools should be set up in such a way to ensure that the most gifted can move to the top and that the greatest number of individuals will achieve basic knowledge as efficiently as possible. For that reason, there should be the same curriculum for all students, the same methods of teaching, and the same "standardized" methods of assessment. Students, teachers, administrators, school districts, states, and even the whole nation should be judged in terms of the efficiency and effectiveness with which these common standards are achieved. Paying attention to individual differences is at best a luxury, at worst a dangerous deviation from essential educational priorities.

Of course, it is an oversimplification to band together under one slogan the whole gamut of critics of education in America today. There are clear differences among E. D. Hirsch, Allan Bloom, Mortimer Adler, William Bennett, and the representatives of municipal, state, and federal agencies, not to mention such private-interest groups as the Council for Basic Education and the Twentieth Century Fund. What unites these individuals, and justifies their grouping beneath one ample neoconservative umbrella, is their dissatisfaction with "progressive" ideas in American education, their hunger for a capacious store of common knowledge and skills, and their impatience with approaches that cherish the individuality of each student, teacher, and school building.

It would be wrong, and in any case it is unnecessary, to dispute every paragraph of the neoconservative critique. Along with many others who are unsatisfied with the "uniform view," I certainly believe that the literacies of American students ought to be improved, that every student ought to have the opportunity to master certain basic disciplines, and that much of the educational program of the 1960s (and of earlier decades) was not well considered. Yet I am equally convinced that many of the cures suggested by the neoconservative reformers are worse than the disease; and that in any case the proposed cures will not heal the patients.

My fundamental quarrel with the uniform view comes from my conviction that it is based on a fundamentally flawed view of human cognition—one that I call "IQ-style thinking." As is well known, nearly a century ago, the first intelligence tests were designed, with the reasonable goal of predicting which students were likely to encounter difficulties with standard school curricula. Over the years, psychologists have in fact been able to identify a set of "short-answer" items that predicts school performance with some success.

In the last eighty or so years, however, this line of thinking has burgeoned to an extent that is completely out of keeping with its legitimate scope. Where there was once a single instrument used for a circumscribed purpose, we now embrace hundreds of paper-and-pencil standardized tests that are used for a variety of purposes, from special education to college admission to "wall-chart" comparisons among nations. Where these tests were once introduced as embellishments to an ongoing curriculum, we now have schools and programs especially designed to improve performances on these instruments, with little attention to the meaning of such improvements in performance. It is not an exaggeration to say that we have let the testing tail wag the curricular dog. Nor is it an exaggeration to say that the IQ test has led the way inexorably to the current intoxication with the uniform school.

Paradoxically, at the very time when IQ-style thinking has made unprecedented inroads into thinking about educational programs, the slender scientific base on which it was erected has almost completely crumbled. From a number of disciplines interested in human cognition has come strong evidence that the mind is a multifaceted, multicomponent instrument, which cannot in any legitimate way be captured in a single paper and pencil–style instrument. As this point of view gains plausibility, the need to rethink educational goals and methods becomes profound.

The evidence that has challenged IQ-style thinking has come from the range of academic disciplines that probe the human mind. Neurobiologists have documented that the human nervous system is highly differentiated. Proceeding quite independently, research in artificial intelligence has moved steadily away from uniformist thinking. Two decades ago, computer scientists quested for general problem-solving mechanisms that could deal with the full range of intellectual domains, from scientific discovery to chess. However, recent advances have occurred almost entirely through the development of "expert systems," which contain highly detailed knowledge about specific domains, such as medical diagnosis, and which exhibit little or no "transfer" to other domains of knowledge.

And what of my own discipline of psychology? A generation ago most psychologists believed in general laws of learning, perception, memory, and attention that are applicable across diverse content; what was true of the college sophomore would be true for the Norwegian rat, as well as all other species in between. Behaviorist psychologists believed as well that the human mind could be adapted to deal with any kind of information in an equally skilled way. But with every year further evidence accumulates as to the deep constraints in the human mind. Certain patterns of growth are easy to achieve, while others are elusive; the basic cognitive processes at work in one area, say language, are quite distinct from those at work in other areas, such as spatial cognition or social understanding.

In an effort to make sense of these parallel trends across disparate disciplines, I undertook a major survey about a decade ago. As a result of this wide-ranging survey, I finally arrived at a list of several human intelligences (see chapters 1 and 2). All normal human beings have all of these potentials, but for both genetic and environmental reasons, individuals differ remarkably among themselves in the particular profiles of intelligence that they happen to exhibit at any given moment of their lives.

It turns out that cultures profit from these differences in intellectual proclivities found within their population. We are able to "staff" our numerous roles and niches more effectively because people exhibit different profiles of intelligence. Even within a particular profession like the law, one finds individuals with different blends of strength in such areas as language, logic, and interpersonal understanding. Now that the reasons that lead to these differences in skill and inclination have become clearer, a uniform approach to education makes even less sense than it did before.

My belief in the importance—indeed, the necessity—of individual-centered education derives from two separate but interlocking propositions. First of all, it has now been established quite convincingly that individuals have quite different minds from one another. Education ought to be so sculpted that it remains responsive to these differences. Instead of ignoring them, and pretending that all individuals have (or ought to have) the same kinds of minds, we should instead try to ensure that everyone receive an education that maximizes his or her own intellectual potential.

The second proposition is equally compelling. It may once have been true that a dedicated individual could master the world's extant knowledge or at least some significant part of it. So long as this was a tenable goal, it made some sense to offer a uniform curriculum. Now, however, no individual can master even a single body of knowledge completely, let alone the range of disciplines and competences. The period of the Renaissance Man or Woman is long past. Inasmuch as choices of emphasis and scope *must* be made, it becomes an issue only to choose which path an individual should follow. The theory of multiple intelligences ought not to be used to dictate a course of study or career, but it constitutes a reasonable basis on which to make suggestions and to choose electives.

Once we decide to move away from uniform schooling, we need models that take seriously individual profiles of intelligence and seek to maximize the educational achievements of each person. I have in recent years devoted thought to how such an individual-centered school might be designed; and I have become involved in a number of experimental investigations that should ultimately indicate which of these models have merit. A convenient way to sketch an individual-centered school is to delineate a set of roles that would be carried out within the school or school system.

A first role I have termed the *assessment specialist*. It is his or her task to provide a regular, updated view of the particular strengths, inclinations, and weaknesses of the children in the school. Such an assessment cannot be based primarily on standardized tests. According to my analysis, such instruments are inevitably biased in favor of two kinds of individuals: those with a particular blend of linguistic and logical intelligences; and those who can succeed with instruments that are administered in a neutral or decontextualized setting.

I believe that any new form of assessment needs to meet three criteria. It should be intelligence-fair—presented in such a way that the potency of an intelligence can be monitored directly and not through the "lens" of logic and mathematics. It should be developmentally appropriate—using techniques appropriate to the child's developmental level in the particular domain of knowledge at issue. It should be linked to recommendations—any score or description should be linked to recommended activities for a child with that particular intellectual profile.

To accomplish such assessment, and to update it regularly, is obviously a major undertaking. Successful deployment depends upon teachers who are sensitive to the dimensions being examined and who can make pertinent observations while students are engaged in meaningful activities and projects. There remains a place for more focused interventions, using standardized instruments, but these should never again be allowed to dominate assessment.

The assessment specialist shares findings and recommendations with students, parents, teachers, and the occupant of a second role called the *student-curriculum broker.* Based on a current view of the student's intellectual profile, this broker recommends which courses the student should elect; and, in the event of a uniform curriculum, recommends how these materials are most likely to be mastered by the student.

To the extent that there are electives, it is pertinent for students to know their own proclivities. This knowledge should not be used to dictate electives (in itself a contradiction in terms!). Rather, knowledge of one's own strengths can help one to choose courses that might be particularly congenial to one's learning style. In the case of a uniform or required curriculum, such information is equally important. For even if the courses themselves are mandated, there is no reason why they need to be taught in the same way to all.

In most areas of the curriculum, materials can be presented in a plethora of ways—by teachers or through books, software, hardware, or other media. The choice of mode of presentation can in many cases spell the differences between a successful and an unsuccessful educational experience. A history lesson can be presented through linguistic, logical, spatial, and/or personal modes of knowing, even as a geometry class can draw upon spatial, logical, linguistic, or numerical competences. Ofttimes some kind of cognitive prosthetic (for example, a computer program that allows one to create a variety of spatial configurations) can help a student to master material that is difficult for her to envisage in her own head. Now that we know something about teaching styles, learning styles, and individual intelligences, it is simply inexcusable to insist that all students learn the same thing in the same way.

A third role in the individual-centered school is called the *school-community broker.* Just as the student-curriculum broker attempts to intercede on the student's behalf within the school walls, the school-community broker searches for educational opportunities for the student within a wider community.

In my own view nothing is more important in a student's educational career than the encountering of a discipline or craft that fits a particular blend of intelligences—a pursuit worthy of a student's efforts for years or even a lifetime. Individuals of accomplishment often attribute enormous importance to "crystallizing experiences" where they first confronted a pursuit that fit their learning strengths and styles. All too often, these matches occurred completely by chance.

The goal of the school-community broker is to increase the likelihood that students will discover a vocational or avocational role that matches their own profile of intelligences. To accomplish this goal, the broker assembles information about apprenticeships, mentorships, community organizations, and the like; each of these learning opportunities should exemplify a particular blend of intelligences. This information is stored in some kind of a data base and made available to interested students and parents.

Of course, the information culled by the school-community broker could be drawn on by any student. In practice, however, it is particularly important for students who exhibit an unusual, nonscholastic profile of intelligences. After all, those students with a blend of linguistic and logical intelligences are likely to do well in school, to evolve a positive self-image, and thus to feel less need for special counseling and for pursuing out-of-the-ordinary opportunities. On the other hand, for those students with unusual intellectual configurations, the school-community broker can provide the perhaps life-changing opportunity to engage in an activity that matches a specific configuration of talents.

It should be stressed that none of these roles is designed in any way to minimize or circumvent the role of the individual teacher. Indeed, such roles should free teachers to focus on their chosen subject matter and to present it in a way that is most comfortable in light of their own intellectual strengths. I envisage a special role for master teachers who would make sure that the possibly idiosyncratic needs of individual students are being well served by the specialists and brokers who make educational recommendations.

In speaking of an individual-centered classroom or school, it is important to indicate what I do *not* mean. No connotation of egocentricism, self-centeredness, or narcissism is intended. Indeed, approaches involving cooperative learning are often at a premium in an individual-centered educational environment. What I do intend to stress is the importance of taking seriously each child's own proclivities, interests, and goals, and, to the maximum extent possible, helping the child to realize those potentials.

Were such an individual-centered education to be pursued, it should lead to a happy situation—one in which an increasing percentage of students find their métier, feel better about themselves, and are perhaps more likely to become positive members of their community. Where there is only one standard of competence, it is virtually inevitable that most students will end up feeling incompetent; and this is particularly true when that standard happens to favor a narrow band of intelligences. By openly embracing a wider range of end states, and seeking to match intellectual profiles with educational opportunities, the individual-centered school increases the likelihood that students will achieve their maximum intellectual potential. I am pleased that these ideas fit comfortably with the long-term American ideals of progressive education—a form of education that is nowadays much maligned but, when well practiced, is most consistent with societal values of pluralism, individuality, and cooperation for the greater good of all.

These, then, are three of the institutional roles or structures that I would like to see incorporated into a school of the future. But what might such a school look like? And how can one build school communities of this sort? Tina Blythe and I have sketched the dimensions of one such school.

The school we envision commits itself to fostering students' deep understanding in several core disciplines. It encourages students' use of that knowledge to solve the problems and complete the tasks that they may confront in the wider community. At the same time, the school seeks to encourage the unique blend of intelligences in each of its students, assessing their development regularly in intelligence-fair ways. To achieve these goals, the school draws inspiration from the educational successes of nonschool enterprises. Modeling the fresh and engaging approach of children's museums, the school creates an atmosphere in which students feel free to explore novel stimuli and unfamiliar situations. In the spirit of traditional apprenticeships, it promotes students' sustained and guided efforts on individual projects. Students and teachers collaborate in an environment that is at once unconstrained and purposeful.

Our school day reflects these ideals. In the morning, students study the traditional subject areas but in untraditional ways. Almost all the work in mathematics, social studies, reading and writing, and science takes the form of student projects. Students explore particular aspects of material in depth, addressing problems that confront professionals in the discipline. For instance, they might attempt to make sense of conflicting reports about a single historical event or to define a scientific problem and then informatively explore it by carrying out small-scale experiments (Gardner, 1989b).

Our Arts PROPEL collaboration (see chapter 9) provides a model for this kind of learning via projects. The domain projects developed for this study provide a rich series of exercises to help students focus on a particular aspect of an art form (composition in the visual arts, characterization in playwriting, rehearsal in music). Students work through these projects, keeping their drafts, revisions, final products, and observations in a portfolio (a better name might be "processfolio"). This documentation of the student's creative growth serves as a catalyst for her own reflections on herself as learner and fledgling artist. The student's work is assessed by examining the final product, her thinking informing it, and her plans for subsequent projects.

The second half of our school day is a natural extension of the first. During this time, students and teachers venture out into the community for further contextual exploring and learning. The younger children and their teachers often travel to a children's museum, a playground, or a special participatory demonstration at the local theater, symphony, or art museum. These excursions differ from typical field trips because classes return to the same spots many times over the course of the year. Students can continue projects begun in previous visits (perhaps working on a sculpture at the local art museum or continuing study on the life cycle of the crabs at the aquarium) or hone their skills in favorite activities (examining butterfly specimens at the children's museum or playing the timpani at the symphony demonstrations). Teachers prepare students for these experiences by planning related in-class projects and discussions, and debrief them afterward in parallel ways.

Such educational bridges could be constructed with programs like a current Project Spectrum initiative (see chapter 6), which seeks to create thematic ties between preschool curricula and museum exhibits through the use of kits. Organized around topics that intrigue young schoolchildren, these kits provide activities that can be used in school, museum, and home settings to stimulate a range of intelligences. The "Night and Day" kit, for example, includes a game board (featuring children's usual night and day activities), which facilitates exploration of number concepts. Books and related storyboards stimulate language skills, and "shadow games" encourage students' active investigation of the concepts of "light" and "dark."

Whether at the museum or our enriched school environment, children are allowed to explore freely and encouraged to ask questions. Teachers, aides, and other adults (including those who staff the field trip sites) jot down notes (or make mental ones to be written down later) about the children they are watching. Which students show interest or skill in particular activities or exhibits? What sorts of questions do students ask? What tasks do they have difficulty with?

Project Spectrum employs a similar in-school technique for compiling information about a student's intellectual proclivities. In a Spectrum classroom, students are provided with a variety of rich materials designed to stimulate particular intelligences. A treasure hunt game helps to develop children's abilities to make logical inferences. Assembly activities involving simple mechanical objects draw upon their fine motor skills. A storyboard composed of an ambiguous landscape and imaginative figures and objects (a king, a dragon, a jewel box) fosters children's skills in using descriptive language, dialogue, and narration. Over the year, teachers and observers make notes about the activities students gravitate toward and the progress they make in working with the materials. At the end of the year, parents receive a Spectrum Report: a short essay detailing the child's intellectual profile, along with suggested home or community activities that might foster growth in areas of particular strength or weakness.

These reports play a prominent role in the MI-based school. Teachers and parents observe how the child carries out tasks and projects in the classroom, on field trips, and at home and put their notes into the files the school's assessment team keeps on each child. Video documentation of the student's projects, activities, and personal observations and preferences is also a possibility—and is in fact being carried out at the Key School, an Indianapolis public school strongly influenced by MI theory (see chapter 7). A record of the student's own preferences completes the collection. When a student reaches third grade, he and his parents meet with a member of the assessment team to review the variety of strengths and preferences he has exhibited thus far. Together, they choose the three apprenticeships he will pursue within the school and community in the coming years.

Like the Key School, our school not only takes its students into the community but also brings the community to its students. Community members volunteer to share their expertise in some craft or occupation by working with a small group of students who have expressed interest in it. In addition, a "flow period" gives students time to play with games, activities, and ideas that appeal to them (while observers take note of their preferences and strengths). The important point here is that students can explore interests and abilities not necessarily tapped by the typical school curriculum.

In our school, older students carry on this intellectual exploration in a more structured way. While continuing to spend mornings carrying out the projects of the basic core curriculum, they devote their afternoons to the apprenticeships they chose as third graders. They study intensively with "master" teachers, members of the community who possess expertise in a particular area. Each student pursues an academic discipline, a physical activity, and an art or craft. Just as in the early years, when their school encompassed numerous exploratory opportunities in the wider community, now the workplaces and studios of their various masters become another richly contextualized extension of the classroom.

Adults in the community can participate in two ways. Some become masters; they devote time to working intimately with a young apprentice. Others, while not working directly with apprentices, provide ideas for particular projects that advanced apprentices can carry out with minimal guidance from their masters. Such projects might include designing and painting murals for particular buildings or businesses, developing a more efficient record-keeping system for the public library, or composing music for a school event. Each adult meets with a member of the school's community liaison team, which keeps names of potential masters and projects in the community/school opportunities bank. These are shared with the assessment team as it guides students in selecting their apprenticeships. In addition, the community liaison team monitors the progress of the apprenticeships and projects, intervening constructively if problems arise.

I am open to criticisms and reservations about individual-centered education. But there is one critique that I unequivocally reject. That is the claim that individual-centered education is utopian. As such a critique is customarily expressed, it is simply too expensive and unwieldy to try to construct education around the particular strengths and inclinations of individual children.

According to this view, even if there are some principled merits to the individual-centered approach, they must be set aside in favor of an approach that is cost-efficient, "competitive," or practical. And thus, on pragmatic if not scientific or value grounds, we must embrace a uniform approach to education.

To my mind, the real obstacles to individual-centered education are not financial constraints or knowledge limitations, but rather questions of will. So long as we choose to believe that the individual-centered approach is not valid, or, even if valid, simply not practical, it will appear utopian. If, however, we decide to embrace the goals and the methods of individual-centered education, I have no doubt that we can make significant progress in that direction.

Any vision, no matter how appealing, is of little value in the absence of a plan for achieving it. Most discussions of school reform have focused sharply on the learner or student, be she a young child in preschool or an adolescent bent on acquiring a new skill. It is clarifying to have such a focus and, indeed, efforts at reform are doomed to fail unless they keep their eye on the properties and potentials of the individual learner. Yet, after several years of active involvement in educational reform attempts, I am convinced that success depends upon the active integration of at least four factors.

Assessment. Unless one is able to assess the learning that takes place in different domains, and by different cognitive processes, even superior curricular innovations are destined to remain unutilized. In this country, assessment drives instruction. We must devise procedures and instruments that are "intelligence-fair" and that allow us to look directly at the kinds of learning in which we are interested.

Curriculum. Far too much of what is taught today is included primarily for historical reasons. Even teachers, not to mention students, often cannot explain why a certain topic needs to be covered in school. We need to reconfigure curricula so that they focus on skills, knowledge, and above all, understandings that are truly desirable in our country today. And we need to adapt those curricula as much as possible to the particular learning styles and strengths of students.

Teacher education and professional development. While most teacher education and professional development institutions make an honest effort to produce teaching candidates of high quality, these institutions have not been at the forefront of efforts at educational improvement. Too often they are weighted down by students of indifferent quality and by excessive—and often counterproductive—requirements that surround training and certification. We need to attract stronger individuals into teaching, improve conditions so that they will remain in teaching, and use our master teachers to help train the next generation of students and teachers.

Community participation. In the past, Americans have been content to place most educational burdens on the schools. This is no longer a viable option. The increasing cognitive demands of schooling, the severe problems in our society today, and the need for support of students which extends well beyond the nine-to-three period each day, all make it essential that other individuals and institutions contribute to the educational process. In addition to support from family members and other mentoring adults, such institutions as business, the professions, and especially museums need to be involved much more intimately in the educational process.

Many individuals have now entered into discussions of school reform; some are drawn from the domain of educational research, others from the practical world of classrooms. Too often, the gulf between educational theory and practice remains unchallenged. In the long run, there is nothing so practical as a good theory, but a theory without the opportunity for real-life implementation will soon fade away.

Too often, Americans have responded to educational needs only in times of crisis. This is an unacceptable approach. Education works effectively only when responsibility is assumed over the long run. We have made significant progress in this regard over the past decade. There is reason to be optimistic for students of the future, as dedicated individuals continue to collaborate in solving the challenging educational problems of our time.

The Two Rhetorics of School Reform: Complex Theories versus the Quick Fix

D espite the plethora of reports and articles about school reform during the past decade, there has been distressingly little genuine dialogue between the two principal participants in the discussion. On the one hand are the educational researchers and policy experts, who are pleased that at last the nation has become interested in the plight of its schools. On the other side are arrayed the government, business, and community "opinion leaders," who are equally concerned about the schools, but whose analyses and recommendations are decidedly different from those of the educational leaders.

Unless the reasons for the lack of communication can be identified and dealt with satisfactorily, it is most unlikely that the critical problems of American precollegiate education can be dealt with effectively.

Among educators, a surprising degree of consensus exists about the nature of schools' problems and the kinds of solutions that are likely (and unlikely) to work. They believe schools' difficulties arise from a variety of sources, including the sharp rise in the incidence of broken homes, the lessening of respect for parents' and teachers' authority, the huge amount of time youths spend passively watching television, and the alarming decline of the quality of life in our cities. Over the decades, such factors have greatly complicated the process of delivering quality education; they cannot be alleviated by a "quick fix."

Nearly all educators also acknowledge the failure of the entrenched factory model of education, in which students are all served the same curriculum in the same assembly-line fashion and teachers are cogs in a massive bureaucratic apparatus. A "constructivist" approach, which involves children in active, hands-on learning, is widely admired; most educators believe that "less is more" and that it is better to know a few things well than to add on courses and requirements ad nauseam.

Short-answer, multiple-choice tests stifle students' and teachers' initiative, they believe, and should be replaced by more probing, open-ended forms of assessment. Voucher programs allowing families to transfer government funds to the school of their choice may work in limited contexts, but they are unlikely to address the severe educational problems in our big cities. If anything, such programs are a diversion from the problem. Genuine educational changes will take several years, if not decades, to achieve.

Of course, there are disputes about each of these topics, and skeptics can be detected on the left and the right. But at the very least, none of the assertions above would be seen as particularly contentious by most of my fellow educators.

However, the "opinion leaders" in business, politics, and the general public—whatever they identify as the cause of educational problems—dearly desire a quick fix. And so they look to solutions like merit pay, voucher systems, the enunciation of higher standards, a voluntary or required national examination for all students. These leaders do not know if such solutions can be put into effect, but, examined from a distance, they sound as if they might do the trick. Because our educational institutions are seen as inefficient and undemanding, schools—rather than the larger society—are seen as causing the problems.

Punitive attitudes and language abound when the schools are being castigated. The "first wave" of educational reform in the early 1980s, calling for skills and standards, has been aptly (if cruelly) summarized as "getting the little buggers to work harder." The second, "restructuring wave" in the late 1980s reflected a business-influenced belief that if schools could simply manage themselves properly, all would work out.

Overall, little appreciation exists among outside critics of the complexity of the problems of school failure, little appreciation of the many steps needed to place American schools on a stronger footing. Again, there are admirable exceptions to the above characterization, particularly certain business leaders like David Kearns, formerly of Xerox and now deputy secretary of education under Lamar Alexander, and certain governors like Roy Romer of Colorado. But they turn out to be as atypical as educators who enthusiastically endorse vouchers or a national examination.

It may sound as though I, as an educator, have offered a stacked deck: a reasonable and penetrating analysis by school people, a peremptory and ill-advised set of nostrums doled out by those who are ignorant of the facts of school life and the obstacles to school reform. But I have little difficulty in sympathizing with the rhetorical picture sketched by opinion leaders: school folks endlessly spinning complex theories and refusing to make demands of their own ranks, in contrast to government and business representatives generously offering new resources and promising ideas in a laudable effort to improve American education.

Indeed, rhetoric becomes the issue here: a major stumbling block to school reform has been the construction and pursuit of rival rhetorics.

People who work in schools or who are familiar with current research are overwhelmed by the realities of American schools today. As Jonathan Kozol has shown in his new book *Savage inequalities*, many American schools are faced with a physical reality (crumbling facilities, drug- and crime-infested neighborhoods) and a cohort of youngsters (homeless, without love or hope) so dispossessed that they are more reminiscent of Dickensian London than of a developed nation on the cusp of the twenty-first century.

Educators are aware of pervasive institutional lethargy and of the fact that reform efforts are time consuming, involve a large investment of resources, and have a distressing tendency to backslide. Absent sustained application of human and financial resources over a significant period of time, efforts to change seem doomed. As a consequence, educators embrace a rhetoric of *woe and complexity*—one devoid of realistic first and second steps and remote from American-style pragmatism.

Opinion leaders know little of these deteriorating physical and social conditions firsthand and are disinclined to probe, because such probing thwarts the possibility of quick solutions. Of necessity or choice, they espouse an economic, political, or organizational model, rather than one rooted in the social realities of school, the psychological processes of learning, or the social psychology of group change.

Not surprisingly, then, they argue for—and believe in—the same "moves" that have worked in the political and business realms with which they are familiar: incentives for pay, changing the chain of command at the workplace, negative sanctions for poor performance, the adoption of standardized forms of evaluation. Opinion leaders propose "sound bite" solutions—a rhetoric of *culprits and quick cures*.

What, then, to do? I believe that it is imperative to create an effective new discourse of educational reform. Such a way of speaking must draw on analogies and stories that make sense to those who want to "do right" by American schools but who are not fully aware of the distressing range of problems that schools must overcome. So, for example, when it comes to assessment, educators need to make it clear that merely taking a temperature over and over again does not heal a patient and that a person who can only spit back facts cannot be expected to solve an unfamiliar problem or to create something new.

When it comes to site-based management, in which individual schools gain more autonomy, educators must point out that mere redistribution of money is of no help if the supply of money is too meager or if the teachers and administrators on-site have no experience in managing a complex facility or if they do not know how to achieve consensus on goals and means of reaching them.

No single comparison, metaphor, or argument can work for a phenomenon as complex as the school. That said, I believe that the most appropriate model for talking about school change is the idea of *building a new community*. Many educators today are adopting the metaphor of a community to distinguish schools from older organizational models—for example, those based on factories and industrial organizations—in which administrators imposed the agenda from the top down. They point out that in a community, everyone has a voice.

For a community to be viable, its members must work together over time to develop reasonable goals and standards, work out the means for achieving such goals, have mechanisms to check whether progress is being made, and develop methods for changing course—sometimes dramatically—if progress is not being achieved. In a viable community, members recognize their differences and strive to be tolerant, while learning to talk constructively with one another and perennially searching for common ground.

If school reform is to progress, educators and opinion leaders must adopt a common vision—and a common metaphor or way of speaking—of the sort that I have sketched. Were such a vision to be adopted, it would represent a considerable stretch for both parties in the current debate. Educators would need to recognize the genuine differences about ideology and the learning process within their ranks but temper those differences for the sake of establishing a cooperative atmosphere. They would also have to commit themselves to the difficult tasks of setting and maintaining locally relevant standards and altering strategies and personnel when progress is not being achieved.

Opinion leaders, for their part, would need to acknowledge that the various aspects of school reform are interconnected; that changes require time, leadership, and guidance; and that the atmosphere of schools is affected by that of their localities and the nation. Far from representing sentimental rhetoric, a commitment to community reveals a recognition of the hard realities required for effectiveness in today's world.

In fact, the most effective current efforts in school reform have attempted to delineate some of the processes involved in creating such communities. These include identifying key staff members willing to dedicate themselves to a long-term process of change, discovering strengths and weaknesses, involving students and parents throughout the planning and evaluation process, cooperating with other schools involved in similar reform efforts, and developing advisers who can draw on their own experiences to aid in the bumpy process of community building and school change. Such promising experiments make it possible for all parties interested in school reform to move beyond rhetoric and to become actively involved in building more effective environments for learning.

But so long as the rhetorics about school reform remain widely divergent, little progress is likely. An important, if not decisive, step will have been taken when educational experts and opinion leaders come to speak of—and think about—school reform in terms of the same images. Then perhaps they can forge solutions superior to those that either group could develop on its own.

Chapter 6

The Emergence and Nurturance of Multiple Intelligences in Early Childhood: The Project Spectrum Approach

Coauthored by Mara Krechevsky

Standardized tests were invented, in part, as one way to identify unusual talents, and they are certainly capable of revealing scholastic prodigies. But consider the individuals who do not perform well on such assessments. How can we assess their strengths, and what would it mean to do so?

Jacob is a four-year-old boy who was asked to participate in two forms of assessment at the start of the school year: the Stanford-Binet Intelligence Scale (4th ed.) and a new approach to assessment called Project Spectrum. Jacob refused to be tested on the Stanford-Binet. Three subtests were attempted and partially completed, after which Jacob ran out of the testing room, left the building, and climbed a tree. On the Spectrum battery, which includes fifteen different tasks spanning a wide range of domains, Jacob participated in most of the activities, and demonstrated outstanding strength in the areas of visual arts and numbers. He revealed a consuming love of different materials, and worked with every possible medium in the art area. On other activities, even when he resisted engaging in the task at hand, he always expressed interest in the materials out of which the games were made, for example, the small figures on a storytelling board, the metal of the bells for the music activity, and so on. This passion for the physicality of materials extended to almost every area: his exploration of the discovery or natural science area focused at one point on an examination of bones and how they fit together, and led to a remarkably accurate sculpture of a bone fashioned from clay.

Of all the activities in the Spectrum battery, Jacob was least interested in movement and music. At first, he also resisted participating in a numbers task embedded in a bus game. However, when he at last became engaged, he seemed to take special delight in figuring out the correct number of people boarding and leaving the bus. Tapping Jacob's understanding of numbers in a context that was meaningful and familiar to him seemed to help elicit abilities that might otherwise have remained hidden.

The above comparison suggests that while the Spectrum and Stanford-Binet assessments can reveal similar qualities, there are distinct advantages to an assessment conducted over time with rich materials in the child's own environment. The example of Jacob indicates four ways in which the Spectrum assessment system might benefit children. First, Spectrum engages children through games that are meaningful and contextualized. Second, Spectrum blurs the line between curriculum and assessment, thereby integrating assessment more effectively into the regular educational program. Third, the Spectrum approach to assessment makes the measures "intelligence-fair" by using instruments that look directly at the intelligence in operation, instead of through a linguistic or logical-mathematical lens. Fourth, Spectrum suggests how a child's strength may provide access to more forbidding areas (areas in which the child shows less promise).

In this chapter, we consider the possibility that children's exceptional talents can be identified at an early age and that the profile of abilities exhibited by preschoolers can be clearly distinguished from one another. We also consider some of the educational implications of an approach that focuses on the early identification of areas of strength and weakness. After a brief introduction to the theoretical background and framework of the Spectrum approach to assessment, we discuss some of the research findings and offer some preliminary conclusions.

Recently a number of researchers working in the cognitive and neural sciences have offered new support for a pluralistic view of cognition, suggesting that the mind is organized into relatively discrete realms of functioning (Ceci, 1990; Feldman, 1980; Fodor, 1983; Gardner, 1983; Keil, 1984, 1986). I, for example, define intelligence as the ability to solve problems or fashion products that are valued in one or more cultural settings. In my theory of multiple intelligences (hereinafter referred to as MI theory), I propose that all normal individuals are capable of at least seven relatively autonomous forms of intellectual accomplishment (see chapters 1 and 2).

Each intelligence is based, at least initially, on a biological potential, which then gets expressed as a result of the interplay of genetic and environmental factors. Although one may view an intelligence in isolation in exceptional individuals such as idiots savants, in general, individuals exhibit a blend of several intelligences. Indeed, after early infancy, intelligences are never encountered in pure form. Rather, they are embedded in various symbol systems, such as spoken language and picturing systems; notational systems, like maps and musical or mathematical notation; and fields of knowledge, such as journalism and mechanical engineering. Thus, education at any point in time represents the cultivation of intelligences as they have come to be represented over time in a variety of culturally fashioned systems.

These intelligences are best thought of as biopsychological constructs: they constitute cognitive resources by virtue of which an individual may effect a meaningful connection to a content area. However, to round out this perspective of intelligences as they are espoused in any culture, we need to consider two additional components as well: the epistemological perspective of the domain and the social perspective of the field. The structure of a domain of knowledge represents the organization of a particular area of study or competence at a given historical moment. These domains undergo reorganization at different points in time, as, for example, the advent of jazz or the twelve-tone system in music. A field, on the other hand, includes the range of roles (composers, performers, critics) and institutions (conservatories, orchestras, professional competitions) that make up the culturally defined realms in which learning and performance necessarily take place.

Nearly all cultural roles and tasks in any domain or field require a combination or blend of intelligences. For example, becoming a successful concert violinist requires not only a high degree of musical intelligence, but both bodily-kinesthetic dexterity and the interpersonal skills of relating to an audience and, in a different way, of choosing a manager. To become an architect requires skills in spatial, logical-mathematical, bodily-kinesthetic, and interpersonal intelligences in varying degrees. If Jacob goes on to become a sculptor, he will probably need to draw on spatial, bodily-kinesthetic and interpersonal intelligences.

The Spectrum Approach to Assessment

O nce these intelligences have been identified, the question arises of how to assess them in an ecologically valid way. In the following pages, we describe Project Spectrum, an innovative attempt to measure the profile of intelligences and working styles of young children. Spectrum is a long-term, collaborative research project undertaken by several researchers at Harvard Project Zero with our colleague, David Feldman at Tufts University (see Feldman & Gardner, 1989; Malkus et al., 1988; and Ramos-Ford et al., 1988). Spectrum begins with the assumption that every child has the potential to develop strength in one or several areas. The project's focus on preschool children has both a scientific and a practical thrust. On the scientific side, we address the question of how early individual differences can be reliably detected, and the predictive value of such early identification (see also, Lewis, 1976). On the practical side, parents and teachers are likely to benefit most from information about their children's cognitive competences during this time when the young child's brain is especially plastic, when schools are likely to be more flexible and where a free-choice component is typically built into most curricula.

Although Spectrum started out with a search for the early indices of the seven intelligences, it soon became apparent that many more competences warranted examination. To be sure, we identified a number of core capacities in each intelligence; but rather than attempting to look at intelligences in pure form, we looked at the domains of accomplishment of the culture through those forms taken up by children (Feldman, 1986). For example, we address both production and perception in music; both invented and descriptive narrative in language; and expressive and athletic movement in the bodily-kinesthetic realm. We also used the notion of adult end states to help us focus on those skills and abilities that are relevant to achieving significant and rewarding adult roles in our society, rather than just focusing on skills that are useful in the school context. Thus, instead of looking at logical-mathematical skills in the abstract, we examine competences that may culminate in scientific inventiveness; instead of examining competence at repeating a series of sentences, we look at the child's ability to tell a story or provide a descriptive account of an experience.

In order to capture fully a child's approach to a task, we found it important to look at cognitive or working styles as well as sheer intellectual capacities. Working styles describe the way a child interacts with the materials of a content area, such as ability to plan an activity and to reflect on a task, and level of persistence. While some individuals exhibit working styles that determine their approach to any task, no matter what the content area, others have styles that are much more domain-specific. Such information may be particularly important for fashioning an effective educational intervention for a child. At the present time, we address fifteen areas of cognitive ability and eighteen stylistic features (see tables 6.1 and 6.2).

Implementation of the Spectrum Approach

How does Spectrum work in practice? In a Spectrum classroom, children are surrounded each day by rich and engaging materials that evoke the use of a range of intelligences. We do not attempt to stimulate intelligences directly using materials that are labeled "spatial" or "logical-mathematical." Rather, we employ materials that embody valued societal roles or end states, drawing on relevant combinations of intelligences. So, for example, there is a naturalist's corner, where various biological specimens are brought in for students to examine and to compare with other materials; this area draws on sensory capacities as well as logical analytic power. There is a story-telling area, where students create imaginative tales using an evocative set of props and where they have the opportunity to design their own storyboards; this area evokes linguistic, dramatic, and imaginative facility. There is a building corner, where students can construct a model of their classroom and manipulate small-scale photographs of the students and teachers in the room; this area draws on spatial, bodily, and personal intelligences. Numerous other intelligences, and combinations of intelligences, are tapped in the remaining dozen areas and activities in a Spectrum classroom.

It is highly desirable for children to observe competent adults or older peers at work—or at play—in these areas. Provided with the opportunity for such observation, youngsters readily come to appreciate the reasons for the materials as well as the nature of the skills that equip a master to interact with them in a meaningful way. It is not always feasible to provide such an apprentice-master setting, however, and so learning centers have been constructed in which children can develop some facility from regular interactions with these materials even by themselves or with only other novice-level peers. In this sense, our entry-level environment is a self-sustaining one that harbors potential for cognitive and personal growth.

Over the course of a year or more spent in this nourishing environment, children have ample opportunity to explore the various learning areas, each featuring its respective materials and its unique set of elicited skills and intelligences. Reflecting the resourcefulness and curiosity of the mind of the five-year-old, most children readily explore the majority

TABLE 6.1.
Areas of Cognitive Ability Examined in Project Spectrum

NUMBERS

Dinosaur Game: designed as a measure of a child's understanding of number concepts, counting skills, ability to adhere to rules, and use of strategy.

Bus Game: assesses a child's ability to create a useful notation system, perform mental calculations, and organize number information for one or more variables.

SCIENCE

Assembly Activity: designed to measure a child's mechanical ability. Successful completion of the activity depends on fine-motor skills and visual-spatial, observational, and problem-solving abilities.

Treasure Hunt Game: assesses a child's ability to make logical inferences. The child is asked to organize information to discover the rule governing the placement of various treasures.

Water Activity: used to assess a child's ability to generate hypotheses based on observations and to conduct simple experiments.

Discovery Area: includes year-round activities that elicit a child's observations, appreciation, and understanding of natural phenomena.

MUSIC

Music Production Activity: designed to assess a child's ability to maintain accurate pitch and rhythm while singing, and to recall a song's musical properties.

Music Perception Activity: assesses a child's ability to discriminate pitch. The activity consists of song recognition, error recognition, and pitch discrimination.

LANGUAGE

Storyboard Activity: measures a range of language skills including complexity of vocabulary and sentence structure, use of connectors, use of descriptive language and dialogue, and ability to pursue a story line.

Reporting Activity: assesses a child's ability to describe an event with regard to the following criteria: ability to report content accurately, level of detail, sentence structure, and vocabulary.

VISUAL ARTS

Art Portfolios: reviewed twice a year, and assessed on criteria that include use of lines and shapes, color, space, detail, and representation and design. Children also participate in three structured drawing activities. The drawings are assessed on criteria similar to those used in the portfolio assessment.

MOVEMENT

Creative Movement: the ongoing movement curriculum focuses on children's abilities in five areas of dance and creative movement: sensitivity to rhythm, expressiveness, body control, generation of movement ideas, and responsiveness to music.

Athletic Movement: an obstacle course focuses on the types of skills found in many
   different sports, such as coordination, timing, balance, and power.

SOCIAL

Classroom Model: assesses a child's ability to observe and analyze social events and
   experiences in the classroom.

Peer Interaction Checklist: a behavioral checklist is used to assess the behaviors in which
   children engage when interacting with peers. Different patterns of behavior yield
   distinctive social roles such as facilitator and leader.

of these areas, and children who do not cast their nets widely are
encouraged to try out alternative materials or approaches. For the most
part the teacher can readily observe a child's interests and talents over
the course of the year, and no special assessments are needed. For each
domain or craft, however, we have also devised specific games or
activities that allow a more precise determination of the child's intelligences in that area.

At the end of the year, the information gathered about each child is
summarized by the research team in a brief essay called a Spectrum
Report. This document describes the child's personal profile of strengths
and weaknesses and offers specific recommendations about what might
be done at home, in school, or in the wider community to build on
strengths as well as to bolster areas of relative weakness. Such informal
recommendations are important. In our view, psychologists have traditionally been far too concerned with norming or ranking; comparable
efforts throughout the school years should help individual students and
their families make informed decisions about their future course, based
upon a survey of their capacities and options.

What of the actual measures that we devised? In order not to con-
found competences, we tried as much as possible not to rely exclusively on logical and linguistic measures; instead we used measures
that were "intelligence-fair" (Gardner, 1991). We also tried to avoid
hypothetical situations and abstract formulations. Instead, we provided
children with something concrete to manipulate no matter which domain was being assessed. For example, the aforementioned classroom
model provides children with small figures of their peers and teachers,
offering a tangible structure within which to consider children's knowledge of friends, social roles, and classroom dynamics. The music perception task provides children with Montessori bells with which they
can play a pitch matching game.

As table 6.1 indicates, Spectrum measures range from relatively structured and targeted tasks (for example, in the number and music domains) to relatively unstructured measures and natural observations (in the science and social domains). These measures are implemented throughout the course of a year—one part of a classroom is equipped with engaging materials, games, puzzles, and learning areas. Documentation takes a variety of forms, from score sheets and observation checklists to portfolios and tape-recordings. Although most teachers will not find it practical to administer formally all fifteen measures to each child, we have used such a procedure for research purposes.

In addition to drawing up a Spectrum Report, we have also prepared a Parent Activities Manual with suggestions for activities in the different domains addressed by Spectrum. Most of the activities use readily accessible and affordable materials; however, a cautionary note to parents is added regarding premature streaming or fasttracking of a child: the idea is not to make each child a prodigy in the area of greatest strength. Rather, Project Spectrum stresses the notion that every child is unique: parents and teachers deserve to have a description faithful to the child, as well as suggestions for the kinds of experiences appropriate to the child's particular configuration of strengths and weaknesses.

PRELIMINARY RESULTS

Having provided a general overview of the Spectrum assessment model, we now turn to a discussion of the results of our research to date. Because Project Spectrum is still under development, the following comparisons should be regarded as preliminary and suggestive, rather than definitive. Given the limited scope of our sample population, we are not prepared to draw general conclusions about four-year-old children. The major part of the analysis centers on the 1987–88 sample on whom more complete data were gathered. However, we do report on the 1986–87 sample wherever it seems instructive to do so.

AREAS OF STRENGTH

The analyses presented in this section are based on data collected during the 1986–87 and 1987–88 school years. We were primarily interested in the following questions:

1. Do young children have domain-specific as well as more general strengths?
2. Is there any correlation between performances in different activities?
3. Does a child's strength in one domain facilitate or hinder performance in other domains?

We now report on each question in turn.

1. The Spectrum battery was administered in two preschool classrooms at the Eliot-Pearson Children's School at Tufts University in Medford, Massachusetts. The 1986–87 class consisted of nineteen children between the ages of three and four, drawn chiefly from a relatively homogeneous, white, middle- and upper-income population. Except where otherwise noted, we restrict the present discussion to our population of four-year-olds. (Although three-year-old children yielded distinctive intellectual profiles as well, we decided to limit the 1986–87 sample to the thirteen four-year-olds in the class, given that it was the age for which most of our activities were developed.) Ages of the subjects in the 1986–87 class ranged from forty-eight to fifty-nine months at the start of the school year; the mean age was fifty-two months. Eight of the fifteen Spectrum activities were included in the analysis (the remaining activities did not yet have complete scoring systems).

The 1987–88 class was comprised of twenty children, also drawn primarily from a white, middle- and upper-income population. The children ranged in age from forty-two to fifty-eight months at the beginning of the school year; the mean age was fifty-three months. Ten of the fifteen Spectrum activities were included in this part of the analysis.

In each of the two samples, we looked at a child's strengths and weaknesses, both in relation to the group and to the self. Children who scored one standard deviation or more above the mean on the Spectrum measures were considered to have a strength in a domain, while children who scored one standard deviation or more below the mean were considered to demonstrate a weakness. The majority of the children in the 1986–87 class revealed a strength in at least one domain (ten out of thirteen children), and a weakness in at least one domain (nine out of thirteen). Four children exhibited one or more strengths across Spectrum activities and no weaknesses, and three children exhibited no strengths and one or more weaknesses. Finally, every child exhibited at least one strength and one weakness relative to him or herself.

In the 1987–88 sample, fifteen of the twenty children demonstrated a strength in at least one domain, and twelve children demonstrated a weakness in one or more domains. Seven children in the sample revealed strengths in one or more areas and no weaknesses, and four children demonstrated a weakness in one or more areas and no strengths. One child was also identified as having no strengths or weaknesses. (Her scores ranged from -0.985 to $+0.87$ standard deviations from the mean, with an average of -0.03.)

The results from the two samples are strikingly similar. For the majority of children, strengths and/or weaknesses were identified in relation to the group, and in all cases, areas of relative strength and weakness were identified for each child.

2. In order to determine the degree of correlation between performances on the different activities, we created a matrix of correlations between pairs of the ten activities used with the 1987–88 sample. The results indicated that there was very little correlation between the activities, reinforcing the notion that the Spectrum measures identify a range of nonoverlapping capabilities in different content areas. Only one pair was significant at the $p < 0.01$ level: the two number activities, the Dinosaur Game and the Bus Game ($r = 0.78$). In contrast, the two music and the two science activities included in the sample were not significantly correlated ($r = -0.07$ and $r = 0.08$, respectively).

3. There was also some evidence that a child's strength in one area might facilitate performance in another. For example, one child exhibited a keen sensitivity to color, and demonstrated both interest and ability in the area of visual arts. While playing the treasure hunt game, which focuses on logical inference skills, this child's attentiveness to colors seemed to help her identify the rule governing the placement of treasures under color-coded flags. Another child, who was identified as having a strength in music production (singing), found it easier in the creative movement sessions to synchronize his movements to the underlying rhythm of a piece of music if he sang while he moved. His musical talents also characterized his performance on the invented narrative task: he created both a theme song and a death march for the characters in his story.

A third child, who exhibited outstanding ability in story-telling, yet remained motionless in the creative movement sessions, moved with uncharacteristic expressiveness when storyboard props were used as a catalyst in one of the exercises. She also transformed tasks in visual arts, social analysis, and mathematics into occasions for further story-telling (see Renninger, 1988, on the effect of children's interests on their attention and memory for tasks and types of play). Her drawings in art often served to illustrate accompanying narratives. Her mother reported that she often made puppets and dolls at home, modeling them on characters from the books she was "reading." She also used the classroom model as a reality-based storyboard, creating vignettes with the figures of her classmates. On the bus game, however, she became so involved in the motivations for the different figures boarding and leaving the bus, that she was distracted from recording the correct numerical information.

It seems that strength in an area can also interfere with one's performance. One child exhibited outstanding strength in visual arts, demonstrating an unusual sensitivity to line, color, and composition. However, his sensitivity to visual cues led him to misinterpret directional signs when using dice that had a + and − on their sides. He interpreted the crossing lines (+) to mean that the player could move in two directions, while the single horizontal line (−) meant that the player could proceed in only one direction.

TABLE 6.2.
Stylistic Features Examined in Project Spectrum

The child is:

---

easily engaged/reluctant to engage in activity
confident/tentative
playful/serious
focused/distractible
persistent/frustrated by task
reflects on own work/impulsive
apt to work slowly/apt to work quickly

The child:

---

responds to visual (auditory, kinesthetic) cues
demonstrates methodical approach
brings personal agenda (strength) to task
finds humor in content area
uses materials in unexpected ways
shows pride in accomplishment
shows attention to detail (is observant)
is curious about materials
shows concern over "correct" answer
focuses on interaction with adult
transforms task (material)

WORKING STYLES

As noted earlier, in addition to recording a child's performance, we also recorded "working style" or the way in which each activity was approached (see table 6.2). We were primarily interested in the following two issues:

1. Do children utilize distinctive working styles when solving problems from different domains? (And if so, what is the nature of the differences in a child's areas of strength and weakness?)
2. Are some working styles more effective than others in particular domains?

We now answer each of these questions.

1. With regard to the first issue, it seemed that for the majority of children, while one or two working styles usually obtained across domains, other working styles depended more on the content of the area being explored. Approximately three-quarters of the children in the sample exhibited general working styles that, in specific instances, combined with one or two others to yield domain-specific configurations. For example, one girl displayed attention to detail only on the classroom model activity, her one area of strength, and was impulsive only in the music perception activity, her area of weakness. Another child was easily engaged and confident, even in areas of weakness, as long as the task involved a performance aspect.

Not surprisingly, performances in an area of strength were typically characterized by "easy to engage," "confident," and "focused" working styles. In contrast, weak performances were characterized by "distractible," "impulsive," and "reluctant to engage" working styles. "Playfulness" characterized both strengths and weaknesses. Also, a number of children showed reflectiveness and attention to detail in their area of strength. Three of the five children who exhibited no strengths relative to their peers never reflected on their own work, and eight children only reflected on their work in areas of strength.

Five of the children demonstrated working styles that were highly domain-specific. One child found it very difficult to remain focused on most of the Spectrum and classroom activities. However, when she was presented with the materials for the assembly activity, she worked in a focused and persistent manner until she had completely taken apart and reassembled the objects. This result gave the teacher valuable information about how she might use this child's strength to engage her in focused work in the classroom. Also Jacob, the boy described in the introduction, exhibited confidence, attention to detail, seriousness, planning skills, and reflectiveness *only* in the visual arts and numbers domains—his areas of strength.

2. Some of the children who exhibited a consistent working style were clearly helped by their content-neutral style, whereas others were probably hindered by it. One child worked in a serious and focused manner across domains, which helped him to complete activities in which he experienced difficulty as well as those where he exhibited competence. Every child exhibited confidence in at least one activity, and one girl, who revealed no strengths relative to her peers, nonetheless demonstrated "pride in accomplishment" on more tasks than any other child, perhaps indicating a resilience that augurs well for her scholastic prospects. Ironically, it may be that too general a confidence inhibits successful performance across tasks. The child who was identified as having the most weaknesses of any child (five) and no strengths relative to her peers, never showed any tentativeness, whereas all but three of the rest were tentative in their approach at least once.

One child brought his own program of ideas to every Spectrum activity. Although his ideas were often compelling, his unwillingness to attend to the task caused him to perform poorly on many of the activities. On the music perception activity, for example, he was most interested in how the metal bells, which looked exactly the same, could produce different sounds. To explore this phenomenon, he examined the differences in their vibrations after hitting them with his mallet. He also invented new rules for the dinosaur game, and tried to fashion tools out of the parts of the two food grinders in the assembly activity. Because he was so interested in exploring his own ideas, he often resisted exploring the ideas of others. When he experienced difficulty with an activity, he would become frustrated and turn to his sense of humor to distract the adult from the task at hand.

It also appeared that the structure of the tasks (or sometimes their lack of structure) served to inhibit the performances of some children. In the less structured environment of the classroom, the boy just described demonstrated great experimental ability, and constantly formulated and tested hypotheses to find out more about the world around him. Jacob was another child who required very little structure, so immersed in the materials did he become. Unfortunately, his intense focus on materials to the exclusion of other people—whether child or adult—is likely to present problems for his future scholastic performance.

A Comparison of Views: Parents, Teachers, and Spectrum

While it seemed clear that the Spectrum measures identified domain-specific strengths in the children, it also seemed important to determine whether we were uncovering abilities hitherto unrecognized by teachers and parents. To address this question, we asked parents and teachers of the 1987–88 class to fill out a questionnaire indicating the level of ability shown by each child in a number of different areas. We also sent response forms to parents to solicit their reactions to the Spectrum profiles.

Seventeen of the twenty sets of parents returned a completed questionnaire. In general, parents were quite generous in identifying their child as demonstrating outstanding ability in an area. The average number of areas checked by parents for their child was eight out of thirty. On the other hand, the teachers rarely scored a child as exhibiting outstanding ability in any area, averaging one out of thirty. This discrepancy between parent and teacher ratings may reflect the broader frame of reference available to teachers who see each child in the context of his or her peer group. While parents may understandably be biased, they also have fewer opportunities to view the strengths of a large number of children. These factors should be kept in mind in the following comparison. A child was considered to have an outstanding strength by Spectrum only if the score in a given domain of activity was at least one standard deviation above the mean.

The comparison revealed that Spectrum identified outstanding strengths that had not otherwise been identified in eight of the seventeen children. In all, Spectrum identified twelve strengths that had not been identified by *either* parent *or* teacher. The domains of strength included science, visual arts, music, and social understanding. Also, seven children were identified as exhibiting outstanding strengths by parents and teachers, but not by Spectrum. In most of these cases, although Spectrum identified relative strengths, they were not considered outstanding in relation to the group. For a number of other children, strengths scoring close to, but less than, one standard deviation above the mean were identified by Spectrum, but not by parents or teachers. Finally, parents, teachers, and Spectrum identified the same areas of outstanding ability in nine of the seventeen children in the comparison.

It appears that some areas, like language and numbers, can be relatively easily identified regardless of whether the child is at home or at school, but other areas are not so easily noticed, like music perception, mechanical skills, or social analysis. In fact, Spectrum never identified language or numbers as outstanding strengths, where they were not already identified by parent or teacher. However, even in a commonly recognized area of ability like language, Spectrum provides a breakdown of the area into component skills (vocabulary, sentence structure, use of descriptive language, and so on) employed in the service of a meaningful endeavor (story-telling).

Of course, many competent preschool teachers simply cannot provide experiences in all areas, especially those with which they may be relatively unfamiliar, like music perception and logical inference tasks. The assembly activity, in particular, helps to break down gender preconceptions by providing girls with the same opportunity as boys to reveal a strength and become engaged in an area traditionally considered masculine. The profile response forms also revealed that the areas where parents were most surprised to learn of strengths included music perception, mechanical ability, and creative movement. Because the information in the profiles is generated from contextualized tasks, it may be easier for parents to translate it into meaningful follow-up activities.

A Comparison of Spectrum Results with Stanford-Binet Intelligence Scale

A professional diagnostician administered the Stanford-Binet Intelligence Scale (4th ed.) to nineteen of the twenty children in the 1987–88 Spectrum class. Two of the nineteen children did not complete the measure, and are therefore not included in the analysis. The results from this sample, while useful for providing a very general sense of how the two measures compare, should be read with the following caveats in mind.

First, Spectrum addresses seven domains of ability through fifteen activities, ten of which are included in the analysis, whereas the Stanford-Binet focuses on four areas or factors (verbal reasoning, abstract/

visual reasoning, quantitative reasoning, and short-term memory) through eight subtests. Second, the battery of Spectrum activities is administered in a series over the course of a year, whereas the Stanford-Binet is administered in a one- to two-hour session. Finally, the Stanford-Binet is a standardized measure and Spectrum is not. Thus, the findings presented in the following comparison should be considered tentative.

The seventeen children in the sample who completed the Stanford-Binet assessment scored in the low-average to very superior range, with composite scores ranging from 86 to 133. The average score was 113. As with the preceding analysis, a child was considered to demonstrate a strength and/or weakness on a Spectrum activity only if he or she scored one or more standard deviations above or below the mean of the group.

To determine whether Stanford-Binet composite scores were predictive of performance on some or all Spectrum activities, we ranked the composite scores of the children to see how the top five children (with composite scores from 125 to 133) and the bottom five children (with scores from 86 to 105—the low-average to average range) performed on the Spectrum battery. Of the five children earning the highest Stanford-Binet composite scores, one child demonstrated a strength on three of the ten Spectrum activities in the analysis, three displayed strengths in two of the activities, and one child exhibited one strength. The areas Spectrum identified as strengths for these children are as follows: two in narrative language; four in music perception and production; two in the visual arts; one in social understanding; and one in science (logical inference).

The movement, numbers, and mechanical component of the science domains were not identified as strengths for any of the children and, in fact, movement and numbers were identified as areas of weakness for two of them. Moreover, only one of the three children who displayed three or more strengths on the Spectrum measures was among the top five scorers on the Stanford-Binet. One of the top three Spectrum scorers was also the top scorer on the combined Spectrum mathematics activities.

It seems that the Stanford-Binet Intelligence Scale did not predict successful performance either across or on a consistent subset of Spectrum activities. The one qualification is the possibility of a connection between the Stanford-Binet composite scores and performance on the Spectrum music tasks. Four of the five strengths in music identified by the Spectrum measures were displayed by the children receiving the highest Stanford-Binet composite scores. However, in general, no correlation was found between Stanford-Binet subscores and the individual Spectrum activities. Of course, without a much larger sample, no firm conclusions can be drawn.

The Stanford-Binet also did not seem to predict lack of success across Spectrum tasks, although it did identify three of the lowest-scoring children (children with no strengths and zero to five weaknesses). Of the five children with the lowest Stanford-Binet composite scores, one child exhibited one strength (social understanding) and one weakness (music perception), and another exhibited no weaknesses and three strengths (mechanical ability, language, and music perception). The remaining three children displayed no strengths on the Spectrum activities, and between zero and five weaknesses.

The child who received the lowest composite score in the group (eighty-six) was also identified by the Spectrum battery as the lowest-scoring child across tasks: she exhibited no strengths and five weaknesses on the Spectrum activities (two more weaknesses than any other child). However, Spectrum did identify two relative strengths displayed by this child in the domains of social understanding and creative movement. The Stanford-Binet subtests also revealed some scatter (the verbal reasoning skills and memory for sentences subscores were in the fifty-third and forty-ninth percentiles, respectively, while bead memory and pattern analysis scores fell in the thirty-ninth and fortieth percentiles).

These data suggest that although the Stanford-Binet Intelligence Scale does yield a range of factor scores and subtest variability within factors, the Spectrum measures produced more jagged profiles. Part of this difference can be attributed to the number of domains addressed by each measure: eight tasks in four content areas for Stanford-Binet versus fifteen tasks (ten in the current analysis) in seven areas for Spectrum. But Spectrum does more than simply expand the areas addressed by the Stanford-Binet. All of the Stanford-Binet subtests can be considered either good or fair measures of g, the general intelligence factor (see Sattler, 1988, for a full discussion). Spectrum, however, does not postulate g as a general intelligence factor that is present in a wide range of mental abilities, and that accounts for children's performances in different content areas. Rather, the Spectrum model suggests that the jagged profiles represent domain-specific abilities, which reflect real world problem-solving in the context of meaningful activities: for example, analysis of one's own social environment, assembling a mechanical object, telling a story, et cetera. The information gained from the Spectrum inventory may therefore be potentially more useful in designing appropriate educational interventions for children.

A Preliminary Look at Follow-up Data from the Class of 1986–87

A preliminary look at longitudinal data collected on seventeen of the nineteen children in the 1986–87 class (including five three-year-olds) suggests that strengths and working styles in the Spectrum cohort remained constant, at least during a one- to two-year follow-up period. Follow-up information on the children in the 1986–87 group was gathered from interviews with parents and teachers, and second-year participation in a Spectrum classroom. Of the nineteen children in the 1986–87 sample, six remained in a Spectrum-related classroom at the Eliot-Pearson Children's School the following year, six were in a non-Spectrum kindergarten class at Eliot-Pearson, and seven attended other kindergarten programs.

Five of the children participated in an expanded set of the year-long activities for a second time in the 1987-88 Spectrum class. Four of the five children demonstrated strengths consistent with those identified by Spectrum the previous year, with one child exhibiting an additional strength in the language domain. The fifth child, who had not exhibited any strengths during the first year, was identified as having a relative strength in experimental science (through the newly added water activity).

The working styles for the five children remained relatively consistent over the one- to two-year follow-up period. One child, who seemed serious and focused on many of the tasks in his first year, only became more so during year two, continuing to show great concern with task demands. Another girl took the same uncharacteristically forward-thinking, focused, and reflective approach to the assembly activity that she had exhibited during the first year, in contrast to her more distractible style on other tasks.

For the remaining twelve children in the sample, information in the Spectrum profile was compared to information obtained through interviews with parents and/or teachers. Eleven of the twelve children were identified by their parents or teachers as having abilities consistent with those identified by Spectrum in the first year. One girl, who had demonstrated a strength in logical inference, continued to be fascinated with things logical: she made up her own rules for backgammon and other games, and reportedly derived great satisfaction from trying to figure out how different relatives were related to her. At a subsequent two-year follow-up conducted on seven of the eleven children (through teacher and parent questionnaires and checklists), the majority of strengths remained unchanged. (One girl, who identified "snack" as the activity she enjoyed the most during Year One of Spectrum, reported to her mother that one of the activities she did best two years later was "eating lunch.")

Of note for the social domain, two teachers considered their students' social skills to be areas where they exhibited least ability, although both Spectrum and parents had identified the areas as strengths. The definition of social ability provided to teachers was "knowledge of one's own and others' abilities, interests, likes, dislikes, and feelings." In the teachers' descriptions of the two girls, it was clear that the girls exhibited such knowledge; however they put it to inappropriate use. One was a quite successful and subtle manipulator of others, as well as an effective leader in her group; while the other, also an effective leader, often attempted to control those around her. Unlike other domains, the social realm seems to be an area where ability does not always take on a neutral cast. One's judgment is influenced by concern for how such ability is used.

The twelve children also exhibited relatively consistent working styles from year to year. The children who were serious, focused, and forward thinking across tasks remained so. Likewise, the more impulsive and stubborn children remained the same. Again, this consistency was also true for the seven children in the two-year follow-up. Sometimes, the particular configuration of a child's working style and areas of strength determined whether or not a strength would resurface. For example, one girl who "liked to shine," according to her teacher, was not the most able in her group at the writing table or book area. Consequently, she frequented the art and construction areas where she would be more likely to stand out. Given the context of her relative standing within the group, there was less chance that her previously identified ability in language would re-emerge and develop during the year.

Furthermore, if a child's interests did not match his or her strengths, or if an individual chose to focus on the same set of materials or to explore new skill areas, opportunities to observe ability in other domains would be correspondingly reduced. One girl who had demonstrated both interest and ability in art while in the Spectrum classroom, in kindergarten became much more interested in learning how to read and avoided the art area. On the other hand, a child who had been an outstanding storyteller was very reluctant to start writing, and experienced difficulty both with his fine-motor coordination and sound-letter connections. At the two-year follow-up, he was reported still to love listening to stories and performing in class plays. It should also be noted that written language may well involve a different set of skills from spoken language (Olson, 1977).

Responses from parents in the sample revealed that the area that they seemed to have encouraged most at the one-year follow-up was drama. This activity seems to have been considered an effective way to combine ability in the story-telling and social domains with the performance aspect of the movement domain. Music perception and production was another area where many parents were surprised and pleased to discover the enjoyment their child showed in the domain. Music appeared to be an area that enriched a child's life, regardless of level of ability. A number of parents also spoke of the usefulness of having a written document to which they could refer and compare more recent views of their child.

Thus, a number of factors and conditions seem to work in concert to determine whether a strength will ultimately resurface and have a chance to develop in a given year: the range of areas provided and emphasized in the classroom; family knowledge and interest in an area; the child's own fluctuating interests (which depend on the areas to which he or she is exposed as well as the context of the child's peer group); and the nature of the domain at the particular point in the child's development.

Some Limitations and Long-term Implications of Project Spectrum

At this point, it may be worthwhile to raise explicitly several issues that are likely to be on the reader's mind. Clearly, the current study has limitations. Because of the small sample that received the Spectrum battery, the study should be regarded as generating hypotheses rather than as conclusive in any sense.

However, we can identify some of the potential benefits of Spectrum in comparison with other assessment approaches, such as the Stanford-Binet. First, Spectrum provides an opportunity to involve children more actively in the assessment, giving them a chance to reflect on their experience and their own sense of their interests and strengths. Children also become actively involved in helping to collect and document their work in the Spectrum model: saving their work for the art portfolios, taping stories and songs, and bringing in items for the discovery or natural science area. Such involvement conveys to children the sense that their products are being taken seriously, and includes them in the process of monitoring their own growth.

For children who are unusually sensitive about performance issues, Spectrum may have information to offer that a one-session, decontextualized, heavily verbal measure does not (Gardner, 1991). For example, as part of the intrapersonal component of the social analytic activity, children are shown pictures of the different Spectrum activities and asked which activities they consider their favorite, their best, and the hardest. One boy who had remained unengaged in either Spectrum activities or the Stanford-Binet subtests (the Stanford-Binet testing had to be discontinued because of his great anxiety about his performance), showed a surprising degree of interest in answering questions about his reactions to the different activities. He seemed to have an accurate sense about his areas of relative interest and strength. He identified the storyboard as his best activity and, indeed, it was the only one of the eight tasks he completed where his score was above the group mean. He selected the water activity as his favorite, and although he was reluctant to try out his ideas for sinking and floating experiments during the task, he became so excited about a discovery he made at one point, that he called his teacher over to the area in an uncharacteristic display of enthusiasm.

Of course, the Stanford-Binet Intelligence Scale has advantages as well. It is a standardized measure, with excellent internal consistency and high reliability. The measure is easily and efficiently administered, and the areas examined map readily on to the standard school curriculum. While we do not yet know whether a Spectrum assessment can predict scholastic success with the reliability of standardized forms of assessment, the Spectrum measures do identify distinctive areas of strength with immediate implications for further avenues to explore, both inside and outside school. The Spectrum battery also allows teachers and parents to perceive individual differences in areas traditionally considered important only with regard to passage through universal stages of development (Feldman, 1980) or as a reflection of general intelligence.

However, the Spectrum approach contains its own risks. The danger of premature streaming of children must be weighed against the benefits of giving every child a chance to do well. There is also the potential for achievement-oriented parents to push their children to excel not just in the traditional academic areas, but in all seven domains, increasing an already powerful pressure on children to achieve. Moreover, families outside the mainstream culture may quite properly be less concerned with performance in domains like visual arts and music, and more concerned with those areas that continue to be valued most by those in power—language and logic.

Clearly, family environment determines in part both the use and the usefulness of the information contained in the Spectrum profile. As one parent reported, because the family members were either not interested in music, or were simply non-musical, her child's musical capabilities might never have surfaced without Spectrum, or even if they had, they would not have been recognized as talent. This result can be contrasted with the case of a mother who considered music to be an important part of her son's life and greatly encouraged his interest in it. At the one-year follow-up, she reported that he loved watching musical and operatic performances, and would sit through them attentively, without talking or moving. While no one really knows the exact relationship between early talents and later achievements, the identification of strengths early on may become a self-fulfilling prophecy.

Could a Spectrum perspective lead to a reasonable curriculum for the primary years? Our data suggest the potential influence of the structure of the environment on the particular qualities that can be discerned in children. They emphasize the importance of continuing to provide a rich set of stimulating materials across diverse curricular areas. Creative movement and mechanical skills cannot be recognized in a kindergarten that does not offer these areas in the curriculum. Also, starting in first grade, many children are taught subjects like art, music, movement, and science by specialists once or twice a week. Unless these specialists communicate with the classroom teachers, the latter may be unaware of a child's abilities in a particular area. At a minimum, teachers may find it easier to be good teachers in the Spectrum framework, both in terms of documenting their observations and individualizing their curriculum.

The emphasis on end states may also provide a more direct link between identification of a strength and a decision on what to do once it has been identified. An apprenticeship model emerges as a particularly attractive alternative educational approach. Once an end state has been defined, the possibility arises for staking out an educational regimen towards its realization. Apprenticeships embed the learning of skills in a social and functional context, with well-defined stages of mastery. In our view, the apprenticeship model, where students receive frequent and informal feedback on their progress in highly contextualized settings, holds much promise educationally. Thus, in the case of a child like Jacob, we would recommend that if he continues to exhibit interest in his chosen domain, he could well benefit from the guidance of an expert in a variety of rich, hands-on learning situations.

Finally, although Spectrum reflects in part a value system of pluralism associated with the middle class, it may also have something to offer children from a less privileged background. The Spectrum assessment system has the potential for revealing unsuspected areas of strength and bringing about enhanced self-esteem, particularly for those children who do not excel in the standard school curriculum.

Extensions of the Project Spectrum Approach

Until this point, we have been focusing on the original Project Spectrum, which was developed for use in a middle-class American preschool setting. Both the tasks described and the data analyzed reflect this history and this particular milieu.

The question naturally arises about the extent to which Spectrum could be extended to other settings. Our first effort to do this involved the utilization of Spectrum in several preschool, kindergarten, and first-grade classes in Somerville, Massachusetts, a working-class suburb of Boston with a high incidence of social and economic problems. Allaying our doubts about transportability, Spectrum materials were found most attractive by the children, who looked forward eagerly to their time in a Spectrum environment. Indeed, it turned out to be parents and teachers who had concerns about Spectrum, either because they feared that the students would not be comfortable with such open-ended tasks, or because they themselves had a different, far more regulated view of what school should be like.

In such a setting Spectrum has shown particular power in identifying talents and inclinations that are typically missed in the regular school. Donnie (as I'll call him) was a six-year-old who was highly at risk for school failure. The product of a broken home with more than its share of violence and substance abuse, he was having such difficulty in the tasks of first grade that by the second month, his teacher had reluctantly concluded he would have to be retained.

In Project Spectrum, however, Donnie excelled at the assembly tasks. He had greater success in taking apart and putting together common objects, like a food grinder and a doorknob, than any other student his age. (Indeed, most teachers and researchers failed to match Donnie's skilled and seemingly effortless achievements in these mechanical tasks.) We videotaped Donnie's impressive performance and showed it to his teacher. A thoughtful and dedicated person, she was overwhelmed. She had difficulty believing that this youngster, who experienced such trouble with school-related tasks, could do as well as many adults on this real-world endeavor. She told me afterwards that she could not sleep for three nights; she was distraught by her premature dismissal of Donnie and correspondingly eager to find ways to reach him. I am happy to report that Donnie subsequently improved in his school performances, possibly because he had seen that there were areas in which he could excel and that he possessed abilities that were esteemed by older people.

In addition to identifying unexpected strengths in young students, Spectrum can also locate surprising difficulties. Gregory was an excellent student in first grade, apparently destined for a bright scholastic future; he displayed skill in the acquisition of notational and conceptual knowledge. He performed poorly, however, across a number of Spectrum areas. His teacher felt that Gregory was able to perform well only in situations where there is a correct answer and where a person in authority had somehow indicated to him what that answer is. The Spectrum materials posed problems for Gregory because many of the activities are open-ended and do not harbor any evident correct answers; he was thus frustrated and looked to the teacher or to other students for clues about what he should do. As a result of his participation in Spectrum, Gregory's teacher began to look for ways to encourage him to take risks, to try things out in new ways, to acknowledge that there are not always correct answers, and to appreciate that any response entails certain advantages as well as certain costs.

Over the last several years, Spectrum has evolved from a means of assessing strengths to a rounded educational environment. In collaboration with classroom teachers, we have developed curricular materials in the form of theme-related kits that draw on the range of intelligences as they may figure in the development of a broad theme such as "Night and Day" or "About Me." With younger children, these curricula are used primarily in an exploratory mode. With older children, they are tied more closely to the traditional goals of school, promoting preliteracy or literacy attitudes, approaches, and skills. Thus children encounter the basics of reading, writing, and calculating in the context of themes and materials in which they have demonstrated interest and an emerging expertise. As they gain proficiency in a board game, for example, children can be introduced to numerical tally systems, and as they create adventures at the storyboard, they can begin to write them down as well as recite or dramatize them.

The adaptability of Spectrum has proved to be one of its most exciting features. Teachers and researchers from several regions of the country have used Spectrum as a point of departure for a variety of educational ends. The Spectrum approach has been adapted with children ranging in age from four to eight, for purposes of diagnosis, classification, or teaching. It has been used with average students, gifted students, handicapped students, and students at risk for school failure, in programs designed for research, for compensatory purposes, and for enrichment. Just recently it has been made the center of a mentoring program, in which young children have the opportunity to work with adults from their neighborhood who exemplify different combinations of intelligences in their jobs. One of my delights as a researcher-turned-implementer has been to sit in on discussions among people who have never met each other but who have adapted Spectrum to their varied needs. It seems clear from such conversations that the Spectrum school-museum blend is appropriate for young children of very different interests, backgrounds, and ages.

In our own work we have made explicit the ties to the children's museum. Working with the Boston Children's Museum, we have transformed our theme-based kits so that they can be used at home and in the museum as well as at school. The home and school furnish regular stimulation, while the museum provides the opportunity to encounter a related display in an awe-inspiring setting, such as the moon and the stars viewed in a planetarium. It is our hope that encountering a similar cluster of themes, materials, and skills in disparate settings will help children to make this cluster their own; we speak of a "resonance" among these milieus that ultimately leads to the child's internalization of important understandings.

Naturally this kind of cross-fertilization works best when children have the opportunity to visit the museum regularly. Thus we are excited by the installation directly in the Washington, D.C., Capital Children's Museum of a Spectrum-inspired Model Early Learning Preschool Classroom—an ambitious melding of school and museum. But even when visits are less frequent, a well-prepared class of students can profit from the opportunity to interact with skilled professionals at a children's museum, particularly if they then have the opportunity to revisit related experiences and lessons on a more leisurely basis at home or at school.

In a number of respects, Project Spectrum epitomizes the way in which the theory of multiple intelligence has been able to catalyze the creation of effective educational interventions—in this case, with young children. Beginning with a scholarly interest in the existence and identification of talents in very young children, we have seen Spectrum evolve naturally over a decade into a full-scale approach to early education. This approach has been inspired by aspects of MI theory, but in no way has MI theory dictated the exact contents or the precise steps in the implementation of Spectrum. Indeed, our program has itself altered considerably over the decade, in response to our own observations, feedback from parents, teachers, researchers, and students, and the changing conditions within which we have attempted to implement the approach. Add to that the very different uses made of Spectrum ideas by researchers and practitioners in different parts of the country, and one encounters a family, indeed a "spectrum" of variations of Project Spectrum. It is fitting that a program rooted in the celebration of individual differences among young children should itself generate a family of highly individualized approaches.

Chapter 7

The Elementary Years:
The Project Approach in
the Key School Setting

About two years after *Frames of mind* was published, I was scheduled to give a talk near my place of birth in Scranton, Pennsylvania. Shortly before my voyage to northeastern Pennsylvania, I received a phone call from a teacher in Indianapolis, who said that she and some of her fellow teachers had read *Frames of mind* and wanted to speak with me about some of the ideas expressed therein. Was I available for a meeting in Kutztown?

Unbeknownst to me, a group of eight teachers from the Indianapolis Public Schools drove for fourteen hours in order to have a relatively brief meeting with me in Kutztown. At that prophetic meeting they showed me a videotape that they had recently completed, and indicated to me that they were interested in starting their own K–6 elementary school, inspired in part by the ideas of MI theory. I was as surprised as I was delighted.

While I was becoming increasingly interested in educational applications of the theory, it had never dawned on me that someone might take these ideas so seriously as actually to plan a school based upon them. I told the "Indianapolis 8" quite frankly that I would be happy to help them but that I knew little about schools. "You are the school people," I insisted, and "it will have to be your school."

Few groups of teachers can have worked harder than did the "Indianapolis 8" over the next two years. Under the guidance of the energetic and visionary Patricia Bolanos, who eventually became the principal, they raised funds, lobbied, planned curricula, and after many moments of suspense and some disappointments, were eventually allowed to have their own inner-city public "options" school in downtown Indianapolis (Olson, 1988; Winn, 1990). While I deserve no credit for launching this project, I have met regularly with the teachers to talk with them about what they are doing; and in the way of these things, I have been given excessive credit in the popular media for having inspired the Key School.

Now in its sixth year, the Key School has in many ways proved to be a remarkable success. One of its founding principles is the conviction that each child should have his or her multiple intelligences ("MI") stimulated each day. Thus, every student at the Key School participates on a regular basis in the activities of computing, music, and "bodily-kinesthetics," in addition to theme-centered curricula that embody the standard literacies and subject matter.

While an "MI curriculum" is its most overtly innovative aspect, many other facets of the school also suggest an education that strives toward diverse forms of understanding. Three practices are pivotal. First, each student participates each day in an apprenticeshiplike "pod," where he works with peers of different ages and a competent teacher to master a craft or discipline of interest. Because the pod includes a range of ages, students have the opportunity to enter into an activity at their own level of expertise and to develop at a comfortable pace. Working alongside a more knowledgeable person, they also have what may be a rare opportunity of seeing an expert engage in productive work. There are a dozen pods, in a variety of areas ranging from architecture to gardening, from cooking to "making money." Because the focus of the pod falls on the acquisition of a real-world skill in an apprenticeship kind of environment, the chances of securing genuine understandings are enhanced.

Complementing the pods are strong ties to the wider community. Once a week, an outside specialist visits the school and demonstrates an occupation or craft to all the students. Often the specialist is a parent, and typically the topic fits into the school theme at that time. (For example, if the current theme is protection of the environment, visitors might talk about sewage disposal, forestry, or the political process of lobbying.) The hope is that students not only will learn about the range of activities that exist in the wider community but in some cases will have the opportunity to follow up a given area, possibly under the guidance of the visiting mentor. One way of achieving this end is through participation in a Center for Exploration at the local Indianapolis Children's Museum; students can enter into an apprenticeship of several months, in which they can engage in such sustained activities as animation, shipbuilding, journalism, or monitoring the weather.

The final, and to my mind most important, avenue for growth at the Key School involves student projects. During any given year, the school features three different themes, introduced at approximately ten-week intervals. The themes can be quite broad (such as "Patterns" or "Connections") or more focused ("The Renaissance—Then and Now" or "Mexican Heritage"). Curricula focus on these themes; desired literacies and concepts are, whenever possible, introduced as natural adjuncts to an exploration of the theme.

As part of school requirements, each student is asked to carry out a project related to the theme. Thus students execute three new projects each year. These projects are placed on display at the conclusion of the theme period, so that students have an opportunity to examine what everyone else in the school has done (and they are very interested in doing so!). Students present their projects to their classmates, describing the project's genesis, purpose, problems, and future implications; they then answer questions raised by classmates and by the teacher.

Of special importance is the fact that all project presentations are videotaped. Each student thus accumulates a video portfolio in which his succession of projects has been saved. The portfolio may be considered as an evolving cognitive model of the student's development over the course of his life in the Key School. Our research collaboration with the Key School has centered on the uses that might be made of these video portfolios.

In the course of their careers in the American schools of today, most students take hundreds, if not thousands, of tests. They develop skill to a highly calibrated degree in an exercise that will essentially become useless immediately after their last day in school. In contrast, when one examines life outside of school, projects emerge as pervasive. Some projects are assigned to the individual, some are carried out strictly at the individual's initiative, but most projects represent an amalgam of personal and communal needs and ends. Although schools have sponsored projects for many years and the progressive era featured an educational approach called the "project method," such involvement in projects over the years has been virtually invisible in records of a child's progress.

Here our research team has sought to make a contribution. We believe that projects are more likely to be taken seriously by students, teachers, parents, and the wider community if they can be assessed in a reasonable and convenient way. We have therefore sought to construct straightforward ways of evaluating the developmental sophistication as well as the individualized characteristics of student projects. At present we are viewing projects (and student portfolios) in terms of the following five separate dimensions that can be assessed (see Seidel & Walters, 1991):

Individual profile. At issue here is what the project reveals about the specific cognitive strengths, weaknesses, and proclivities of the student. The profile includes the student's disposition toward work (taking risks, persevering) as well as the student's particular intellectual propensities (linguistic, logical, spatial, interpersonal, and the like).

Mastery of facts, skills, and concepts. Projects can be quite marvelous to behold and yet remote from what is being taught in school or even directly at odds with it. When invoking this dimension, one is able to look at the student's capacity to showcase her command of factual knowledge, mastery of concepts, and skills in deploying the standard curriculum. Customarily a bargain is struck between student and teacher: the teacher can ask the students to draw on school knowledge and understanding in creating a project; the student has the opportunity to select from her schoolwork those facts, skills, and concepts she wants to include in a project.

Quality of work. Each project is an instance of a certain genre—a comic play, a mural, a science experiment, a historical narrative. These genres harbor within them certain specific criteria of quality that can be invoked in their evaluation—skits are not assessed in the same way as lectures. Among the aspects of quality that are customarily examined are innovation and imagination; aesthetic judgment and technique; the development of a project in order to foreground a particular concept; the execution of a performance. As a student continues to create in a genre, she gains greater familiarity with the criteria of that genre and learns increasingly to think *in* that domain.

Communication. Projects offer an opportunity for students to communicate with a wider audience; with peers in collaborative efforts; with teachers and other adults; and with themselves. Sometimes the communication is quite overt, as in a theatrical or musical performance; but even in a more "desktop" science or history project, the student needs to communicate his findings skillfully, and that process proves to be distinct from the work of conducting the experiment or the library research.

Reflection. One of the most important, but most neglected, features of intellectual growth is the capacity to step back from one's work, to monitor one's goals, to assess what progress has been made, to evaluate how the course can be corrected, how to make use of knowledge that has been obtained in the classroom or from others, and the like. Projects provide an excellent occasion for such "metacognitive" or reflective activity. Teachers and students can review work together, ponder how it relates to past work, conceive of it in terms of longer-term goals, working styles, and so on. Equally important, the student can come to internalize these reflective practices, so that he is able to evaluate his work even in the absence of outside agents.

It should be stressed that there is nothing magical or final about these dimensions. They reflect a distillation of much discussion in our group and can be expected to evolve further in the years ahead. Despite our belief that these dimensions constitute a powerful set of lenses for the examination of student work, we do not believe that it is efficacious simply to impose them on a school or a school system. Rather, we believe that a consideration of such dimensions will arise naturally, as teachers (and students) learn to look at work together and begin to think about its distinctive qualities and its evolution over time.

Still, there is a distinct place for a research team in such an effort. As researchers, we can be of help in presenting teachers with rich examples for discussion and in helping to guide the discussion in what appears to be fruitful ways—for example, helping to avoid terminological dead ends or the confounding of dimensions. In the end, we believe that groups of teachers who are engaged in serious evaluation of student efforts will eventually come up with an ensemble of dimensions much like the one that I've just described. In that sense, the five dimensions can serve as a kind of "super-matrix"—what we have humorously dubbed "the mother of all scoring systems." Should this be the case, it will be possible for schools to compare the works of students with one another—a very desirable outcome if such scoring systems are to achieve a more enduring stature in American assessment.

Naturally, part of the evaluation of student projects focuses on the quality of the projects. But we are also interested in two other facets. One is the extent to which the project reveals something about the student herself—her own particular strengths, limitations, idiosyncracies, and overall cognitive profile. The other is the extent to which the project involves cooperation with other students, teachers, and outside experts as well as the judicious use of other kinds of resources, such as libraries or computer data bases.

Students are not graded up or down if projects are more individualistic or more cooperative. Rather we describe projects in this way because we feel that these features represent important aspects of any kind of project in which a person will ever participate, aspects that should be noted rather than ignored. In particular, in working with others, students become sensitive to the varying ways in which a project can be conceived and pursued; moreover, in reflecting upon their own particular styles and contributions, students receive a preview of the kinds of project activities in which they are most likely to become involved following completion of school.

The other form our involvement has taken concerns the preparation of projects. Somewhat naively, researchers and teachers originally thought that students could readily create and present projects on their own. In the absence of help, however, most projects either are executed by parents or, if done by children, are pale imitations of projects already carried out before or observed elsewhere. Particularly common are book reports or television-style presentations in front of displays resembling weather maps. If students are to conceptualize, carry out, and present their projects effectively, they need to be guided—"scaffolded" is the term of choice—in the various phases and aspects of this activity.

Far from undermining the challenge of making one's own projects, such support actually makes participation in projects possible and growth in project-execution abilities likely. Just as students benefit from apprenticeships in literacy or in a craft, discipline, or pod, so too they benefit from an apprenticeship in the formulation and execution of projects. Some students are fortunate enough to have had this apprenticeship at home or in some community activity, such as organized sports or music lessons. But for the vast majority who have not had such opportunities, elementary school is the most likely place where they can be apprenticed in a "project" way of life—unless they happen to go to graduate school fifteen years later!

The course of project construction gives rise to opportunities for new understanding. A project provides an opportunity for students to marshal previously mastered concepts and skills in the service of a new goal or enterprise. The knowledge of how to draw on such earlier forms of representation or understanding to meet a new challenge is a vital acquisition. Planning the project, taking stock along the way, rehearsing it, assembling it in at least tentatively final form, answering questions about it, and viewing the tape critically should all help to enhance the student's understanding of the topic of her project, as well as her own contributions to its realization.

These features of the Key School point up some aspects of effective education during the period of middle childhood. To an immersion in a richly furnished environment one now adds a more or less formal apprenticeship; skills are acquired in a domain-appropriate form, and the purposes and uses of these skills remain vivid in the consciousness of the apprentice. At the same time disciplines are encountered not in an isolated form that provides little motivation but rather as part of a continuing involvement in encompassing themes that reverberate throughout the curriculum of the school. The student's emerging knowledge and skills are mobilized in the course of executing a project of her own devising, which has meaning for herself, for her family, and within the wider community. Such skills and projects are assessed as much as possible within the context of daily school activities, the assessment involving not only the teacher but also peers and, increasingly, the student herself. The student comes to view the project from a variety of perspectives, as it speaks to a variety of audiences and as she observes it evolving, often in unpredictable ways, over the course of time.

It would be a mistake to consider projects as a panacea for all education ills, or as the royal road to a nirvana of knowledge. Some materials need to be taught in more disciplined, rote, or algorithmic ways. Some projects can become a license for fooling around, while others may function as a way of hiding fundamental deficiencies in the understanding of vital disciplinary content. At their best, however, projects can serve a number of purposes particularly well. They engage students over a significant period of time, spurring them to produce drafts, revise their work, and reflect upon it; they foster positive cooperativeness, in which each student can make a distinctive contribution; they model the kind of useful work that is carried out after the completion of school, in the wider community; they allow students to discover their areas of strength and to put their best feet forward; they engender a feeling of deep involvement or "flow," substituting intrinsic for extrinsic motivation (Csikszentmihalyi, 1990); and, perhaps most importantly, they offer a proper venue in which to demonstrate the kinds of understandings that have (or have not) been achieved in the course of the regular school curriculum.

Though the Project Method has a lengthy history within American educational circles, I am not alone among my contemporaries in being in debt to the Key School for clarifying these possibilities during the present moment.

Chapter 8

Approaching School Intelligently: Practical Intelligence at the Middle School Level

Coauthored by Mara Krechevsky

Educational interventions grounded in theory exhibit a distinctly different flavor from those that grow out of practice. Consider, for example, the difference between Boole's *Laws of thought* (1854) and Edwards's *Drawing on the right side of the brain* (1979). Boole's volume was designed to help people think; yet, it reflects the aesthetics of the logician rather than the kinds of practical problems that the ordinary rational (or irrational) person must confront in daily life. Edwards's book offers a promissory note that one may invoke a typically underutilized set of brain structures in becoming a better artist. But the appeal of the book inheres in its set of exercises, which are quite effective in helping nascent drawers observe and depict their subjects in a representationally faithful fashion.

The distance between a textbook on human memory and the "method of memory" devised by Simonides in the Classical era may seem slimmer, but the difference in accent is parallel. The theorist whose work is summarized in the text is trying to flesh out the basic laws of memory. These principles should explain the slavish recall of nonsense syllables as well as reconstruction of the gist of a story. Simonides, in contrast, wanted simply a method that could help him to recall the identities of a large number of guests gathered around a table at a fateful dinner.

Reverberations of these tensions are found today in the flood of materials being devised to improve thinking skills. On the one hand, nearly every psychologist or cognitive scientist who has ever uttered the word "thinking" has at least asked him- or herself whether he or she might have something useful to contribute to the current intellectual malaise in American schools. On the other hand, a large number of current teachers, former teachers, and other "practitioners" have drawn on *their* lore. They too hope to popularize methods that will improve the thinking processes and/or the thought-filled products of school children. While each of these "interest groups" is comfortably rooted in its own history, there is a certain hankering for the other perspective. Scientific theorists wish that their methods could be instantly transferred to the untidy and unpredictable classroom, while practitioners search for the generative power of an appropriate theoretical base for their techniques.

As members of the research community, we presumably suffer from the same limitations of experience and perspective. The particular slant that we have taken on issues of thinking grows out of the theory of multiple intelligences, on which we have been working for the last decade. Yet, it is a cardinal principle of this theory that thinking does not and cannot occur apart from interaction with real materials in a living context. At the same time, we would argue, an approach to thinking that aspires to have an effect in the schools must reflect the perceived needs of the students for help in various scholastic tasks and the reality of conditions inside ordinary schools, where twenty-five or thirty students inhabit the same room with the same teacher for several hours a day. In what follows, as we put forth the theoretical rationale for our approach to thinking, we seek to bear in mind these important contextual factors.

A New Conception of Intelligence

Traditionally, intelligence has been considered a general ability found in varying degrees in all individuals and especially critical for successful performance in school. Since the time of Plato, this unitary view of the mind has been a dominant influence in Western thought. In recent years, however, an alternative view has been put forth, which suggests that the mind is organized into relatively independent realms of functioning (Feldman, 1980, 1986; Fodor, 1983; Gardner, 1983). The theory of multiple intelligences (hereafter, MI theory), discussed in detail in *Frames of mind* (Gardner, 1983), represents one such pluralistic approach to the notion of intelligence (see chapters 1 and 2).

Intelligences are always negotiated within the context of the current array of fields and disciplines represented in the schools and society at large. Although based initially on a biological potential, intelligences are inevitably expressed as a result of intersecting genetic and environmental factors. They do not ordinarily function in isolation, except in certain exceptional populations, such as idiots savants. Each culture emphasizes a different set of intelligences and combination of intelligences. These intelligences are embedded (or perhaps embodied) in the employment of the various symbol systems, notational systems, such as musical or mathematical notation, and fields of knowledge, for example, graphic design or nuclear physics (Csikszentmihalyi & Robinson, 1986).

In most Western cultures, the task of learning the notational systems is carried out in the relatively decontextualized setting of schools. Many students cannot connect their more commonsense knowledge to cognate concepts presented in a school context. To take one well-known example, when a group of students was presented the problem of how many buses would be required to transport 1,128 soldiers if each bus held thirty-six soldiers, most replied "thirty-one, remainder twelve." These students correctly applied the appropriate arithmetic operation, but without regard for the meaning of their answer (Schoenfeld, 1988; Strauss, 1982).

Although school knowledge is often dissociated from real-world contexts, it is in rich, situation-specific contexts that intelligences are typically and productively deployed. The kind of knowledge required in workplaces and in one's personal life usually involves collaborative, contextualized, and situation-specific thinking (Gardner, 1990; Resnick, 1987; Rogoff & Lave, 1984). Schools do provide some group activities, but students are usually judged on their individual work. By contrast, in many social and occupational settings, one's ability to communicate effectively and work productively with others is critical to a successful outcome. Furthermore, whereas school learning often features the manipulation of abstract symbols and the execution of "pure thought" activities, most of the thinking required outside of school is tied to a specific task or goal, whether it be running a business, calculating a batting average, or planning a vacation. In these situations, intrapersonal intelligence—or the ability to recognize which skills are required, and to capitalize on one's strengths and compensate for one's limitations—may be especially important.

Of course, the institution of school itself is a complex one for children to negotiate. School features its own disciplines, codes, notations, and expectations that, for better or worse, are critical to survival in the West.

Children who find it difficult to "decode" school are likely to be at risk for future problems, in or outside of school. While a great deal of research has focused on the "academic" intelligences of language and logic and on the other main academic disciplines, less effort has been devoted to what it takes to survive and thrive in the environment of school more generally. Because school plays such a central role in our culture, it is important to examine those intelligences and skills needed for students to survive and flourish in the system.

The Practical Intelligence for School (PIFS)
Project

As one turns one's attention to a specific setting like school, the question arises of how best to aid students in adjusting to and mastering that environment. In our view, a comprehensive effort to enhance a student's "school intelligences" must address at least several factors. For example, such an effort has to address conditions particular to that environment, ranging from the physical setup of classes to the demands of particular disciplines. It also has to consider the particular skills that students initially bring to the tasks and the general environment of school, as well as the optimal pedagogical means for helping students to enhance or alter their current skills and attitudes, so that they are more appropriate for the demands of the school context. Finally, the production of a set of measures that can indicate the way in which a prescribed intervention achieves (or fails to achieve) its effect is also needed. In all probability, no single current theoretical framework is adequate to incorporate all of these factors, though important components of such an account can be found in the works of Bruner et al. (1966), Scribner & Cole (1973), and Wagner & Stevenson (1982).

Two recent approaches have a dual concern with the development of intelligence in general and practical survival in specific contexts such as school. The first, Sternberg's (1985, 1988) triarchic theory of intelligence, defines intelligence in terms of: (1) the internal world of the individual (the information-processing components of metacognitive, performance, and knowledge-acquisition components); (2) the external world of the individual (the individual's ability to adapt to and shape existing environments, or select new ones); and (3) the experience of the individual in the world (how the individual copes with novelty and automatizes information processing). As already noted, the second approach—MI theory—stresses the importance of skills being used in specific cultural contexts. In addition, particular intelligences are keyed to particular school subject matters; for example, English and history stress linguistic intelligence, whereas math and science draw on logical-mathematical intelligence. Adaptation to the social environment of school calls upon interpersonal intelligence, while having a sense of oneself as a learner, with particular strengths, weaknesses, and stylistic features, draws upon intrapersonal intelligence.

In collaborative research, my colleagues and I have sought to identify how best to prepare students "at risk for school failure" for successful performance in school and subsequent institutional and occupational settings. The project was designed to develop and test a multifaceted model of *practical intelligence for school* (PIFS), drawing on both the MI and the triarchic theories of intelligence. In particular, it seemed important to determine how the academic intelligences work together with the more practical inter- and intrapersonal intelligences to produce a successful scholastic experience. We also wanted to examine the relationship of academic success to the functions of adaptation to, selection of, and shaping of environments, outlined in Sternberg's "contextual subtheory." Our underlying premise was that students who thrive in school need to learn, apply, and integrate both academic knowledge about subject domains and practical knowledge about themselves, academic tasks, and the school system at large.

As we initially formulated it, PIFS requires knowledge in three broad areas: (1) one's own intellectual profile, learning styles and strategies; (2) the structure and learning of academic tasks; and (3) the school as a complex social system. These categories can also be articulated in MI terms: The first represents intrapersonal intelligence. The second represents the manifestation of academic intelligences and combinations of intelligences in particular domains. (For example, science involves logical-mathematical competence more than linguistic ability, and some spatial ability; social studies draws upon its own blend of linguistic and logical competences.) The third category reflects primarily interpersonal intelligence.

The PIFS intervention efforts target the middle-school population for a number of reasons. The sixth and seventh grades (ages eleven to twelve), in particular, are a time when students should have already developed considerable practical knowledge about the school environment, and a time after which lack of such knowledge proves increasingly deleterious to scholastic performance. Youths in early adolescence are starting to undergo major physical, intellectual, and emotional growth and change. They are becoming increasingly independent, which is reflected in the activities and projects they will be asked to carry out. Thus, the middle-school years represent an important transition between the elementary grades and high school.

In light of these concerns, we embarked on a multipronged attack on the issue of practical intelligences. Our approach involved identification of students' own knowledge about the topic, determining students' and teachers' understanding of the sources and nature of the trouble spots, designing rich and inviting curricula to address the problem areas directly and imaginatively, piloting and implementing PIFS curricular units in a number of settings, and devising appropriate evaluation schemes.

THE PIFS INTERVIEWS

As indicated, we wanted to determine what the students themselves understood about their roles as students. Thus, we conducted a series of in-depth interviews with fifty fifth and sixth graders (ten to eleven years old) from a variety of socioeconomic backgrounds in five schools in the Boston area. The interviews elicited student views on such topics as study habits, the evaluation process, subject matter differences, the demands of academic tasks, the roles of teachers and administrators, peer interactions, and the nature of the school system. After transcribing and analyzing the responses, we outlined a hierarchical taxonomy of PIFS profiles, dividing students into categories based on whether they exhibited characteristics of a "high," "middle," or "low" PIFS profile.

We focus here on the three main factors that differentiated low from high PIFS profile students—elaboration of responses, awareness of strategies and resources, and sense of self as learner. However, an important similarity emerged in the limited understanding exhibited by both high and low PIFS students regarding similarities and differences among different subject matters. These factors had direct implications for the infusion approach and were incorporated into the themes and guiding principles for the curriculum.

Elaboration of responses. Low-profile students seemed restricted by the limited vocabulary that they could draw on for discussion of the PIFS issues. They found it difficult to explain why they found certain subjects hard or easy or why they preferred one subject to another. High-profile students were more likely to offer reasons spontaneously for their answers and were better able to differentiate among courses, academic tasks, and personal strengths and weaknesses. However, "verbal molecules" (Strauss, 1988), or truisms, were common among both low- and high-profile students, such as, "A good student is one who pays attention" or "Anyone can do better if she tries." In fact, the majority of students could be considered "incremental" rather than "entity" theorists (Dweck & Elliott, 1983), at least at the rhetorical level. Incremental theorists view intelligence as a set of skills that can be improved through effort, whereas entity theorists consider intelligence to be more global and stable. Yet, although both lows and highs espoused an incrementalist view in their responses, few lows were able to articulate more specifically how academic performance might be improved. Finally, fifth graders seemed significantly more literal than sixth graders in their thinking ("A bad teacher is one who is absent a lot"; "A bad textbook is one with a page ripped out"; "A good school is not dirty"); this result helped to motivate our decision to focus on the latter grade.

Strategies and resources. Highs and lows also varied greatly in their awareness and use of strategies for studying, as well as their resourcefulness in seeking help. Highs understood their strengths and weaknesses and varied their approaches to different subjects accordingly. They were also able to call upon teachers, friends, parents, and older siblings for encouragement, critique, instruction, and motivation. Lows, in contrast, advocated a more global, all-encompassing strategy: "Try harder and study more." As one boy explained, "Everything helps a little, but not that much." When asked what his "resource period" was, he said, "I don't know, I never asked." His responses suggested helplessness, passivity, and magical thinking. School was a mystery to him.

Self as learner. Finally, highs evinced a strong sense of themselves as learners. They related their various school tasks to both long-term and personal goals. Lows often espoused a "disciplinarian" viewpoint: "You do homework because you have to"; "A good test is a hard one"; "A good teacher is a strict one." "Good" means "hard," and "learning" means "suffering." While most lows seemed to have a limited or negative identity as learners, they usually revealed at least one area in which they could make appropriate discriminations and value judgments. For example, one student, in discussing team sports, was able to articulate the qualities of a good coach, the connections between practice and performance, the nature of his time commitments, and so forth. Such topics, ranging from dancing and designing to athletics and auto mechanics, represented areas in which students had interest and, usually, felt capable. These potential "hooks" might be used to exploit student interest and confidence in one domain of knowledge as a means to facilitate growth in other domains.

Subject matter differences. An unexpected similarity between highs and lows was the limited understanding they displayed of the kinds of skills and underlying reasoning processes entailed in different subject matters. In fact, without explicit training, youngsters at this age appear oblivious to cross-disciplinary similarities and differences. Most students defined subjects in terms of content:

> In science you learn about nature; in English, they are teaching about how to talk properly—like "I learned about frogs today, ain't that nice"—that's not good English, but it's okay to say in science.

Moreover, students could articulate little, if any, understanding or appreciation of the differing status of knowledge within and across content areas. Many considered facts more important than fiction; textbooks were "real," and stories were "fake" and "just for fun." One high PIFS student, however, articulated the difference as follows:

> Stories . . . take you into a different world—and you're off fighting dragons and being in love. And textbooks, you're right down, in earth, this time, this place, doing math . . .

Through our interviews, we identified the following themes that permeate each of the PIFS curriculum units: ability and willingness to take an active role as learner; understanding of the learning process involved in different academic activities; and ability to take a pluralistic view of school tasks and roles. We elected to present these themes primarily through an "infusion" approach. That is, rather than teaching students how to be practically intelligent in school through a separate "stand alone" set of lessons, we infuse these themes throughout the course of the students' daily work in the major subject matter areas or disciplines.

THE INFUSION CURRICULUM

The aim of the PIFS infusion curriculum is to promote transfer by explicitly directing students' attention to how problems in different domains relate to each other and by providing students with the tools and techniques for self-monitoring in different subject matters. The approach is based on two fundamental assumptions of MI theory: (1) one learns information best when it is presented in a rich context; and

(2) it is difficult to secure transfer from separate courses or isolated definitions and skills to the kinds of problems that arise unexpectedly in the course of school work or life (Brown & Campione, 1984; Perkins & Salomon, 1989).

The infusion approach can be thought of as a "metacurriculum" that serves as a bridge between standard curricula (math word problems, geography, vocabulary, et cetera) and a decontextualized thinking or study-skills curriculum that purports to be applicable across subject matter. The curriculum consists of a set of infusion units intended to help students better understand the reasons for the types of tasks they are assigned in school, and how best to accomplish them. The units try to foster a self-monitoring and a self-reflectiveness directly related to the nature and problems of the specific content area in which a student is working (Hyde & Bizar, 1989). This self-understanding, a constituent of intrapersonal intelligence, is directly related to the themes noted above. In particular, the units build on those areas identified by both students and teachers as difficult for students, such as the process of revision, and organizing and presenting one's work.

The infusion units currently cover topics in social studies, mathematics, reading and writing, and more general topics such as organizing and presenting work and taking tests, that draw on specific subject matter instantiations. Two examples of units follow.

Choosing a project. The objective of this unit is to help students choose and plan school projects more effectively. Projects represent a rich alternative to work sheets, comprehension questions, and standardized tests. They provide students with the opportunity to study a topic in depth, to raise questions and explore answers, and to determine the best form for demonstrating newly acquired expertise. However, while students are often absorbed in a variety of extracurricular projects such as writing rap songs and building skateboard ramps, they are often less engaged in executing school projects. Many find it difficult to get started; or they may choose topics that are either too narrow or too broad, or topics in which they exhibit scant interest.

The "Choosing a Project" unit includes three sets of activities: "Understanding Projects," "Choosing a Project Appropriate to You," and "Planning a Project Appropriate to the Audience and Resources." The first set of activities encourages students to examine the similarities and differences between personal and school projects and between school projects and other school assignments. They also address the definition, goals, and criteria for success of various projects. The remaining activities encourage students to use their past experiences with projects to plan new projects that: (1) relate to their abilities, interests, and relative expertise; and (2) can be carried out within the constraints of the assignment.

Finding the right mathematical tools. The goal of this unit is to familiarize students with a range of mathematical resources and to help students apply resources appropriate to particular problem types. Part 1 invites students to consider the resources with which they are already familiar in their daily life: books, television, recipes, maps, and the like. The second part of the unit introduces resources specific to math: calculators, textbooks, measuring tools, tables and charts, et cetera. The advantages and shortcomings of different types of resources are identified and discussed through a variety of classroom activities. Focus is on choosing the appropriate resource for a problem type, rather than on generating the final solution. In the last section, students reflect on their own patterns of error as well as their skills in using the various resources.

PIFS INFUSION PRINCIPLES

Each PIFS infusion unit reflects some of the following principles:

Practical intelligence skills are most fruitfully nurtured in domain-specific contexts. The topics addressed by the PIFS units are always explored in the context of the subject matter; thus, the types of resources that are important for mathematics are considered separately from those useful for social studies. These differences are further highlighted and contrasted in order to sensitize students to the nature of various subject matters. In the "Mathematical Tools" unit, students study the general characteristics, relevance, and reliability of the different types of mathematical resources for specific categories of math problems. In a "Reliability of Sources" unit, students examine potential causes of unreliability specific to the domain of social studies—lack of corroboration or expertise, observer bias, perceptual inaccuracy, and so forth.

Concepts that present difficulties for students should be analyzed and clarified in focused activities. Each problem area is analyzed in order to identify specific sources of difficulty, which are then addressed in manageable chunks via short exercises. The problems are worked through in the context of an actual assignment, rather than in isolation. In the "Choosing a Project" unit, such identified trouble spots as choice of topic, planning within the constraints of time and resources, monitoring one's progress, and responding to feedback are each considered in turn. A "Notetaking" unit includes brief exercises intended to let students know that taking notes can be quickly and easily accomplished. A note can be as simple as a single "key word" that triggers other information. Students begin by identifying key words in single sentences, moving on to longer pieces of text. Of course, establishing the right kind of classroom atmosphere and providing appropriate follow-up activities are also important to ensure that the benefits of the core activities are reinforced.

Concepts taught in the PIFS units are most effectively implemented when used in service of a particular purpose. The units highlight and exemplify the fact that most tasks, projects, assignments, indeed most of work, are undertaken for a particular purpose. In the "Mathematical Tools" unit, students compare the purpose of resources used in their personal lives and in math class. They are also asked to write problems for which particular resources would be appropriate. One of the goals of the unit is to increase students' independence and resourcefulness by explicitly linking different math resources to situations in which students typically have difficulties. In a geography unit, students engage in a number of activities which illustrate that maps are always drawn for a specific purpose, with a particular audience in mind.

Students acquire knowledge best when it is related to their own sets of abilities and interests. Each PIFS unit is individualized in order to: (1) enrich assignments by bringing in students' own interests from their scholastic or nonscholastic experience; (2) draw on students' strengths by reflecting their unique sets of intelligences; and (3) connect students' prior projects and work (old papers or tests, habitual sources or patterns of error, et cetera) to current assignments. As already noted, the "Projects" unit addresses each of the above points. The "Discovering Your Learning Profile" unit is comprised of activities that explicitly encourage students to contemplate their various "intelligences" and learning styles. If a student recognizes that she has limited linguistic intelligence, she may need to put extra effort into studying for a vocabulary test. If she is aware of her strong spatial intelligence, she may be able to study vocabulary more effectively by memorizing words and their definitions in terms of their location on a study sheet or translating definitions into concrete images.

Practical intelligence skills are most powerfully integrated when presented in both scholastic and real-world contexts. The PIFS skills addressed by the units are situated in both academic and real-world settings to help students establish connections to their own experience. For example, students consider how mathematical resources are useful not just for their homework assignments, but when planning a trip, baking cookies, or justifying an increase in one's allowance. The "Notetaking" unit identifies situations in which notetaking occurs, perhaps without students recognizing it as such, for example, phone messages and shopping lists. The "Why Go To School" unit encourages thought about the function of school, its effect on quality of life, alternative methods of education, and the reality and myths (often fostered by television portrayals) of the working world. Metaphors and analogies are also used where helpful to demystify difficult concepts and facilitate understanding. These metaphors help make a concept like revision more accessible and memorable by tying it to an image students can readily recognize and understand, such as movie-making, sports practice, or choosing an outfit. Trying to solve math problems without the right resources is compared to a mechanic trying to get the job done without a box of tools.

Students benefit from a focus on process as well as product. While final products and correct answers are clearly important, practical intelligence involves knowing what to do when one gets stuck and how to seek appropriate help. Therefore, the PIFS units often emphasize the process of carrying out an assignment or solving a problem, with reduced emphasis on the actual solution. As mentioned earlier, the "Mathematical Tools" unit contains many exercises that do not require completion. Rather, students are asked to identify the mathematical resources appropriate for different problems. In the "Understanding Fiction" unit, students focus on pinpointing the source of their misunderstanding in a work of fiction so that they will be able to ask more precise questions and identify areas requiring further help.

Self-monitoring helps students to take active responsibility for their own learning. Self-monitoring is explicitly encouraged in all of the units before, during, and after the activities. It is not enough simply to learn the skills of practical intelligence; students must also practice overseeing and monitoring their use so that reliance on the teacher is reduced. In mathematics, both the advantages and disadvantages of particular resources are highlighted in an effort to encourage students to think more critically and reflectively about when and how to use different mathematical tools. In the "Projects" unit, projects undertaken both in and outside of school are examined, compared and evaluated. Students are asked to compare reports written in areas about which they know a great deal to reports written in areas where they have little or no knowledge. As a general rule, students are provided with exemplars illustrating successful and unsuccessful performances in order to provoke more evaluative thinking.

EVALUATION OF PIFS UNITS

We find that practical intelligence skills can be most effectively evaluated by a focus on metacognitive issues as well as on actual task performance. The PIFS evaluation measures assess students' ability-in-context. The measures fall into three categories—definitional, task-oriented, and metatask. The definitional component addresses students' understanding of the problem; for example, do they understand the issues addressed by the PIFS unit and why they are important? Such understanding might be exhibited even without mastery of the skills needed to execute the task effectively. The task component samples the actual skills targeted in the units—students may be asked either to start or to complete a task, or perhaps to work through a problem area. Finally, the metatask component requires students to reflect on the nature of the process or skills involved in a particular task. They are asked to evaluate whether their performances were successful, and if not, how they could be revised or improved.

The following evaluation measures provide examples from the two sample units described earlier. A definitional measure for "Choosing a Project" asks students to list the factors that should be considered when choosing a particular project. In the "Mathematical Tools" unit, students are asked to identify situations in which particular math resources would be helpful. The task measure for the "Projects" unit asks students to complete a planning sheet for a hypothetical project. An equivalent measure for the "Mathematical Tools" unit gives students a problem, while restricting their access to certain resources, and asks them to generate other options for solving the problem. Finally, one of the metatask measures for "Choosing a Project" asks students to critique three completed planning sheets and to make suggestions for improving one of the less promising proposals. In the math unit, students are presented with a scenario in which a hypothetical classmate has used several resources to solve a particularly thorny math problem. They are asked to evaluate the appropriateness of the classmate's work.

The PIFS measures incorporate some of the characteristics of Wiggins's (1989) criteria for "authentic" tests in that the assessments are contextualized. They reflect realistic complexity; content is mastered as a means, not an end; and students are asked to pose and clarify problems, not just to provide solutions. The evaluation measures are intended to be useful not only as assessment of what the students learned in the PIFS unit, but also as examples of good pedagogy (Gardner, 1991).

We have described a new curricular approach, designed to aid students in managing the complex and sometimes conflicting demands of school. The overall PIFS approach identifies three major areas of focus for a "practical intelligence" curriculum and several of the factors critical to such an effort. The PIFS infusion approach reflects, in addition, a number of principles related to the development of an infusion curriculum. While it is too early to indicate whether this approach succeeds in each of its avowed goals, we can state that the several master teachers who have piloted portions of the curriculum find it congenial to their classroom procedures and goals; moreover, students in a PIFS class outperform members of a control group on a variety of measures (Gardner, Krechevsky, Sternberg, & Okagaki, in press).

Our work raises a number of questions to which we can here provide brief answers. A first question is whether a multiple-intelligences approach can be productive, given the schools' perennial focus on linguistic and logical thinking. It seems clear that certain combinations of intelligences (such as linguistic, logical, and certain aspects of interpersonal) are highly prized and rewarded in the scholastic context. It is certainly neither straightforward (nor necessarily desirable) to elevate some of the "fringe" intelligences to the status of the academic competencies, nor to use them as vehicles of instruction in the standard subject areas. However, students experiencing difficulty in the traditional academic areas seem both to perform better and to feel more empowered when given the chance to exhibit their knowledge and understanding through other than linguistic means.

A second question is whether Sternberg and Gardner's theories have been affected by involvement in this project. We believe that they have in at least two ways. First, MI theory stands to benefit from increased attention to the metacognitive aspects of the several intelligences, just as the metacomponents of the triarchic theory are nuanced by application to different domains. Second, like most psychological theories, our accounts of intelligence have been centered on the cognition of the solitary individual. But once one begins to work in the classroom, it becomes evident that one must confront issues of how students work together on projects as well as how assessment and instruction can work most effectively in the context of such a large group of individuals.

A third question is how the PIFS approach might work if it sought to take advantage of the traditional strengths of a "stand-alone" curriculum as well as an "infusion" approach. In current work carried out in conjunction with Robert Sternberg and Tina Blythe, we are in fact combining these usually contrasted approaches. At the beginning of the year, we introduce the specific PIFS ideas and themes in an explicit fashion, and, then, periodically, these PIFS concepts become the subject of special "reminder" lessons.

Nevertheless, the principal means for helping students to become more practically intelligent is to provide them with ample opportunities to use the PIFS approach in their daily work. And so, in this combined approach, much PIFS material is introduced in the course of standard lessons in reading, writing, and other traditional subject matters. Our hopes are that teachers will return to the PIFS materials as needed to supplement the existing subject matter curricula, that students will learn to call upon the techniques during times of difficulty, and, finally, that students will gradually internalize the PIFS techniques and concepts so that they become a standard and readily available part of every child's repertoire. Accordingly, the success of the PIFS approach is assessed by looking for improvements in the students' performances in their customary areas of school work.

A final question arises regarding the extent to which the curriculum might be manipulative in spirit or in operation. Although one of the goals of the PIFS curriculum is to help students in their coursework and assignments, there is a fine line between learning to "psyche out" what teachers want and acquiring the tools to learn on one's own and want to learn more. One criterion of success of the PIFS project is improvement in scholastic performance and student engagement in school. But an even more attractive goal is for students to take responsibility for their own education, even after school is over, so that practical intelligence for schooling becomes practical intelligence for the acquisition of knowledge and understanding throughout life. By expanding the focus of current educational interventions to include practical as well as academic skills, we hope not only to serve a young contemporary Simonides or Boole well, but to help many struggling students become active, planful, and reflective learners.

Chapter 9

Disciplined Inquiry in the High School: An Introduction to Arts PROPEL

A ny long-term participant in arts education in the United States
should take some pleasure in the recently acquired notoriety of
this field. Within a decade of the demise of CEMREL (the
largest federally funded effort in arts education), the virtual cessation of
national efforts by the Department of Education, and the muted recep-
tion to *Coming to our senses* (Arts, Education, and Americans, 1977), there
has been a renaissance of interest in education in the arts. Sparked
primarily by the Getty Center for Education in the Arts, buoyed as well
by support from other federal and private philanthropies, and symbol-
ized by *Towards civilization,* the lavish publication on arts education
issued by the National Endowment for the Arts (1988), arts education
is now an unmistakable participant in national conversations about
educational reform. Such an opportunity is unlikely to arise more than
once in a generation, and thus one is well advised to seize it.

At the rhetorical level, it is easy to find areas of consensus among the
various participants in the rebirth of a national arts education movement.
Nearly all individuals would call for more class time spent on the arts,
better-trained teachers, and some kind of graduation requirement. Yet
lurking beneath the surface agreement, there are vexed issues that
engender sharp controversy (Burton, Lederman, & London, 1988;
Dobbs, 1988; Eisner, 1987; Ewens, 1988; Getty, 1986; Jackson, 1987;
Zessoules, Wolf, & Gardner, 1988).

Some of the questions seem practical in nature. Should we call for specialist teachers or train regular classroom teachers? Should we focus on one or two art forms or provide the whole menu of genres and forms? Should we have a uniform curriculum across cities or states? Should we employ standardized tests? But one soon encounters issues that exceed the "merely practical." To what extent should arts classes be used to foster creativity? Should art be taught separately or infused across the curriculum? Is there a privileged canon of Western art, or does the art of *our* civilization merely take its place among many other equally meritorious traditions? Should art training focus on the productive skills, or should there be a heightened emphasis on connoisseurship? Is artistic knowledge primarily factual, or does it involve unique forms of cognition and metacognition?

None of these questions is new to arts educators, but they take on special significance at a time when major resources are being directed to educational efforts in the schools, in museums, and even on television. Decisions made (or avoided) are likely to have reverberations for a decade or more.

In this essay I introduce a new approach to curriculum and assessment in the arts, principally at the high school level, called Arts PROPEL. While a number of the features of Arts PROPEL are shared with other contemporary initiatives, the approach differs both in terms of its intellectual origins and its particular mix of components. Thus the current essay serves as well as an introduction to the general approach to arts education devised over the past decades at Harvard Project Zero and to a particular form it has currently assumed in the practical arena.

Intellectual Roots of Harvard Project Zero

Project Zero was founded in 1967 at the Harvard Graduate School of Education by the noted philosopher Nelson Goodman. An epistemologist by training, Goodman challenged the widespread notion that linguistic and logical symbol systems had priority over other expressive and communicative systems. Instead, following earlier attempts by Charles Sanders Peirce (1940), Ernst Cassirer (1953–57), and Susanne Langer (1942), Goodman (1976; 1978) formulated a taxonomy of the major symbol systems utilized by human beings. Included in his discussion was a description of those symbol systems of special importance in the arts (such as musical, poetic, gestural, visualgraphic) as well as the modes of symbolization which they embodied (such as representation, expression, metaphor, multiple meanings).

Though Goodman's own work was primarily philosophical in nature, he soon attracted around him investigators interested in the psychological and educational aspects of his "theory of symbols." During the first years of the project, much of the work involved interdisciplinary discussion and analysis of major concepts and processes in the arts. The point of view adopted was unflinchingly "cognitive." That is, whatever else they may be, artistic activities are seen as occasions for mental activities, some shared with other pursuits (such as attention to detail), others of special moments in the arts (sensitivity to compositional patterns, for example). One who would traffic in the arts must become able to "read" and to "write" the symbol systems featured in the arts. An artistic "reader" can discriminate diverse styles in music or discern the allegoric content of a poem or novel. An artistic "writer" is able to use abstract forms and colors to suggest elegaic or triumphant moods; or to vary musical phrases so as to create the impressions of different seasons or psychological states.

In the wake of the pervasive cognitive revolution (Gardner, 1985), it may be difficult to appreciate that this point of view was distinctly iconoclastic in its time. Evident among lay individuals, but also noticeable among art educators and theorists, was the belief that the arts were primarily a realm of emotion, mystery, magic, or intuition. Cognition was associated with science and problem solving, not with the creativity needed to fashion and appreciate artistic masterpieces. And even those who had some sympathy with a cognitive approach questioned whether an analysis in terms of "those little things called symbols" could be productive. Nowadays, however, the battle has been largely won; those who would question the cognitive dimensions of the arts are themselves in a minority.

In the 1970s, under David Perkins's and my codirection, Project Zero became more fully devoted to psychological issues. Perkins directed a "Cognitive Skills Group" with a primary interest in the perceptual and cognitive capacities of adults; I directed a "Developmental Group," which focused on the development of symbol-using skills in normal and gifted children. In more recent times, these psychologically based investigations continue, but the project has also taken a firm educational turn. Well over half of the studies in which we are currently engaged involve more-or-less direct efforts to apply our analyses and insights to programs in schools, ranging from the preschool to the college level. Arts PROPEL exemplifies this shift from philosophical analysis and psychological experimentation to practical efforts in educational settings.

Project Zero has involved well over 100 researchers in the past two decades, and these individuals have made contributions in a variety of corners of the humanities and social sciences. Our collective work has been reviewed in a number of summary publications (Gardner, 1982; Goodman et al., 1972; Perkins & Leondar, 1977; Winner, 1982) and was the subject of an issue of the *Journal of Aesthetic Education* (Gardner & Perkins, 1988). It is therefore not necessary to review our principal research findings here.

But it is appropriate to introduce those lines of analysis within the Development Group that have led most directly to the Arts PROPEL undertaking. In early work, we adapted the path-breaking methods of investigation devised by Jean Piaget (1970) in his study of children to the kinds of symbol-using competences that had been described by Goodman. This focus eventually gave rise to three principal lines of investigation. First of all, we carried out cross-sectional experimental studies of specific capacities (like style sensitivity or metaphoric competence) in order to determine the "natural" developmental trajectory of these important skills (Gardner, 1982). Second, we carried out naturalistic longitudinal studies of the development in early childhood of various kinds of symbol-using capacities (Wolf & Gardner, 1981, 1988; Wolf et al., 1988). Third, in a scientifically related body of work, we investigated the breakdown under conditions of brain damage of the very symbolic skills whose ontogenesis we had been probing (Gardner, 1975; Kaplan & Gardner, 1989).

A number of important and sometimes unexpected findings emerged from these studies undertaken principally during the 1970s.

1) In most areas of development, children simply improve with age. In several artistic spheres, however, evidence suggests a surprisingly high level of competence in young children, followed by a possible decline during the years of middle childhood. This jagged or "U-shaped" curve in development is particularly evident in certain areas of artistic production, though it can perhaps be manifest as well in selective areas of perception (Gardner & Winner, 1982).

2) Notwithstanding certain deficiencies in their performance, preschool children acquire a tremendous amount of knowledge about and competence in the arts. As is the case with natural language, this acquisition can occur without explicit tutelage on the part of parents or teachers. The evolution of children's drawings constitutes a particularly vivid example of this self-generated learning and development (Gardner, 1980). In this respect artistic learning stands in sharp contrast to most traditional school subjects.

3) In nearly every area, an individual's perceptual or comprehension

capacities develop well in advance of productive capacities. Once again, however, the picture in the arts proves far more complex, and at least in some domains, comprehension actually appears to lag behind performance or production capacities (Winner et al., 1983). This finding underscores the importance of giving young children ample opportunity to learn by performing, making, or "doing."

4) According to classical developmental theory, children's competence in one cognitive sphere should predict the child's level of competence in other spheres as well. Along with other investigators, we discovered much less synchrony across areas. Indeed, it was entirely normal for children to be strong in one or two areas (for example, art form *x*) while being average or below average in their attainment in other areas (including art form *y*[Gardner, 1983a; Winner et al., 1986]).

5) It had been thought for some decades that the brain was "equipotential," with each area capable of subserving the range of human capacities. Neuropsychological research called this finding into severe doubt. A better description indicates that specific areas of the cortex have particular cognitive foci, and that, particularly after early childhood, there is little "plasticity" in the representation of cognitive capacities in the nervous system (Gardner, 1975, 1986).

It would be misleading to suggest that we now understand artistic development, even to the same extent that researchers have illuminated scientific development or the development of linguistic competence. As our taunting "zero" reminds us, research on this topic is still in its infancy. Our work has established that artistic development is complex and multivocal; generalizations are hard to come by and often fall by the way. Still, it has been important for us to try to tie together our major findings about artistic development, and this we have attempted in a number of places (Gardner, 1973; Winner, 1982; Wolf & Gardner, 1980).

The Theory of Multiple Intelligences

In my own work, these various insights came together particularly in the "theory of multiple intelligences" (see chapters 1 and 2). In light of a pluralistic view of the intellect, the question immediately arises about whether there is a separate artistic intelligence. According to my analysis, there is not (Gardner, 1983b). Rather, each of these forms of intelligence can be directed toward artistic ends: that is, the symbols entailed in that form of knowledge may, but need not, be marshaled in an aesthetic fashion. Thus, linguistic intelligence can be used in ordinary conversation or for the purpose of authoring legal briefs; in neither case is language being employed aesthetically. The same intelligence can be used for writing poems or novels, in which case it is being deployed aesthetically. By the same token, spatial intelligence can be used by sailors or sculptors, even as bodily-kinesthetic intelligence can be exploited by dancers, mimes, athletes, or surgeons. Even musical intelligence can be used nonaesthetically (as in a communication system based on bugle calls), just as logical-mathematical intelligence can be directed in an aesthetic vein (as when one proof is deemed more elegant than another). Whether an intelligence is mobilized for aesthetic or nonaesthetic ends turns out to be an individual or a cultural decision.

Alternative Accents in Arts Education

Over the course of history, human intelligences have been trained primarily in one of two contrasting ways. On the one hand, individuals have become participants from an early age in activities that mobilize and canalize their intelligences. This process occurs in traditional *apprenticeships* as well as in those informal scholastic activities that feature observation, demonstration, and coaching-in-context (Collins & Brown, 1988; Gardner, 1991a; Resnick, 1987; Schon, 1984). On the other hand, human intelligences have also been trained in more *formal scholastic settings* and formats. Here students attend lectures on various subject matters and are expected to master what they hear, or they read textbooks about these subject matters. They are then expected to memorize and understand this material and to draw on it for homework, examinations, and "later life."

According to my analysis, the scholastic approach has come to dominate our thinking about learning and to exercise a near-stranglehold over activities featured in school. Yet individuals can also train intelligences—including a much wider band of their intelligences—through informal or nonscholastic training regimens.

In few areas of knowledge has the distinction between these two forms been more salient than in the field of arts education. For hundreds if not thousands of years, students have learned much of artistry through apprenticeships; they observe artistic masters at work; they are gradually drawn into these activities; they at first participate in simple, carefully supported ways, and then gradually tackle more difficult assignments, with lessened support from their coach or master. Certainly this was the procedure of choice in the ateliers of the Renaissance, and versions of it have persisted in private art and music lessons until this day. Recent "Artists-in-the-Schools" programs are efforts to exploit the power of these traditional learning schemes, where appropriate intelligences are mobilized directly, without the need for extensive linguistic, logical, or notational interventions.

Over the last few hundred years, however, a "second front" has opened in the area of arts education. With the emergence of fields like art history, art criticism, aesthetics, communications, semiotics, and the like, an ensemble of scholastic understandings about the arts has gained importance in the academy. Rather than being acquired through observation, demonstration, or apprenticeship, however, these "peri-artistic" bodies of knowledge are mastered primarily through traditional scholastic methods: through lecturing, reading, writing, in the same manner as history, economics, or sociology.

Now there is no necessary link between these aspects of the arts and the modes of teaching. Art history could be taught through observation or demonstration, even as painting or fiddling could be taught (if not learned!) through lecturing or reading a textbook. And yet, for evident reasons, each of these artistic disciplines has tended to favor one form of pedagogy over its rival.

The Current Scene in Arts Education

Various surveys of American education undertaken in the past decade or so paint a generally consistent picture. At the younger grades, arts education is close to universal. More often than not, artistic instruction is provided by the regular classroom teacher and, in general, it focuses very much on artistic production. Children paint, draw, model clay, even as they sing, participate in rhythm bands, or, less often, play an instrument, dance, or tell stories. When teachers are gifted and/or inspired, these productions may achieve a high level, but for the most part the artistic productions are not noteworthy. With the advent of middle childhood, arts education declines in frequency; by high school, specialists handle instruction but only a minority of students participate. With few exceptions the accent continues to fall on production. The actual classroom procedures often involve apprenticeship methods, particularly at the older age levels, but not infrequently the initiative for production is placed almost entirely in the students' hands.

In a few school systems, efforts have been made to train children in "peri-artistic" activities like history or connoisseurship. Traditionally there has been little constituency in the community for this activity; only with the advent of the Getty Trust, and parallel bodies, has there been a wider call for training in artistry outside the production sphere.

Within the professions of arts education, however, a consensus has emerged over the last few decades that "production alone" will not suffice. While arts educators differ in their assessment of the importance of artistic production—and its putative connection to creativity, more broadly framed—they concur that, for the majority of the population, such an exclusive emphasis no longer makes sense. Thus, nearly all of the reform efforts cited above call for an arts education that encompasses some discussion and analysis of artworks themselves and some appreciation of the cultural contexts in which artworks are fashioned.

The Project Zero Approach to Art Education

Given our cognitive approach to artistic education, these general trends have been applauded within Project Zero. (Indeed, in our more chauvinistic moments, we claim a bit of credit for some of the recent reorientation in arts education.) We believe that students need to be introduced to the ways of thinking exhibited by individuals involved in the arts: by practicing artists and by those who analyze, criticize, and investigate the cultural contexts of art objects.

Yet, in contrast to some advocates of "discipline-based arts education," we introduce a number of nuances in our position. These points have led us to put forth our own approach to education in the various art forms. While not pretending to speak for all of Project Zero—past or present—I would call attention to the following points:

1) Particularly at younger ages (below, say, ten), production activities ought to be central in any art form. Children learn best when they are actively involved in their subject matter; they want to have the opportunity to work directly with materials and media; and in the arts, these strengths and inclinations almost always translate into the making of something. Moreover, young children have considerable gifts for figuring the crucial components or patterns in an artistic object, and they should have the opportunity to do such "ferreting out" on their own (Bamberger, 1982). This accent is the legacy of the Progressive Era that deserves to endure, even in a more "disciplinary epoch" (see Dewey, 1959; Lowenfeld, 1947).

2) Perceptual, historical, critical, and other "peri-artistic" activities should be closely related to, and (whenever possible) emerge from, the

child's own productions. That is, rather than being introduced in an alien context to art objects made by others, children should encounter such objects in relation to the particular artistic products and problems with which they are themselves engaged—and whenever possible, in intimate connection to the child's own art objects. (Older students and adults can also benefit from such contextualized introductions to "peri-artistic" activities.)

3) Arts curricula need to be presented by teachers or other individuals with a deep knowledge of how to "think" in an artistic medium. If the area is music, the teacher must be able to "think musically"—and not merely introduce music via language or logic. By the same token, education in the visual arts must occur at the hand—and through the eyes—of an individual who can "think visually or spatially" (see Arn-heim, 1969). To the extent that teachers do not already possess these skills, they ought to enroll in training regimens that can develop these cognitive capacities.

4) Whenever possible, artistic learning should be organized around meaningful projects, which are carried out over a significant period of time, and allow ample opportunity for feedback, discussion, and reflection. Such projects are likely to interest students, motivate them, and encourage them to develop skills; and they may well exert a long-term impact on the students' competence and understanding. As much as possible, "one-shot" learning experiences should be spurned.

5) In most artistic areas, it will not be profitable to plan a K–12 sequential curriculum. (I have in mind here simpleminded but all too frequent curricular goals: can provide four color names; can sing three intervals; can recite two sonnets.) Such a formula may sound attractive, but it flies in the face of the holistic, contextually sensitive manner in which individuals customarily gain mastery in crafts or disciplines. Artistry involves a continuing exposure, at various developmental levels, to certain core concepts, like style, composition, or genre; and to certain recurrent problems, like performing a passage with feeling or creating a powerful artistic image. Curricula need to be rooted in this "spiral" aspect of artistic learning. A curriculum may be sequential in the sense that it revisits concepts and problems in an increasingly sophisticated way, but not in the sense that there exists one set of problems, concepts, or terms at grade two, another set at grade three or four.

6) Assessment of learning is crucial in the arts. The success of an arts program cannot be asserted or taken on faith. However, assessments must respect the particular intelligences involved—musical skill must be assessed through musical means, and not via the "screens" of language

or logic. And assessment must probe those abilities and concepts that are most central to the arts. Rather than crafting the curriculum to suit the assessment, we must devise assessments that do justice to what is most pivotal in an art form.

7) Artistic learning does not merely entail the mastery of a set of skills or concepts. The arts are also deeply personal areas, where students encounter their own feelings as well as those of other individuals. Students need educational vehicles that allow them such exploration; they must see that personal reflection is a respected and important activity; and their privacy should not be violated.

8) In general, it is risky—and in any case, it is unnecessary—to teach artistic taste or value judgments directly. However, it is important for students to understand that the arts are permeated by issues of taste and value that matter to anyone who is seriously engaged in the arts. These issues are best conveyed through contact with individuals who do care about these issues, who are willing to introduce and defend their values, but who are open to discussion and who countenance alternative points of view.

9) Art education is too important to be left to any one group, even that group designated as "art educators." Rather, art education needs to be a cooperative enterprise involving artists, teachers, administrators, researchers, and the students themselves.

10) While ideally all students would study all art forms, this is not a practical option. There are simply too many subjects—and, in my terms, too many intelligences—competing for attention on the calendar, and the school day is already excessively fragmented. In my view no art form has any intrinsic priority over others. Thus, at the risk of offending an audience of visual-art educators (and many others!), I assert that students should all have extended exposure to some art form—but that it need not be one of the visual arts. Indeed, I would rather have an individual well versed in music, dance, *or* drama than one with a smattering of knowledge across the several lively arts. The former student will at least know what it is like to "think" in an art form and will retain the option of assimilating other arts forms in later life; the latter individual seems consigned to remain a dilettante, if not to become a drop-out.

At Last, Arts PROPEL

The above points could give rise to any number of programs in arts education. In the present instance, they have contributed to a new approach called Arts PROPEL. In 1985, with encouragement and support from the Arts and Humanities Division of the Rockefeller Foundation, Harvard Project Zero joined forces with the Educational Testing Service and the Pittsburgh Public Schools. The goal of the resulting multiyear project has been to devise a set of assessment instruments that can document artistic learning during the later elementary and high school years. The ideas of Arts PROPEL have been worked out in collaboration with the partners I've just named.

As anyone involved in educational experiments can readily appreciate, it has proved easier to state, than to implement, our one-sentence goal. We began by attempting to delineate the kinds of competences that we sought to measure in our students. We decided to work in three art forms—music, visual art, and imaginative writing. And we decided to look at three kinds of competences: *production* (composing or performing music; painting or drawing; engaging in imaginative or "creative" writing); *perception* (effecting distinctions or discriminations within an art form—"thinking" artistically); and *reflection* (stepping back from one's own perceptions or productions, or those of other artists, and seeking to understand the goals, methods, difficulties, and effects achieved). PROPEL captures acronymically this trio of competences in our three art forms, with the final *l* emphasizing our concern with *learning*.

Ideally, we would have liked simply to devise adequate assessment instuments and administer them to students in the target age groups. However, we soon arrived at a simple but crucial truth: there is no point in assessing competences or even potentials unless the student has had some significant experience in working directly with relevant artistic media. Just as baseball scouts look at students who are already playing baseball, it is necessary for educational assessors to examine students who are already engaged in artistic activities. And just as baseball rookies need well-trained and skilled coaches, so, too, art students require teachers who are fully acquainted with the goals of an educational program and able to exemplify the requisite artistic skills and understandings.

To bring about these goals, therefore, we have elected to devise curriculum modules and link these to assessment instruments. We have implemented a careful procedure of curriculum-and-assessment development. In each art form we have assembled an interdisciplinary team, which together defines the central competences in an art form. In writing, we are looking at students' capacities to create instances of different genres—writing a poem, creating dialogue for a play. In music, we are examining the ways in which students learn from rehearsals of a work-in-progress. And in the area of visual arts (from which I will draw most of my examples here), these competences include sensitivity to style, appreciation of various compositional patterns, and the ability to plan and create a work such as a portrait or a still life.

Two Educational Vehicles

For each of these nominated competences, we then generate a set of exercises called a "domain project"—a set that must feature perceptual, productive, *and* reflective elements. Domain projects do not in themselves constitute an entire curriculum, but they must be curriculum-compatible: that is, they should fit comfortably into a standard art curriculum.

The domain projects are first explored and critiqued by teachers. Following revision, they are administered in pilot form to students. A preliminary assessment system is then tried out by the teachers. An iterative process is invoked until the domain project is considered adequate from the perspective of each of its audiences. Once the project has been completed, it can be used "as is" by teachers, or adapted in various ways to fit a particular curriculum or the teaching style or goals of a specific teacher. Part of the assessment procedure is rough-and-ready— simply giving students and teachers a feeling for what the student is learning. However, it is also possible to make more fine-grained analyses (for research purposes), even as it is possible to produce a summary score for use by the central school administration.

As one example, let me briefly describe the "composition" domain project, which has already been used quite widely in Arts PROPEL. This project is designed to help students notice how arrangements and interrelationships of shapes affect the composition and the impact of artistic works. Students are given an opportunity to make compositional decisions and to reflect on the effects of such decisions in their works and in works created by acknowledged artistic masters.

In an initial session, students are given a set of ten odd black geometric shapes. They are asked simply to drop those shapes on a piece of white paper. The exercise is then repeated except that on the second trial students are asked to put together a set of shapes which they find pleasing. They are then asked to reflect on the differences between the "random" and the "deliberate" work. In a notebook they record the differences that they see and state the reasons that motivated their own "deliberate" choices. Most students find this exercise fun, though at first they may not quite know what to make of it.

In a second session, students encounter informally certain principles of composition. The teacher introduces the students to a number of artistic works of different styles and periods that differ significantly from one another in the kinds of symmetry or balance which they epitomize or violate. Students are asked to describe the differences among these works as they appear to them and to develop a vocabulary that can capture these differences and convey them effectively to others. Achievements (or violations) of harmony, cohesion, repetition, dominant forces, radial patterns, surprise, or tension are noted. At the conclusion of the session, students are asked to jot down in a notebook similarities and differences in a contrasting set of slides. They are also given an assignment. During the next week, they should search in their daily environment for instances of different compositions—both those compositions already achieved by an artist and those that they can themselves create by "framing" a scene in nature.

In a third session, students report on the "compositions" they observed in their own environment and discuss them with reference to those observed in the art class. The students then return to the deliberate composition of session one. Now they are asked to make a "final work." Before proceeding, however, they are asked to indicate their plans for this work. Then they go about realizing, and, if they wish, revising their final composition. On a work sheet they indicate what they found most surprising about their composition and what further changes they might want to make in a future work.

In addition to the student's own compositions, perceptual discriminations, and reflections, the teacher also has his or her own assessment sheet. There the teacher can evaluate the student in terms of the kinds of compositions attempted or achieved. Other kinds of learning—for instance, the student's success in discovering interesting compositions in his environment or his ability to connect his own compositions with those of well-known artists—can also be assessed. This domain project can be repeated, in its initial or in altered form, to determine the extent to which the student's grasp of compositional issues has developed over time.

The "composition" domain project works with a traditional element of the visual arts—the arrangement of form—and seeks to tie this element to the students' own productive and perceptual experiences. A quite different approach is taken in a second domain project called the "biography of a work." In this instance our goals are much broader.

Indeed, we want to help students synthesize their learning from previous domain projects in composition, style, and expression, and to do so through tracing the development of a complete work.

In the "biography of a work" students first observe a large set of sketches prepared by Andrew Wyeth, prior to his completion of *Brown Swiss*. They then survey a companion set of sketches and drafts of Picasso's *Guernica*. Following these perceptual explorations of masterworks, students are asked to draw their room at home in a way that expresses something about themselves. They are given a range of media (paper, pencil, charcoal, pen and ink, and so on) as well as some pictorial material like magazines and slides. In an initial session students are asked to choose any element(s) of their room and to add whatever props or objects that might be revealing about themselves. They are asked to use these in preparing a preliminary sketch. Their focus should fall on composition, but they are encouraged to think about how the range of artistic elements can express *themselves* and not just what is represented literally in the picture. A few examples are given of how aspects of form can convey metaphorically a property of an individual.

In a second session students begin by examining slides that show how artists have used objects metaphorically in their work and also how particular objects or elements can carry a multiplicity of meanings. They are also shown slides of artists' studios or rooms and asked how these rooms might bring out something about the artists' view of their particular world. Students then return to their own preliminary sketches and are asked to make provisional decisions about the media that they wish to use and the style, color, line, texture, and so on they plan to employ. As in the earlier session, students fill out worksheets in which they are asked to reflect on the choices they have made, the reasons for them, and their aesthetic consequences.

In a third session, students review all of their preliminary sketches and "trial sheets," think about whether they are satisfied with them, and then begin their final work. Students discuss their works in progress with other students. Then, in a final session during the following week, the students complete their works, critique one another's efforts, and review their sketches, trial sheets, and reflections. The activities in this final week serve as a model for the kinds of reflections that are used as well in the student portfolio compilations (as will be discussed).

In Arts PROPEL we have sought to create an ensemble of domain projects for each art form. These prototypes should encompass most of the important concepts in an art form. We expect as well that we can develop a *general theory* of domain projects: what set of exercises qualifies as a domain project, what kinds of learning one can expect to take place, how best the student can be assessed within and across domain projects.

In addition to the ensemble of domain projects, we have also introduced a second educational vehicle. While this vehicle is often called a portfolio, I prefer the term *processfolio*. Most artists' portfolios contain only the very best works by an artist, the set by which the artist would wish to be judged in a competition. In contrast, our processfolios are much more like works in progress. In their processfolios, students include not just finished works but also original sketches, interim drafts, critiques by themselves and others, artworks by others that they admire or dislike and that bear in some way on the current project. Students are sometimes asked to present the whole folder of materials; at other times they are asked to select out those pieces that appear particularly informative or pivotal in their own development (see N. Brown, 1987; Wolf, 1988a, 1988b, 1989).

The maintenance of high standards, so crucial to the success of any arts education program, is heavily dependent at the outset upon the stance that the teacher takes vis-à-vis artistic performance and productivity; with time, students' effects on one another may well become the chief means of conveying and maintaining standards (Berger, 1991). The teacher's role in a processfolio environment differs from her role in a classical apprenticeship, in that no single model of progress—no set of discrete levels—underlies the instruction; but in the sense that the teacher serves as an exemplar of productive artistry, and as an embodiment of the standards of the community, an Arts PROPEL classroom does resemble a classical atelier.

Given our initial charge, much of the energy in Arts PROPEL has gone into the construction of assessment systems. Domain projects each feature a set of self-assessment procedures, which can be used during the course of the life of that project. In the case of the composition project, students have the opportunity to step back and reflect on the strengths and weaknesses of each composition, the expressive effects achieved in each composition, and just *how* these effects are (or are not) fully realized. In the case of the biography of a work, students reflect about the changes they have made, the reasons motivating the changes, and the relation between the early and late drafts. The student's drafts and final product, along with her reflections, are then assessed along a variety of qualitative dimensions, such as engagement, technical skills, imaginativeness, and critical evaluative skills. While the primary assessment for the domain project occurs within the class, it is also possible to assess these projects off-site; such assessment sessions have been carried out with reasonable success by "external" arts educators brought together under the auspices of the Educational Testing Service.

While domain projects lend themselves to a number of familiar forms of assessment, the assessment of processfolios is a more challenging and delicate operation. Processfolios can be assessed on a large number of dimensions. Some of them are straightforward: the regularity of the entries, their completeness, et cetera. Others are more complex and subjective, but still familiar: the overall quality of the final products, on technical and imaginative grounds. Of special interest to us are those dimensions that help to illuminate the unique potential of processfolios: students' awareness of their own strengths and weaknesses; capacity to reflect accurately; ability to build upon self-critique and to make use of critiques of others; sensitivity to one's own developmental milestones; ability to use lessons from domain projects productively; capacity to find and solve new problems; ability to relate current projects to those undertaken at earlier times and those that one hopes to undertake in the future; capacity to move comfortably and appropriately from one aesthetic stance or role to another and back again. The goal is not only to assess along a variety of potentially independent dimensions, but also to encourage students to develop along these dimensions. Such an assessment system has the potential to alter what is discussed, and what is valued in the classroom.

Recently, the Arts PROPEL team, under the direction of Ellen Winner, has attempted to set down those dimensions of production, perception, reflection, and "approach to work" that can be applied to student processfolios and the projects contained therein. The four dimensions are summarized in table 9.1. While the taxonomy is tentative, and will typically be altered in the light of local conditions, it captures well the considerations we deem most important.

Even to list these dimensions is to convey something of the difficulty of the assessment task and the extent to which it breaks new ground. It would be misleading to suggest that we have solved the problems involved in any of these facets of assessment: indeed, as we sometimes jest, we simply have several years more experience than others in recognizing what does *not* work! It is sobering to note that it has taken a century to take standardized tests to their present, hardly stupefying status; it is unreasonable to expect domain projects and processfolios to mature in a few years time, with the still modest resources we have at our disposal. Still, our progress to date, and our belief that we are

TABLE 9.1
Processfolio Assessment System
(Currently based on art, music, and writing. To be expanded to other domains.)

I. PRODUCTION: Thinking in the domain

Evidence: The evidence for assessing work on the dimension of production lies in the work itself. Thus, these dimensions can be scored by an outsider looking at drafts and final works, as well as by the classroom teacher.

A. *Craft:* The student is in control of the basic techniques and principles of the domain.

B. *Pursuit:* The student develops works over time, as evidenced by revisions which are productive and thoughtful. She pursues the problem in depth. She returns to a problem or theme from a variety of angles.

C. *Invention:* The student solves problems in a creative manner. She experiments and takes risks with the medium. She sets her own problems to solve.

D. *Expression:* The student expresses an idea or feeling in the work (or in the performance of the work, as in music).

II. REFLECTION: Thinking about the domain

Evidence: The evidence for assessing reflection comes from the student's journals and sketchbooks, and from observations of the kinds of comments that the student makes in class. Thus, these dimensions need to be scored by a classroom teacher, who knows the student.

A. *Ability and proclivity to assess own work:* The student can evaluate her own work. She can articulate and defend the perceived strengths and weaknesses of her own work. She can engage in "shop talk" about her own work.

B. *Ability and proclivity to take on role of critic:* The student has developed the ability to evaluate the work of others (peers, published artists). She has a sense of the standards for quality work in the domain. She can engage in "shop talk" about others' work.

C. *Ability and proclivity to use criticisms and suggestions:* The student can consider critical comments about her own work, and can incorporate suggestions where appropriate.

D. *Ability to learn from other works of art within the domain:* The student can use work by artists for ideas and inspiration.

E. *Ability to articulate artistic goals:* The student has a sense of herself as an artist, as evidenced by the ability to articulate goals for a particular work, or more general artistic goals.

III. PERCEPTION: Perceiving in the domain

Evidence: The evidence for assessing a student's perceptual skills comes from the student's journal entries, and from observations of the student's comments made in critique sessions. Thus, only a classroom teacher can assess a student on this dimension.

TABLE 9.1 *(continued)*

III. PERCEPTION: Perceiving in the domain

A. *Capacity to make fine discriminations about works in the domain:* The student can make discriminations in works from a wide variety of genres, cultures, and historical periods.

B. *Awareness of sensuous aspects of experience:* The student shows heightened sensitivity to physical properties of the environment related to the domain in question (for example, she responds to visual patterns made by shadows, to sounds of cars honking in different pitches, to patterning of words on a grocery list, and so on).

C. *Awareness of physical properties and qualities of materials:* The student is sensitive to the properties of the materials that she is working with as she is developing a work (for example, textures of different papers; timbres of instruments; sounds of words).

IV. APPROACH TO WORK

Evidence: The evidence for assessing a student's approach to work lies in observations of the student in classroom interactions, and from the student's journal entries. Thus, a student's approach to work can only be assessed by the classroom teacher.

A. *Engagement:* The student works hard and is interested in what she is doing. She meets deadlines. She shows care and attention to detail in the presentation of the final project.

B. *Ability to work independently:* The student can work independently when appropriate.

C. *Ability to work collaboratively:* The student can work collaboratively when appropriate.

D. *Ability to use cultural resources:* The student knows where to go for help: books, museums, tools, other people.

assessing in a way that is worthy of the subject matter, emboldens us to continue our work.

Even if we should fall short of our goal of adequate psychometric measures of processfolios, our effort may still have utility. As noted earlier, an important aspect of artistic learning is the opportunity to become involved in meaningful projects, in which one's own understanding and growth can come to the fore. It is already clear to us that both students and teachers find these processfolio activities engaging, exciting, and useful in their own right. Their classrooms come alive. By encouraging the development of processfolios, and by looking at them sympathetically and systematically, we may be able to increase the use of these materials and activities in schools. While it may be too much to expect that colleges will ever base admissions decisions chiefly on such processfolio information, we hope that such educational vehicles may allow students to put forth their own cognitive strengths.

Educators and educational critics frequently lament the gap between theory and practice—and between theorists and practitioners. It is no doubt true that the professional goals of the two groups *are* different—that the theorist's triumph often leaves the practitioner untouched; while the practitioner's pleasures seem uninteresting to the theorist.

For some time, it was fashionable to criticize Project Zero for its remoteness from educational practice. That remoteness had two senses: (1) our work focused more on "natural" development than on what could be explicitly taught in the classroom; (2) our ideas, whether or not they were considered generally appealing, had little or no direct implication for what happens in the classroom on Monday morning.

While these charges sometimes left us a bit offended and made us a tad defensive, we are on the whole comfortable with them as characterizations of our youth and early adolescence. We feel that it is important to look at "natural" development before one examines interventions; and we believe that it is important to establish the psychological facts and to develop one's educational philosophy before one attempts to influence practice—especially since it is always possible that one might influence practice for the worse!

Having had the luxury of two decades of relatively "ivory tower" exploration in arts education, it has certainly been opportune for us to become more directly involved in educational experimentation. The fact that this is a time in which arts educational practice is being so widely discussed only heightens the need for us to "get our hands wet." Arts PROPEL represents one concerted effort to do just that. It is too early to know how successful this effort will prove to be; and even if successful in its "hothouse" atmosphere, whether it can be successfully transported to more remote soils. But it is not premature to indicate that researchers can learn a great deal from attempting to implement their ideas in a school setting. So long as we are on the alert for any disruption that we may cause, this intermingling of theory and practice should redound to the good of all those involved in arts education.

As is the case with Project Spectrum, Arts PROPEL has been adopted for use by a variety of school systems around the country. In Cambridge, Massachusetts, for example, an adaptation of Visual Arts PROPEL is now being used in classes for kindergarten and first-grade children. There has been tremendous interest in the work done in Music PROPEL: domain projects and processfolios have proved of interest not only to classroom teachers around the country but also to educational departments associated with symphony orchestras and operas. All of us on PROPEL were honored when Arts PROPEL was selected by *Newsweek* in December 1991 as one of only two "model" educational programs in the world situated in the United States: the other was graduate science education at the California Institute of Technology! (Chideya, 1991).

Even more surprising, and especially gratifying, is the fact that the ideas undergirding PROPEL have proved attractive to educators in other subject matters. Though the notion of projects and processfolios has a long history in the arts, teachers and curriculum supervisors in domains ranging from history to mathematics have come to appreciate the usefulness of rich and engaging projects and the desirability of that systematic cast of thought involved in reflecting upon one's work and keeping a regular journal. As a long-time arts educator who is used to seeing his field treated as a backwater, I gain special satisfaction from the present circumstance: our ideas and practices may actually provide inspirations to areas of the curriculum that have traditionally been more prestigious.

Interlude

On Implementing Educational Programs: Obstacles and Opportunities

W hen teachers, administrators, and researchers join forces to implement a new educational project, a number of considerations typically arise. Having been involved in a number of such programs, including the ones described in part II, I now have a sense of what to expect when embarking on such a collaboration. Recently I was reviewing progress and problems that have characterized one of our newest projects: an after-school program in which children are encouraged to develop their literate and thinking skills through their participation in engaging projects. I was struck by the following points which turn out to be applicable across our range of projects:

Difficulties of innovation. It is very difficult to initiate an effective new program. Unexpected obstacles arise frequently; team members find themselves working at cross-purposes; sudden setbacks are almost the rule. Participants swing from optimism to pessimism, sometimes seeing the glass as half full, sometimes as half empty. I can convey the mood by describing a conversation that I overheard between two colleagues who were involved in setting up our innovative after-school program:

Optimist (speaking with glee, at the end of a day where students had become fully engaged in the staging of a play): "Boy, this is the best day we've ever had!"
Pessimist (looking down at the ground, speaking despondently): "Yeah, yeah, pal, that's the problem."

Identification of goals. Any program needs a statement of goals—what is desired, what is good. But these aspirations must be flexible and emergent: generally speaking, it is not prudent to articulate a goal and then adhere to it, in indifference to what happens on site.

For example, at the beginning of our after-school program, we discovered the existence of at least five different goals. The parents wanted a place for youngsters to do their homework; the children wanted to have fun; the teachers wanted the children to develop self-esteem; the principal wanted to develop new curriculum; the researchers wanted to answer certain questions about learning that grow out of their earlier investigations. Needless to say, such goals can turn out to be at cross-purposes with one another; and such a vexed outcome is particularly likely when the different groups neither share their goals with one another nor take pains to explain their special perspectives.

The need for team spirit. A sine qua non for progress is the forging of effective human relations among the participants. Members of the different groups must be able to speak to one another, to agree, to disagree, to interact as peers, to have relationships as equals. In the case of our after-school project, it has proved important for the teachers to understand the goals and concerns of the researchers—why, for example, we wish to have a control group even though we have a "treatment" that seems to be effective. It is equally important for the researchers to appreciate the teachers' strengths, constraints, and goals: what it takes to run a smooth classroom, how important it is that students feel good about themselves, what demands are being made by the supervisors at the city and at the state level.

Common conception and language. Gradually a common conception of the project needs to emerge. While it is not necessary that there be a single goal, there must be a view and a set of practices that allow complementary goals to be pursued in a smooth way. Collaborators must be able to manage the project together, forge a common terminology, converge on an agreed-upon set of markers of progress. Indeed, only if some kind of community can emerge is there any chance that the implementation will take hold.

"Getting it." Ultimately a time comes when the various participants in the project understand one another's goals sufficiently that they can move from a shared conception to an actual working program. No longer do the participants think about a "kit," a "cookbook," a "foolproof" procedure. They now have evolved a sufficiently common approach that they trust one another to carry out activities that exemplify the program's philosophy. Thus, for example, instead of calling for

PROPEL or PIFS units that are prepackaged, teachers begin to experiment with the units, adapting them, infusing them into the regular part of the educational day. It is not any longer "The Harvard Program" or "The Project Zero Program"—it is simply what we do because we believe that it suits our purposes.

Looking inward. After one has a sense of what one wants to accomplish and how one is accomplishing it, an impulse naturally arises to become reflective about the program. How is it working, how could it be improved, how can its course be documented? One has sufficient distance from the program that one can identify productive and disruptive occasions without feeling threatened.

Looking outward. After one has a sense of the program as a whole, one may well wish to share the program with others by describing it publicly, having visitors look at it critically, traveling to other sites, promulgating the program, or even "giving it away." At this point, researchers prove superfluous; they can move on to carry on research at other sites, as other educators announce that they wish to adopt the program at "their place."

The points just reviewed denote an ideal sequence of events. In real life, there will be regressions, problems, obstacles, crises, as well as moments of euphoria and documentation of real gains. Every program is different but, as a researcher, I have noted some trouble spots: (1) teachers who say "This is impossible," or "We're already doing this," and, not infrequently, utter both statements without being aware of the contradiction; (2) the absence of early leaders, early adaptors—individuals who are willing to take a risk and are not afraid of failure; and (3) silence, a lack of eye contact, and everyone looking down on the ground. On the other hand, there are hopeful signs: (1) administrators who are well briefed about the program; (2) parents who ask to come and observe; and (3) teachers who raise questions that they themselves would like to investigate, and who criticize constructively.

On occasion there may be a tremendous brouhaha among the participants, perhaps teachers versus researchers, perhaps within the teacher or the researcher group. Sometimes this fight spells the end of the program; but sometimes it is cathartic, allowing all the participants to bracket their differences and get on with the program.

Note that these hopeful signs and trouble spots represent the perspective of the researcher. I am sure that teachers, administrators, parents, and students also develop a sense of when a collaboration with researchers is promising and when it seems earmarked for failure.

Part III

ASSESSMENT AND BEYOND: THE COMPONENTS OF AN MI EDUCATION

Introductory Note

One way to construct a multiple intelligences education is to devise a model program at a specific site. One can then study the program to see whether it has proved effective and if so, why; and determine whether it can then be transplanted to another site. This procedure has been followed with the quartet of projects described in chapters 6 through 9.

An alternative approach involves a consideration of the standard components of an educational system. In my own case, I began by probing the nature of assessment, certainly a mainstay of any scholastic setting. My interest in assessment arose from two disparate sources: (1) the realization that MI theory deserved to be taken seriously only if "fair" means were created for assessing each of the multiple intelligences; and (2) my conviction that, in my own country, the educational system was becoming seriously flawed. A corollary assumption was that a significant part of our educational malaise lay in the mindless instruments that were conventionally used to assess student learning and, not incidentally, to signal what learning *is*. In chapter 10, I detail my general philosophy of assessment; in a short interlude following it I offer some suggestions for how one might approach college admissions in the absence of a standardized test.

While assessment is a key component of education, it is by no means the only one. Indeed, education needs to be approached in the first instance by a consideration of the goals to be achieved, and the means for achieving them. Drawing on work completed well after *Frames of mind* was published, I present in chapter 11 my views about an education that is geared toward the fostering of *understanding*. Such an education cannot be readily achieved but it is, in my view, the only education that is worth striving for. Following the presentation of this educational vision, I consider in turn the major components of an effective educational system: the milieus in which education takes place; the nature of the curriculum; the cadre of teachers responsible for instruction; and the infinitely varied population of students. Chapter 11 concludes with a discussion of how understanding can be achieved in light of the multiplicity of human intellectual capacities.

Chapter 10

Assessment in Context:
The Alternative to
Standardized Testing

A familiar scene almost anywhere in the United States today: Several hundred students file into a large examination hall. They sit nervously, waiting for sealed packets to be handed out. At the appointed hour, booklets are distributed, brief instructions are issued, and formal testing begins. The hall is still as students at each desk bear down on number two pencils and fill in the bubbles that punctuate the answer sheets. A few hours later, the testing ends and the booklets are collected; several weeks later, a sheet bearing a set of scores arrives at each student's home and at the colleges to which the students have directed their scores. The results of a morning's testing become a powerful factor in decisions about the future of each student.

An equally familiar scene in most preindustrial societies over the centuries: A youth of ten or eleven moves into the home of a man who has mastered a trade. Initially, the lad is asked to carry out menial tasks as he helps the master to prepare for his work or to clean up the shop at the end of the day. During this initial phase, the lad has the opportunity to watch the master at work, while the master monitors the youth to discover his special talents or serious flaws. Over the months the apprentice slowly enters into the practice of the trade. After initially aiding in the more peripheral aspects of the trade, he eventually gains familiarity with the full gamut of skilled work. Directed by tradition, but also guided by the youth's particular skills and motivation, the master guides his charge through the various steps from novice to journeyman. Finally, after several years of supervised training, the youth is ready to practice the craft on his own.

While both of these scenes are idealized, they should be readily recognizable to anyone concerned with the assessment and training of young people. Indeed, they may be said to represent two extremes. The first "formal testing" model is conceived of as an objective, decontextualized form of assessment, which can be adopted and implemented widely with some assurance that similar results will be obtained. The second "apprenticeship" model is implemented almost entirely within a naturally occurring context in which the particularities of a craft are embedded. The assessment is based upon a prior analysis of the skills involved in a particular craft, but it may also be influenced by subjective factors, including the master's personal views about his apprentice, his relationship with other masters, or his need for other kinds of services.

It should be evident that these two forms of assessment were designed to meet different needs. Apprenticeships made sense when the practice of various crafts was the major form of employment for nonrural youths. Formal testing is a contemporary means of comparing the performance of thousands of students who are being educated in schools. Yet these forms of assessment are not limited to the two prototypical contexts described earlier. Despite the overwhelmingly agrarian nature of Chinese society, formal tests have been used there for over two thousand years in selecting government officials. And, by the same token, in many art forms, athletic practices, and areas of scientific research (Polanyi, 1958), apprenticeships and the concomitant ongoing, context-determined forms of assessment continue to be used in our highly industrialized society.

Thus, the choice of "formal testing" as opposed to "apprenticeship" is not dictated solely by the historical era or the primary means of production in the society. It would be possible in our society to utilize the apprenticeship method to a much greater extent than we do. Most observers today (myself included) do not lament the passage of the obligatory apprenticeship system, with its frequent excesses and blatant sexism; from several points of view, contemporary formal testing represents a fairer and more easily justifiable form of assessment. And yet, aspects of the apprentice model are consistent with current knowledge about how individuals learn and how their performances might best be assessed.

Our society has embraced the formal testing mode to an excessive degree; I contend that aspects of the apprentice model of learning and

162

assessment—which I term "contextualized learning"—could be profitably reintroduced into our educational system (see Collins, Brown, & Newman, 1989). Following an account of the origins of standardized testing and the one-dimensional view of mentation often implied by such testing methods, I suggest the need for a far more capacious view of the human mind and of human learning than that which informed earlier conceptions.

My task here is to envision forms of education and modes of assessment that have a firm rooting in current scientific understanding and that contribute to enlightened educational goals. In the latter half of the chapter, I will sketch the nature of an "assessing society."

Binet, the Testing Society, and the "Uniform" View of Schooling

The widespread use of formal testing can be traced to the work on intelligence testing carried out in Paris at the turn of the century by Alfred Binet and his colleagues. Binet was asked by city educational leaders to assist in determining which students would succeed and which would likely fail in elementary school (Binet & Simon, 1905; Block & Dworkin, 1976). He hit upon the inspired idea of administering a large set of items to young school children and identifying which of the items proved most discriminating in light of his particular goal. The work carried out by the Binet team ultimately led to the first intelligence tests, and the construct of intelligence quotient, or IQ.

So great was the appeal of the Binet method that it soon became a dominant feature of the American educational and assessment landscape. To be sure, some standardized tests—ranging from the California Achievement Tests to the Scholastic Aptitude Test—are not direct outgrowths of the various intelligence tests. And yet it is difficult to envision the proliferation of these instruments over just a few decades without the widely esteemed examples of the Stanford-Binet, the Army Alpha, and the various Wechsler intelligence instruments (Brown & Herrnstein, 1975).

In the United States especially, with its focus on quantitative markers and its cult of educational efficiency, there has been a virtual mania for producing tests for every possible social purpose (Gould, 1981; Hoffmann, 1962). In addition to standardized tests for students, we have such tests for teachers, supervisors, soldiers, and police officers; we use adaptations of these instruments to assess capacities not only in standard areas of the curriculum but also in civics and the arts; and we can draw on short-answer measures for assessing personality, degrees of authoritarianism, and compatibility for dating. The United States is well on the way to becoming a "complete testing society." We could encapsulate this attitude thus: If something is important, it is worth testing in this way; if it cannot be so tested, then it probably ought not to be valued. Few observers have stopped to consider the domains in which such an approach might *not* be relevant or optimal, and most have forgotten the insights that might be gained from modes of assessment favored in an earlier era.

It is risky to attempt to generalize across the thousands of "formal instruments" that are described in books like Buros's *Eighth mental measurements yearbook* (1978). Yet, at the cost of doing some violence to certain instruments, it is worth indicating the features that are typically associated with such instruments.

There is within the testing profession considerable belief in "raw," probably genetically based potential (Eysenck, 1967; Jensen, 1980). The most highly valued tests, such as IQ tests and the SATs, are thought to measure ability or potential performance. There is no necessary reason why a test cannot assess skills that have been learned, and many "achievement" tests purport to do this. Yet for tests that purport to measure raw ability or potential, it is important that performance cannot be readily improved by instruction; otherwise, the test would not be a valid indicator of ability. Most authorities on testing believe that performance on ability and achievement tests reflects inherent capacities.

Adherents of testing also tend to embrace a view of human development that assumes that a young organism contains less knowledge and exhibits less skill than a more mature organism, but that no qualitative changes occur over time in human mind or behavior (Bijou & Baer, 1965). Making such assumptions enables the testmaker to use the same kinds of instruments for individuals of all ages; and he or she can legitimately claim that descriptions of data at a certain point in development can be extended to later ages, because one is dealing with the same kind of scale and the same property of mind or behavior.

Reflecting general American technological pressures, as well as the desire for elegance and economy, most testmakers and buyers place a premium on instruments that are efficient, brief, and able to be readily administered. In the early days of testing, assessment sometimes took hours and was individually administered; now, group-administered instruments are desired. Virtually every widely used test has spawned a "brief" version. Indeed, some of the staunchest supporters of formal intelligence tests hope to strip them down even further: Arthur Jensen (1987) has embraced "reaction time" measures, Michael Anderson (1987) looks to sensory discrimination, and Hans Eysenck (1979) has called for the examination of patterns of brain waves.

Accompanying a fealty to formal testing is a view of education that I have termed the "uniform view of schooling." This view does not necessarily entail the wearing of uniforms, but it does call for homogenized education in other respects. According to the uniform view, as much as possible students should study the same subject matter. (This may include a strong dosage of the values of the dominant culture or subculture—see Bloom, 1987; Hirsch, 1987; Ravitch & Finn, 1987). Moreover, as much as possible, that subject matter ought to be conveyed in the same way to all students.

In the uniform view, progress in school ought to be assessed by frequent formal tests. These tests should be administered under uniform conditions, and students, teachers, and parents should receive quantitative scores that detail the student's progress or lack thereof. These tests should be nationally normed instruments, so that the maximum comparability is possible. The most important subject matters are those that lend themselves readily to such assessment, such as mathematics and science. In other subjects, value is assigned to the aspects that can be efficiently assessed (grammar rather than "voice" in writing; facts rather than interpretation in history). Those disciplines that prove most refractory to formal testing, such as the arts, are least valued in the uniform school.

In putting forth this picture of Binet, the testing society, and the uniform view of schooling, I am aware that I am overemphasizing certain tendencies and lumping together views and attitudes in a way that is not entirely fair to those who are closely associated with formal testing. Some individuals intimately involved with testing have voiced the same concerns (Cronbach, 1984; Messick, 1988). Indeed, had I put this picture forth fifteen or twenty years ago it might have seemed an outrageous caricature. However, the trends within American education since the early 1980s bear a strong resemblance to the views I have just sketched. At the very least, these views serve as a necessary "contrast case" to the picture of contextualized and individualized assessment and schooling that I present later in the chapter; they should be taken in that contrastive spirit.

Sources for an Alternative Approach to Assessment

While the testing society has responded more to pragmatic needs than to scientific dictates, it does reflect a certain view of human nature. The scientific ideas on which the testing society has been based derive from an earlier era in which behaviorist, learning-theoretical, and associationist views of cognition and development were regnant (see Gardner, 1985 for a summary). According to these views, it made sense to believe in "inborn" human abilities, in a smooth, probably linear curve of learning from infancy to old age, in a hierarchy of disciplines, and in the desirability of assessing potential and achievement under carefully controlled and maximally decontextualized conditions.

Over the past few decades, however, the various assumptions on which this testing edifice was based have been gradually undermined by work in developmental, cognitive, and educational studies, and a quite different view has emerged. It is not possible in this chapter to review all of the evidence on which this shifting psychological conception has been based. But because my alternative picture of assessment builds on the newly emerging picture of human development, it is important to highlight the principal features of this perspective and to indicate where it may clash with standard views of testing.

THE NECESSITY FOR A DEVELOPMENTAL PERSPECTIVE

Owing to the pioneering work of Jean Piaget (1983), it is widely recognized that children are not simply miniature versions of adults. The infant or the toddler conceives of the world in a way that is internally consistent but that deviates in important particulars from a more mature conception. Here are some of the most familiar instances from the Piagetian canon: the infant does not appreciate that an object continues to exist when it has been removed from view; the toddler does not understand that material remains constant in quantity, even when its physical configuration has been altered (for example, squashing a ball of clay); the young school child is unable to reason solely from the implications of one proposition to another but instead proceeds on the basis of knowledge of concrete instances and perceived empirical regularities.

According to Piaget's view, children pass through a number of qualitatively different stages called sensorimotor, preoperational, concrete operational, and formal operational. A child at one stage in one area of knowledge will necessarily be at the same stage in other domains of experience. Few investigators hold any longer to a literal version of this "structured-stage" perspective; there have been too many findings that do not support it (Brainerd, 1978; Gelman, 1978). But most developmental psychologists continue to subscribe to the point of view that the world of the infant or toddler has its own peculiar structures; many developmentalists believe that there are stage sequences within particular domains of experience (for example, language, moral judgment, understanding of physical causality); and nearly all emphasize the need to take into account the child's perspective and level of understanding (Case, 1985; Feldman, 1980; Fischer, 1980).

Another feature of this approach is its assumption that development is neither smooth, nor unilinear, nor free of perturbations. While details differ among theorists, most researchers believe that there may be critical or sensitive periods during which it is especially easy—or especially difficult—to master certain kinds of materials. Similarly, while youngsters tend to improve in most areas with age, there will be periods of more rapid growth and periods of stasis. And a minority of researchers believes that in some domains there may actually be regressions or "U-shapes," with younger children performing in a more sophisticated or integrated fashion than students in middle childhood (Strauss, 1982).

It is possible to construct measurement instruments that reflect the developmental knowledge recently accrued. In fact, some batteries have been devised that build specifically on Piagetian or allied notions (Uzgiris & Hunt, 1966). For the most part, however, American tests have been insensitive to developmental considerations.

THE EMERGENCE OF A SYMBOL-SYSTEM PERSPECTIVE

At the height of the behaviorist era there was no need to posit any kind of mental entity, such as an idea, a thought, a belief, or a symbol. One simply identified behaviors or actions of significance and observed these as scrupulously as possible; so-called thoughts were simply "silent" movements of musculature.

Over the past few decades, however, there has been increasing recognition of the importance in human cognition of the capacity to use various kinds of symbols and symbol systems (Gardner, Howard, & Perkins, 1974; Goodman, 1976; Langer, 1942). Humans are deemed the creatures par excellence of communication, who garner meanings through words, pictures, gestures, numbers, musical patterns, and a whole host of other symbolic forms. The manifestations of these symbols are public: all can observe written language, number systems, drawings, charts, gestural languages, and the like. However, the mental processes needed to manipulate such symbols must be inferred from the performances of individuals on various kinds of tasks. Unexpectedly potent support for the belief in internal symbol-manipulation has come from the invention and widespread use of computers; if these human-made machines engage in operations of symbol use and transformation, it seems ludicrous to withhold the same kinds of capacities from the humans who invented them (Newell & Simon, 1972).

Considerable effort has been expended in the relevant sciences to investigate the development of the human capacity for symbol use. It is widely (though not universally) agreed that infants do not use symbols or exhibit internal symbolic manipulation and that the emergence of symbol use during the second year of life is a major hallmark of human cognition. Thereafter, human beings rapidly acquire skill in the use of those symbols and symbol systems that are featured in their culture. By the age of five or six most children have acquired a "first draft" knowledge of how to create and understand stories, works of music, drawings, and simple scientific explanations (Gardner, 1982).

In literate cultures, however, there is a second level of symbol use. Children must learn to utilize the *invented symbol* (or *notational*) systems of their culture, such as writing and numbers. With few exceptions, this assignment is restricted to school settings, which are relatively decontextualized. Mastering notational systems can be difficult for many students in our society, including students whose mastery of "practical knowledge" and "first-order symbol systems" has been unproblematic. Even those students who prove facile at acquiring notational systems face a nontrivial challenge: they must mesh their newly acquired "second-order" symbolic knowledge with the earlier forms of "practical" and "first-order" symbolic knowledge they brought with them to school (Bamberger, 1982; Gardner, 1986; Resnick, 1987).

Nearly all formal tests presuppose that their users will be literate in the second-level symbol systems of the culture. These tests thus pose special difficulties for individuals who, for whatever reason, have had difficulty in attaining second-level symbol knowledge or cannot map that knowledge onto earlier forms of mental representation. Moreover, it is my belief that individuals with well-developed second-level symbolic skills can often "psych out" such tests, scoring well even when their knowledge of the subject matter that is ostensibly being assessed is modest (Gardner, 1983). At any rate, what the exact relations are among "practical," "first-order," and "second-order" symbolic knowledge and what the best way is to assess these remain difficult issues to resolve.

EVIDENCE FOR THE EXISTENCE OF MULTIPLE FACULTIES OR "INTELLIGENCES"

When intelligence tests were first assembled, there was little attention paid to the underlying theory of intelligence. But soon the idea gained currency that the different abilities being tapped all fed into or reflected a single "general intelligence." This perspective has remained the view-of-choice among most students of intelligence, though a minority has been open to the idea of different "vectors of mind" or different "products, content, and operations" of intellect (Guilford, 1967; Thurstone, 1938). This minority has based its conclusions on the results of factor analyses of test results; however, it has been shown that one can arrive at either unitary or pluralistic views of intellect, depending upon which assumptions guide specific factor analytic procedures (Gould, 1981).

In recent years, there has been a resurgence of interest in the idea of a multiplicity of intelligences. Mental phenomena have been discovered that some researchers construe as evidence for mental *modules*—fast-operating, reflexlike, information-processing devices that seem impervious to the influence of other modules. The discovery of these modules has given rise to the view that there may be separate analytic devices involved in tasks like syntactic parsing, tonal recognition, or facial perception (Fodor, 1983).

A second source of evidence for a multiplicity of intelligences has been the fine-grained analysis of the mental operations involved in the solution of items used in intelligence tests (Sternberg, 1977, 1985). These analyses have suggested the existence of different components that contribute to success on any standard intellectual assessment. Individuals may differ from one another in the facility with which the different components operate, and different tasks may call upon a differential use of the various components, metacomponents, and subcomponents (see chapters 1 and 2). Each of the various "multiple intelligences" perspectives, including my own, concurs on the following proposition: instead of a single dimension called intellect, on which individuals can be rank-ordered, there are vast differences among individuals in their intellectual strengths and weaknesses and also in their styles of attack in cognitive pursuits (Kagan & Kogan, 1970). Our own evidence suggests that these differences may be evident even before the years of formal schooling.

The literature on different individual strengths, as well as the findings on diverse cognitive styles, has crucial educational implications. To begin with, it is important to identify strengths and weaknesses at an early point so that they can become part of educational planning. Striking differences among individuals also call into question whether individuals ought all to be taking the same curriculum and whether, to the extent that there is a uniform curriculum, it needs to be presented in the same fashion to all individuals.

Formal tests can be an ally to the recognition of different cognitive features, but only if the tests are designed to elicit—rather than mask—these differences (Cronbach & Snow, 1977). It is particularly important that instruments used in "gatekeeping" niches (like college admissions) be designed to allow students to show their strengths and to perform optimally. Until now, little effort has been made in this regard and tests are more frequently used to point up weaknesses than to designate strengths.

A SEARCH FOR HUMAN CREATIVE CAPACITIES

During most of the first century of formal testing interest fell heavily on assessment of individual intelligence, and there was relatively little concern with other cognitive capacities. In the post-*Sputnik* era, when scientific ingenuity was suddenly at a premium, American educators became convinced of the importance of imaginativeness, inventiveness, and creativity. They called for the devising of instruments that would assess creativity or creative potential (Guilford, 1950). Regrettably (from my perspective), in their search for creativity measures they repeated most of the mistakes that had been made throughout the history of intelligence testing. That is, they tried to devise short-answer, timed measures of the abilities they thought central to creativity—the capacity to come up with a variety of answers to a question (divergent thinking) or to issue as many unusual associations as possible to a stimulus (ideational fluency).

While the field of intelligence testing is currently filled with controversy, there is consensus that creativity tests have not fulfilled their potential (Wallach, 1971, 1985). These instruments are reliable, and they do measure something other than psychometric intelligence, but they cannot predict which individuals will be judged as creative on the basis of their productions within a domain. Rather than attempting to devise more and better "creativity tests," researchers have instead begun to examine more closely what actually happens when individuals are engaged in problem-solving or problem-finding activities (Gruber, 1981; Sternberg 1988).

These recent studies have yielded two major findings. On the one hand, creative individuals do not seem to have at their disposal mental operations that are theirs alone; creative individuals make use of the same cognitive processes as do other persons, but they use them in a more efficient and flexible way and in the service of goals that are ambitious and often quite risky (Perkins, 1981). On the other hand, highly creative individuals do seem to lead their lives in a way different from most others. They are fully engaged in and passionate about their work; they exhibit a need to do something new and have a strong sense of their purpose and ultimate goals; they are extremely reflective about their activities, their use of time, and the quality of their products (Gruber, 1985).

Except rhetorically, the quest for creativity has not been a major goal of the American educational system. However, to the extent that the fostering of creative individuals is a desirable goal for an educational institution, it is important that this goal be pursued in a manner consistent with current analyses of creativity (Gardner, 1988a).

THE DESIRABILITY OF ASSESSING LEARNING IN CONTEXT

When standardized tests and paradigmatic experimental designs were first introduced into non-Western cultural contexts, they led to a single result: preliterate individuals and others from non-Western societies appeared to be much less skilled and much less intelligent than Western control groups. An interesting phenomenon was then discovered. Simple alterations of materials, test setting, or instructions frequently elicited dramatic improvements in performance. The performance gap between the subjects from another culture and the subjects from our own culture narrowed or even disappeared when familiar materials were used, when knowledgeable and linguistically fluent examiners were employed, when revised instructions were given, or when the "same" cognitive capacities were tapped in a form that made more sense within the non-Western context (Laboratory of Comparative Human Cognition, 1982).

Now a huge body of experimental evidence exists to indicate that assessment materials designed for one target audience cannot be transported directly to another cultural setting; there are no purely culture-fair or culture-blind materials. Every instrument reflects its origins. Formal tests that make some sense in a Western context do so because students are accustomed to learn about materials at a site removed from the habitual application of such materials; however, in unschooled or lightly schooled environments, most instruction takes place in situ, and so it only makes sense to administer assessments that are similarly in context.

Building upon this cross-cultural research, there is also an accumulation of findings about the cognitive abilities of various kinds of experts. It has been shown that experts often fail on "formal" measures of their calculating or reasoning capacities but can be shown to exhibit precisely those same skills in the course of their ordinary work—such as tailoring clothes, shopping in a supermarket, loading dairy cases onto a truck, or defending one's rights in a dispute (Lave, 1980; Rogoff, 1982; Scribner, 1986). In such cases, it is not the person who has failed but rather the measurement instrument which purported to document the person's level of competence.

LOCATING COMPETENCE AND SKILL OUTSIDE THE HEAD OF THE INDIVIDUAL

The research just reviewed has yielded another novel conceptualization. In many cases it is erroneous to conclude that the knowledge required to execute a task resides completely in the mind of a single individual. This knowledge can be "distributed": that is, successful performance of a task may depend upon a team of individuals, no single one of whom possesses all of the necessary expertise but all of whom, working together, are able to accomplish the task in a reliable way (Scribner, 1986). Relatedly, it is too simple to say that an individual either "has" or "does not have" the requisite knowledge; that knowledge may show up reliably in the presence of the appropriate human and physical "triggers" but might be otherwise invisible to probing (Squire, 1986).

It makes sense to think of human cognitive competence as an emerging capacity, one likely to be manifest at the intersection of three different constituents: the "individual," with his or her skills, knowledge, and aims; the structure of a "domain of knowledge," within which these skills can be aroused; and a set of institutions and roles—a surrounding "field"—which judges when a particular performance is acceptable and when it fails to meet specifications (Csikszentmihalyi, 1988; Csikszentmihalyi & Robinson, 1986; Gardner & Wolf, 1988). The acquisition and transmission of knowledge depends upon a dynamic that sustains itself among these three components. Particularly beyond the years of early childhood, human accomplishment presupposes an awareness of the different domains of knowledge in one's culture and the various "field forces" that affect opportunity, progress, and recognition. By focusing on the knowledge that resides within a single mind at a single moment, formal testing may distort, magnify, or grossly underestimate the contributions that an individual can make within a larger social setting.

The foregoing research findings point to a differentiated and nuanced view of assessment, one that, at least in certain ways, might more closely resemble traditional apprenticeship measures than formal testing. An assessment initiative being planned today, in light of these findings, should be sensitive to developmental stages and trajectories. Such an initiative should investigate human symbolic capacities in an appropriate fashion in the years following infancy and investigate the relationship between practical knowledge and first- and second-level symbolic skills. It should recognize the existence of different intelligences and of diverse cognitive and stylistic profiles, and it should incorporate an awareness of these variations into assessments; it should possess an understanding of those features that characterize creative individuals in different domains. Finally, a new assessment initiative should acknowledge the effects of context on performance and provide the most appropriate contexts in which to assess competences, including ones that extend outside the skin of the individual being assessed.

It is a tall order to meet all of these needs and desiderata. Indeed, an attraction of formal testing is that one can bracket or minimize most of the features that I have just outlined. However, if we seek an assessment that is both true to the individual and reflective of our best understanding of the nature of human cognition, then we cannot afford to ignore these lines of thinking.

General Features of a New Approach to Assessment

If one were to return to the drawing board today and lay out a fresh approach to assessment, one might attempt to incorporate the following principal features.

EMPHASIS ON ASSESSMENT RATHER THAN TESTING

The penchant for testing in America has gone too far. While some tests are useful for some purposes, the testing industry has taken off in a way that makes little sense from the point of view of a reflective society. Many who seek to understand the underlying theoretical or conceptual basis of findings of validity are disappointed. It seems that many tests have been designed to create, rather than to fulfill, a need.

While I have ambivalent feelings about testing, I have little ambivalence about assessment. To my mind, it is the proper mission of educated individuals, as well as those who are under their charge, to engage in regular and appropriate reflection on their goals, the various means to achieve them, their success (or lack thereof) in achieving these goals, and the implications of the assessment for rethinking goals or procedures.

I define assessment as the obtaining of information about the skills and potentials of individuals, with the dual goals of providing useful feedback to the individuals and useful data to the surrounding community. What distinguishes assessment from testing is the former's favoring of techniques that elicit information in the course of ordinary performance and its general uneasiness with the use of formal instruments administered in a neutral, decontextualized setting.

In my view, those in the psychological and educational communities charged with the task of evaluation ought to facilitate such assessment (see Cross & Angelo, 1988). We ought to be devising methods and measures that aid in regular, systematic, and useful assessment. In some cases we would end up producing "formal tests." But not in most cases, I expect.

ASSESSMENT AS SIMPLE, NATURAL, AND OCCURRING ON A RELIABLE SCHEDULE

Rather than being imposed "externally" at odd times during the year, assessment ought to become part of the natural learning environment.

As much as possible it should occur "on the fly," as part of an individual's natural engagement in a learning situation. Initially, the assessment would probably have to be introduced explicitly; but after a while, much assessment would occur naturally on the part of student and teacher, with little need for explicit recognition or labeling on anyone's part.

The model of the assessment of the cognitive abilities of the expert is relevant here. On the one hand, it is rarely necessary for the expert to be assessed by others unless competitive conditions obtain. It is assumed that experts will go about their business with little external monitoring. However, it is also true that the expert is constantly in the process of assessing; such assessment occurs naturally, almost without conscious reflection, in the course of working. When I first began to write scholarly articles, I was highly dependent upon the detailed criticism of teachers and editors; now most of the needed assessment occurs at a preconscious level as I sit at my desk scribbling, or typing a first draft, or editing an earlier version of the material.

As assessment gradually becomes part of the landscape, it no longer needs to be set off from the rest of classroom activity. As in a good apprenticeship, the teachers and the students are always assessing. There is also no need to "teach for the assessment" because the assessment is ubiquitous; indeed, the need for formal tests might atrophy altogether.

ECOLOGICAL VALIDITY

A problem with most formal tests is their validity, that is, their correlation with some criterion (Messick, 1988). As noted, creativity tests are no longer used much because their validity has never been adequately established. The predictive validity of intelligence tests and scholastic aptitude tests is often questioned in view of their limited usefulness in predicting performance beyond the next year of schooling.

Returning to our example of the apprenticeship, it would make little sense to question the validity of the judgments by the master. He is so intimately associated with his novice that he can probably predict his behaviors with a high degree of accuracy. When such prediction does not occur reliably, trouble lies ahead. I believe that current assessments have moved too far away from the territory that they are supposed to cover. When individuals are assessed in situations that more closely resemble "actual working conditions," it is possible to make much better predictions about their ultimate performance. It is odd that most American schoolchildren spend hundreds of hours engaged in a single exercise—the formal test—when few if any of them will ever encounter a similar instrument once they have left school.

INSTRUMENTS THAT ARE "INTELLIGENCE-FAIR"

As already noted, most testing instruments are biased heavily in favor of two varieties of intelligence—linguistic and logical-mathematical. Individuals blessed with this particular combination are likely to do well on most kinds of formal tests, even if they are not particularly adept in the domain actually under investigation. By the same token, individuals with problems in either or both linguistic and logical-mathematical intelligence may fail at measures of other domains, just because they cannot master the particular format of most standard instruments.

The solution—easier to describe than to realize—is to devise instruments that are intelligence-fair, that peer directly at the intelligence-in-operation rather than proceed via the detour of language and logical faculties. Spatial intelligence can be assessed by having an individual navigate around an unfamiliar territory; bodily intelligence by seeing how a person learns and remembers a new dance or physical exercise; interpersonal intelligence by watching an individual handle a dispute with a sales clerk or navigate a way through a difficult committee meeting. These homely instances indicate that "intelligence-fairer" measures could be devised, though they cannot necessarily be implemented in the psychological laboratory or the testing hall.

USES OF MULTIPLE MEASURES

Few practices are more nefarious in education than the drawing of widespread educational implications from the composite score of a single test—like the Wechsler Intelligence Scale for Children. Even intelligence tests contain subtests and, at the very least, recommendations ought to take into account the "scatter" on these tests and the strategies for approaching particular items (Kaplan, 1983).

Attention to a range of measures designed specifically to tap different facets of the capacity in question is even more desirable. Consider, for example, the admission standards of a program for gifted children. Conservatively speaking, 75 percent of the programs in the country simply admit on the basis of IQ—a score of 129, and you are out; 131, and you are in. How unfortunate! I have no objection to IQ as one consideration, but why not attend as well to the products that a child has already fashioned, the child's goals and desire for a program, performance during a trial period alongside other "gifted" children, and other unobtrusive measures? I often feel that enormous educational progress would be made simply if the secretary of education appeared in front of the television cameras, not accompanied by a single "one-dimensional" wall-chart, but against the backdrop of a half-dozen disparate graphic displays, each monitoring a distinctly different aspect of learning and productivity.

SENSITIVITY TO INDIVIDUAL DIFFERENCES, DEVELOPMENTAL LEVELS, AND FORMS OF EXPERTISE

Assessment programs that fail to take into account the vast differences among individuals, developmental levels, and varieties of expertise are increasingly anachronistic. Formal testing could, in principle, be adjusted to take these documented variations into account. But it would require a suspension of some of the key assumptions of standardized testing, such as uniformity of individuals in key respects and the penchant for cost-efficient instruments.

Individual differences should also be highlighted when educating teachers and assessors. Those charged with the responsibility of assessing youngsters need to be introduced formally to such distinctions; one cannot expect teachers to arrive at empirically valid taxonomies of individual differences on their own. Such an introduction should occur in education courses or during teaching apprenticeships. Once introduced to these distinctions, and given the opportunity to observe and to work with children who exhibit different profiles, these distinctions come to life for teachers.

It then becomes possible to take these differences into account in a tacit way. Good teachers—whether they teach second grade, piano to toddlers, or research design to graduate students—have always realized that different approaches are effective with different kinds of students. Such sensitivities to individual differences can become part of the teacher's competence and can be drawn upon in the course of regular instruction as well as during assessment. It is also possible—and perhaps optimal—for teachers to season their own intuitive sense of individual differences with judicious occasions of assessment, crafted with the particular domain of practice in mind.

177

USE OF INTRINSICALLY INTERESTING AND MOTIVATING MATERIALS

One of the most objectionable, though seldom remarked upon, features of formal testing is the intrinsic dullness of the materials. How often does *anyone* get excited about a test or a particular item on a test? It was probably only when, as a result of "sunshine" legislation, it became possible for test takers to challenge the answer keys used by testing organizations, that discussion of individual test items ever occupied space in a publication that anyone would voluntarily read.

It does not have to be that way. A good assessment instrument can be a learning experience. But more to the point, it is extremely desirable to have assessment occur in the context of students working on problems, projects, or products that genuinely engage them, that hold their interest and motivate them to do well. Such exercises may not be as easy to design as the standard multiple-choice entry, but they are far more likely to elicit a student's full repertoire of skills and to yield information that is useful for subsequent advice and placement.

APPLICATION OF ASSESSMENT FOR THE STUDENT'S BENEFIT

An equally lamentable aspect of formal testing is the use made of scores. Individuals receive the scores, see their percentile ranks, and draw a conclusion about their scholastic, if not their overall, merit. In my own view, psychologists spend far too much time ranking individuals and not nearly enough time helping them. Assessment should be undertaken primarily to aid students. It is incumbent upon the assessor to provide feedback to the student that will be helpful at the present time—identifying areas of strength as well as weakness, giving suggestions of what to study or work on, pointing out which habits are productive and which are not, indicating what can be expected in the way of future assessments, and the like. It is especially important that some of the feedback take the form of concrete suggestions and indicate relative strengths to build upon, independent of rank within a comparable group of students.

Armed with findings about human cognition and development, and in light of these desiderata for a new approach to assessment, it should be possible to begin to design programs that are more adequate than those that exist today. Without having any grand design to create a "new alternative to formal testing," my colleagues and I at Harvard Project Zero have become engaged in a number of projects over the last several years that feature new approaches to assessment. In part II of this volume, I described several of our current efforts to assess student intellectual strengths in context. Here I attempt to place these efforts within the broader picture of assessment in the schools.

Toward the Assessing Society

This chapter has been an extended essay in favor of regular assessment occurring in a natural fashion throughout the educational system and across the trajectory of lifelong learning. I have reviewed a sizable body of evidence, which, by and large, points up problems with standard formal testing as an exclusive mode of assessment. Many of these findings suggest that it would be more fruitful to create environments in which assessments occur naturally and to devise curricular entities, like domain-projects and processfolios, that lend themselves to assessment within the context of their production. It would be an exaggeration to say that I have called for a reintroduction of the apprentice method. Yet I do claim that we have moved too far from that mode of assessment; contemporary assessment might well be informed by some of the concepts and assumptions associated with traditional apprenticeships.

Indeed, if one considers "formal testing" and "apprentice-style assessment" as two poles of assessment, it could be said that America today has veered too far in the direction of formal testing without adequate consideration of the costs and limitations of an exclusive emphasis on that approach. Even outside the realm of physics, an excessive action calls for a reaction—one reason that this chapter stresses the advantages of more naturalistic, context-sensitive, and ecologically valid modes of assessment. Standard formal tests have their place—for example, in initial screening of certain "at-risk" populations—but users should know their limitations as well.

Some objections to the perspective introduced here can be anticipated. One is the claim that formal testing is, as advertised, objective and that I am calling for a regression to subjective forms of evaluation. I reject this characterization for two reasons. First of all, there is no reason in principle to regard the assessment of domain-projects, process-folios, or Spectrum-style measures as intrinsically less objective than other forms. Reliability can be achieved in these practices as well. The establishment of reliability has not been a focus of these projects; however, the conceptual and psychometric tools exist to investigate reliability in these cases. Moreover, these assessment measures are more likely to possess "ecological" validity.

A second retort to this characterization has to do with the alleged objectivity or non-bias of standard formal tests. In a technical sense, it is true that the best of these instruments avoid the dangers of subjectivity and statistical bias. However, any kind of instrument is necessarily skewed toward one kind (or a few kinds) of individual and one (or a few) intellectual and cognitive styles. Formal tests are especially friendly to those individuals who possess a certain blend of linguistic and logical intelligences and who are comfortable in being assessed in a decontextualized setting under timed and impersonal conditions. Correlatively, such tests are biased against individuals who do not exhibit that blend of intelligences, those whose strengths show up better in sustained projects or when they are examined in situ.

I believe that, especially when resources are scarce, every individual ought to have the opportunity to show her or his strength. There is no objection to a "high scorer" being able to show off a string of College Board 800s to a college admissions staff; by the same token, individuals with other cognitive or stylistic strengths ought to have their day as well.

There are those who might be in sympathy with the line of analysis pursued here and yet would reject its implications because of considerations of cost or efficiency. According to this argument, it is simply too inefficient or expensive to mobilize the country around more sustained forms of assessment; and so, even if formal testing is imperfect, we will have to settle for it and simply try to improve it as much as possible.

This line of argument has a surface plausibility, but I reject it as well. To be sure, formal testing is now cost-effective, but it has taken millions, perhaps billions of dollars expended over many decades to bring it to its current far-from-perfect state. Nor do I think that more money spent on current testing would improve it more than marginally. (I do believe that it is worthwhile to conduct research on diagnostic and interactive forms of testing, but those are not topics that I am treating in the present chapter.)

Our current pilot projects, while dependent on research funds, are modest by any standard. In each instance we believe that the main points of the approach can be taught readily to teachers and made available to interested schools or school districts. We subscribe to Theodore Sizer's estimate that a move toward more qualitatively oriented forms of education (and perhaps also to higher-quality education) might increase costs by 10 to 15 percent but probably not more.

The major obstacle I see to assessment-in-context is not availability of resources but rather lack of will. There is in the country today an enormous desire to make education uniform, to treat all students in the same way, and to apply the same kinds of one-dimensional metrics to all. This trend is inappropriate on scientific grounds and distasteful on ethical grounds. The current sentiment is based in part on an understandable disaffection with some of the excesses of earlier educational experiments but, to a disturbing degree, it is also based on a general hostility to students, teachers, and the learning process. In other countries, where the educational process is held in higher regard, it has proved possible to have higher-quality education without subscribing to some of the worst features of one-dimensional educational thinking and assessment.

It is not difficult to sketch out the reasons for the tentative national consensus on the need for more testing and more uniform schools. Understandable uneasiness with poor student performance in the early 1980s resulted in a general indictment of contemporary education, which was blamed for a multitude of societal sins. Government officials, especially state administrators and legislators, entered the fray; the price paid for increased financial support was simple—more testing and more accountability based on testing. The fact that few students of education were entirely comfortable with the diagnosis or the purported cure was not relevant. After all, political officials rarely pore over the relevant literature; they almost reflexively search for scapegoats and call for the quick fix.

It is unfortunate that few public officials or societal leaders have put forth an alternative point of view on these issues. If significant forces or interest groups in this country were to dedicate themselves to a different model of education, which subscribes to the assessment-and-schooling philosophy outlined here, I have every confidence that they could implement it without breaking the bank. It would be necessary for a wider gamut of individuals to pitch in; for college faculty to examine the processfolios that are submitted; for community members to offer mentorships, apprenticeships, or "special pods"; for parents to find out what their children are doing in school and to work with them (or at least encourage them) on their projects. These suggestions may sound revolutionary, but they are daily occurrences in excellent educational settings in the United States and abroad. Indeed, it is hard to imagine quality education in the absence of such a cooperative ambience (Grant, 1978, 1988).

To my way of thinking, the ultimate policy debate is—or at least should be—centered on competing concepts of the purposes and aims of education. As I have intimated above, the "formal standard testing" view harbors a concept of education as a collection of individual elements of information that are to be mastered and then spewed back in a decontextualized setting. On this "bucket view" it is expected that individuals who acquire a sufficient amount of such knowledge will be effective members of the society.

The "assessment view" values the development of productive and reflective skills, cultivated in long-term projects. The animating impulse seeks to bridge the gap between school activities and activities after school, with the thought that the same habits of mind and discipline can be useful in both kinds of undertakings. Especial attention is paid to individual strengths. According to this view, assessment should occur as unobtrusively as possible during the course of daily activities, and the information obtained should be furnished to gatekeepers in useful and economical form.

The assessment view fits comfortably with the vision of individual-centered schooling that I outlined in chapter 5. Some individuals sympathetic to a focus on assessment might still object to the individual-centered view, seeing it as an impractical or romantic view of education; they would prefer more naturalistic modes of assessment in the service of a rigorous curriculum. To these individuals I would respond, perhaps surprisingly to them, by unequivocally endorsing the importance of rigor. There is nothing in an "individual-centered" approach that questions rigor; indeed, in any decent apprenticeship, rigor is assumed. If anything, it is the sophomoric "multiple-choice-cum-isolated-fact" mentality that sacrifices genuine rigor for superficial conformity. I fully embrace rigorous curricula in an individual-based school: I simply call for a broader menu of curricular options.

Marx hoped that one day the state would simply wither away, no longer needed and hardly missed. In my personal millennial vision, I imagine the apparatus of intelligence testing as eventually becoming unnecessary, its waning unmourned. An hour-long standardized test may at certain points in history have served as a reasonable way of indicating who should be performing better at school or who is capable of military service; but as we come to understand the variety of roles and the variety of ways in which scholastic or military accomplishment can come about, we need far more differentiated and far more sensitive ways of assessing what individuals are capable of accomplishing. In place of standardized tests, I hope that we can develop environments (or even societies) in which individuals' natural and acquired strengths would become manifest: environments in which their daily solutions of prob-

182

lems or fashioning of products would indicate clearly which vocational and avocational roles most suit them.

As we move toward constructing such environments, there will be less need for formal and context-free kinds of evaluations because the distance between what students are doing and what they will need (or want) to do in the society will be correspondingly narrowed. We do not have tests to determine who will become a good leader because leadership abilities emerge under naturally occurring circumstances and this kind of evidence speaks for itself. Nor do we have tests for sex appeal, football playing, musical performance, or legislative powers, for much the same reasons. We designed tests for intelligence because it did not prove easy to observe this alleged global property in the real world; but this is perhaps because intelligence as a single, measurable capacity was never well motivated to begin with.

If the kinds of naturally occurring cognition that I have described are valid, then their several manifestations ought to be readily discernible through judicious observations in the individual's ordinary environment. Far from rendering psychologists or psychometricians unemployable, however, a shift to this kind of subtle measurement would require outstanding efforts from a much larger, more broadly trained, and more imaginative cadre of workers. When one thinks about the enormous human potential currently wasted in a society that values only a small subset of human talents, such an investment seems worthwhile.

In contrast to a "testing society," I think that the assessment approach and the individual-centered school constitute a more noble educational vision. Both are more in keeping with American democratic and pluralistic values (Dewey, 1938). I also think that this vision is more consistent with what has been established in recent decades by scientific study of human growth and learning. Schools in the future ought to be so crafted that they are consistent with this vision. In the end, whatever the forms and the incidence of "official assessments," the actual daily learning in schools, as well as the learning stimulated long after "formal" school has been completed, should be its own reward.

Interlude

A Portfolio Approach to College Admissions

I n my view, there is little need and little advantage to be gained by continuing to require the Scholastic Aptitude Test (I have fewer reservations about the achievement tests). Most colleges are not selective enough to warrant such an instrument, and those that are have sufficient additional sources of information about their candidates. The SAT taps only two intelligences and does so in a relatively narrow way. (One can be a significant scientist or writer without possessing the skills to excel on an SAT.) Teaching for (or to) the SAT wastes much valuable time. I would like to see leading colleges follow the example of Bates College and Franklin and Marshall College: they should dispense with the requirement of the Scholastic Aptitude Test and its counterpart instruments.

What would I urge in place of the SAT? Consistent with my earlier remarks, I would like to see schools look for evidences of several intelligences and do so by collecting information (from the student himself and from others) about the kinds of large-scale projects in which the student has been involved and the kinds of products that were executed. Admissions committees ought to include individuals competent to judge the exercise of less scholastic intelligences and combinations of intelligences.

Collections of projects, in the guise of portfolios, would constitute a revealing part of every student's dossier. I would wager that records documenting successful (and unsuccessful) projects would have equivalent predictive value about success in college and better predictive value for success following college. The time spent by admissions committees in examining portfolios or records of projects would be well spent.

I should mention that my colleagues and I at Harvard Project Zero have been working with colleagues at the Educational Testing Service, trying to develop procedures for evaluating projects and portfolios. I am well aware that the SAT will never be replaced as the result of criticisms like mine but only by devising alternative forms of information that are genuinely useful to colleges.

Even as I feel that college admissions procedures ought to be altered to be sensitive to the range of human intelligences and the varieties of ways in which they can be expressed, I believe that the college experience itself could benefit from a "multiple intelligences" perspective. Instructors ought to reduce their reliance on short-answer tests. Students should receive credit for serious work conducted in a variety of intellectual domains. Advisers ought to be selected with an eye toward the intellectual profiles of a student and should be sensitive to the range of courses and styles of evaluation that are appropriate for a given student. In general, it would be highly desirable for both students and faculty to develop greater awareness (or what is often called "meta-awareness") of the profiles of abilities and difficulties that a student might have and the implications of these profiles for planning a profitable college experience.

Finally, I would like to see college instructors embrace a wider range of evaluation instruments. Projects (and not just term papers) ought to be a regular option for students, and all students ought to have the opportunity to carry out and then evaluate (and have evaluated) some of their own projects. Such projects are not only motivating and educational; I am convinced that they also bear more of a linear relation to the kinds of activities and competences that will be at issue once the student leaves the sheltered walls of the university. To these various suggestions I can envision two equally critical responses.

From the right hand, I expect to hear that these procedures would be too difficult and too expensive. We need SATs and short-answer exams because they are efficient to administer and because only they will tell us whether students are really learning anything. It is hard enough to service two intelligences; any notion of serving seven intellectual masters is utopian. From the left hand, I expect to hear that these ideas are scarcely original and that in fact they are already being carried out at many places. While few have banished the SAT, most consider a victory in the Westinghouse Talent Search or even the State Trombone Competition worth more than 100 additional points on an SAT.

I am not deaf to the merits in each of these counter-arguments. There are risks and expenses involved in a shift to a wider and more flexible set of instruments but to my mind these are worth taking. The very fact that some schools have already taken them—and these are among the very best schools—shows that my vision is not utopian.

Indeed, in careful studies conducted over several years, admissions officers at Bates College document no academic costs, and considerable social gains, consequent to a decision to make SATs optional. As for its originality, I cheerfully concede that none of the above ideas is unique to my perspective. I hope, however, to have provided a firmer rationale for some ideas that have already achieved some currency; and I believe that we are devising methods of evaluation that will allow one to use these new kinds of exercises and approaches with some confidence.

I favor these shifts in assessment, teaching, and evaluation because I believe that they follow logically from new findings in the cognitive and neural sciences. Indeed, I think it should be possible to blur the lines between assessment of potential, teaching of curriculum, and evaluation of learning; and I believe that the theory of multiple intelligences provides a number of clues about how this might be accomplished.

Chapter 11

Beyond Assessment:
The Aims and Means of
Education

A mid the enormous amount of attention directed toward educational reform in America and abroad over the past decade or so, surprisingly little discussion has taken place with respect to the *reasons* that we should educate our children—or ourselves. This "silence with respect to goals" is a largely accurate characterization of earlier parts of this volume, where my focus has fallen on human intellectual potentials; and, equally of the opening chapter of this section, which concentrated on a fresh approach to assessment. In this chapter, I attempt to repair this imbalance, by focusing specifically on the reasons that we should educate, and on some of the most promising means for bringing about an effective educational system.

Understanding: A Straightforward Goal for
Education

F ew would challenge the claim that education should seek to inculcate understanding. However, once one asks What is understanding, and how do we know that it has been achieved?, the difficulties attendant on the concept of understanding readily emerge. Indeed, I would claim that most individuals involved in education do not have a clear sense of the nature of understanding, nor do they know how to document that it has (or has not) been achieved.

In *The unschooled mind*, published in 1991, I argue that an individual understands whenever he or she is able to apply knowledge, concepts, or skills (abbreviated, hereafter, as knowledge) acquired in some kind of an educational setting to a new instance or situation, where that knowledge is in fact relevant. By inference, then, an individual fails to understand if he or she cannot apply that knowledge, or if he or she brings inappropriate knowledge to bear on the novel situation.

As a convenient example, let me refer to the short-lived Gulf War of 1991, in which the United States led a consortium of nations in an effort to wrest Kuwait from Iraqi hands, and, in the process, impose a new kind of balance on that region of the world. An individual with political or historical understanding of the region would be able to predict which kinds of outcomes were likely or unlikely to occur following the completion of the battle—including the unlikelihood of a permanent alteration of the *ante bellum* state of affairs. An individual with understanding of the principles of physics could indicate how to aim a Patriot missile so that it would intercept a Scud missile in flight; and also to make some kind of a prediction about how the resulting debris was likely to distribute itself upon the earth. Finally, an individual who understood the principles of economics could anticipate the effect on the United States economy (and on other economies) of an unanticipated large expenditure of money. It is probably fair to say that the highest degree of understanding was evinced with respect to the interception of Scud missiles; and it may not be coincidental that the necessary calculations were carried out by computers.

By virtue of a considerable amount of research conducted by cognitive researchers in the past few decades, we now know a very dissettling fact: most students in the United States, and, so far as we can tell, most students in other industrialized countries do not understand the materials that they have been presented in school. That is, when confronted with an unfamiliar situation, they are generally unable to mobilize the appropriate concepts from school, even if they have been good students. The "smoking gun" occurs in physics: students who have received high grades in physics at redoubtable institutions like MIT and Johns Hopkins are not able to apply their classroom knowledge to games or demonstrations encountered outside of school. (They often answer in the same way as do "unschooled" five-year-olds.)

But, as documented in *The unschooled mind*, this problem is by no means restricted to the hard sciences. Indeed, whether one looks at student learning in statistics, mathematics, psychology, literature, history, or the arts, one encounters essentially the same situation. Within class, students often appear as if they understand, because they are able to furnish back to their instructors the factual and rule-governed information that they have committed to memory. But once out on their own, once expected to figure out *which* of the school-learned concepts, facts, or skills are actually applicable to a new situation, they show themselves to be incapable of understanding—and, again, often mired at the same level as the proverbial five-year-old. It may be superfluous to add that few adults in our society constitute an exception to this rule: as the above instances from the Gulf War suggest, understanding is not widely distributed in our society.

Needless to say, this is a distressing state of affairs. While our better schools certainly succeed in teaching students the basics of reading, writing, and reckoning, they fail a more stringent—and more fundamental—test. Even our better students by and large can be said not to understand the worlds of the sciences, mathematics, the humanities, and the arts. It is perhaps not too much to say that ten or even twenty years of education fail to achieve the goal that it is most reasonable to expect of "the system."

How to Achieve and Demonstrate Understanding

Unless it becomes a central goal of our entire educational enterprise, understanding is most unlikely to be achieved. For starters, educators must agree about which sorts of understandings they wish their students to have. I believe that it is advisable to have such a conversation at the national or even the international level; while each school needs to wrestle with the problem of understanding, it makes little sense to have every individual school or school system start from scratch in laying out its own preferred understandings. Let me list some plausible candidates for understandings in several disciplines:

- Student of physics should be able to explain the actions of objects and phenomena that they encounter in their everyday world, as well as ones that are staged for various purposes within the physics laboratory.
- Students of mathematics should be able to measure relevant

quantities in their lives, make plausible investments, understand the principles of mortgages and insurance, and be able to fill out their tax returns.

- Students of history should be able to read the daily newspaper or weekly newsmagazine and draw on relevant historical principles both to explain what is happening and to make plausible predictions about what is likely to happen next.
- Students of literature and the arts should be able to create at least simple works in relevant genres, understand and appreciate the qualities of works from their and other cultures, and relate these works to their own lives and concerns, even as they bring those personal agendas to any work that they themselves create or appreciate.

I do not think that these aspirations are particularly controversial, nor do I think that they would be very difficult to achieve. But it is worth noting that very few schools actually articulate such "understanding goals" as these. And even fewer posit the "performances of understanding" that their students should ultimately be asked to exhibit.

It has sometimes been convenient to contrast "performances" with "understanding." In terms of that dichotomy, which I myself used in my 1989 book *To open minds*, some educational systems highlight performances: ritualized, memorized sets of sequences and patterns that are initially exhibited by teachers and that students are expected to model with increasing fidelity. Various sites of traditional education, such as China, are often cited as examples of systems that stress "performance." In contrast, the West is thought to highlight "understanding"—the capacity to probe beneath the surface, to figure out underlying causes, to dissect a text or a work of art and illustrate the principles on which it is built. One can think of Confucius as exemplifying a focus on performance, while Socrates emerges as the exemplar incarnate of understanding.

Upon closer examination, however, it is clear that understandings can only be apprehended and appreciated if they are *performed* by a student. We cannot know whether a student understands a principle of physics unless he can issue a relevant performance: such a performance might include building or repairing an apparatus, correctly employing a formula that explains the relation between two variables, or predicting what will happen when two objects collide under certain circumstances. Each of these are "performances of understanding." By the same token, we cannot know whether a student understands a period of history unless she can issue relevant performances: these might include the capacities to explain that period to someone ignorant of American history, to relate that period to ones that came afterwards, to explain an event in today's newspaper in the light of important historical antecedents, or to illuminate works of art of the period by invoking events or personages of the period that can be thought to have animated those works. These, too, are "performances of understanding."

Work currently carried out in collaboration with David Perkins, Vito Perrone, Rebecca Simmons, and several other researchers at Harvard indicates that it is by no means an easy matter for teachers to define such performances, but that it is possible for them to do so. Following such a delineation, the next step is to share these performances with students, to allow them to become familiar with the kinds of performances that one wants them eventually to be able to carry out alone or in cooperation with fellow students. Far from requiring such performances solely at the end of a course or unit, students need to begin to "practice" these performances from the first days of class. And by the same token, students ought to become partners in the processes of assessment as soon as possible. Rather than having assessment occur at the end of the day, and at the hands of a teacher or an outsider examiner, assessment ought to be an activity of mutual engagement, in which students take regular and increasingly major responsibility for reflecting on the nature of their performances and on the means for improving them.

Implications for Curriculum

The most serious consequence of the decision to educate for understanding is a radical foreshortening of the curriculum. If one wishes to have any chance of securing understanding, it becomes essential to abandon the misguided effort to "cover everything." Broad coverage ensures superficiality: at best, heads become stuffed with facts that are forgotten almost as soon as the short-answer test has been administered. Rather, one must move toward "uncoverage," or, to cite another current slogan, one must embrace the principle that "less is more."

In my own version of education for understanding, it is important to define at the outset the kinds of concepts that one wishes students to understand and the kinds of performances that one wishes students to exhibit upon the completion of school. Once defined, these "end states" or "final exhibitions" become the basis on which curricula and assessments to be used en route are then devised. To the extent possible, students ought to be introduced explicitly to these concepts and performances early in their careers, and have the chance to revisit them numerous times during school. And so, for example, if an understanding of democratic institutions is a major goal for history or social studies, curricula and assessments ought to be directed toward such understandings from the first years of school. By the same token, if an understanding of the processes and principles of evolution is a major goal for biological studies, then primary school children should be involved in activities that begin to acquaint them with the phenomena of evolution and give them practice in issuing the sought-after kinds of performances. In short, education for understanding entails the necessity for a "spiral curriculum" in which rich, generative ideas are revisited time and again across a student's career in school.

One can immediately see that such a process requires intimate intercourse among teachers, and considerable continuity in student learning. I have been astonished how frequently a teacher of one age group has no idea of what the students did the previous year and no idea of what they will be doing the following year; it is as if each year were sacrosanct and one were supposed to begin each fall "from scratch." Students and parents are equally culpable. Quite typically, they do not look for continuities across years, semesters, or even classes. What was done in math or English last year is not considered to be related to the tasks for this coming year; and tips about writing picked up in, say, history class, are rarely thought to be relevant to the tasks of writing posed in English or science classes. Here, again, some kind of curriculum coordination—certainly across the school and possibly across the nation—seems to be indicated.

From the above discussion, it should be clear that I favor some forms of "core knowledge," some materials that all students should know. Note that this preference does not take the form of a canonical list of books or principles: I do not feel that such a mandate is appropriate or well founded. Rather I search for a consensus around certain very rich or generative concepts, like evolution or democracy; and for attention to the kinds of performances that can reveal understanding, such as the application of those concepts to newly encountered biological phenomena or political occurrences. It is reasonable to expect every graduate in our land to be able to understand the significance of a new biological discovery or to anticipate the political implications of an economic downslide or an important judicial opinion.

Balancing Specialized and Comprehensive Knowledge: An Educational Challenge

But how can one mediate between the understandable desire for common forms of knowledge within a society, and the need to recognize individual interests and gifts, which is so central to the notion of multiple intelligences? I believe that part of the answer lies in a sensitivity to what makes pedagogical sense at different stages or levels of development.

It is surely no coincidence that children throughout the world begin schooling "in earnest" at around the age of seven. In my own view, most children have by this age proceeded as far as they can in coming to know the physical and social worlds and the world of symbols through the use of their natural learning processes. For some purposes, this untutored absorption of patterns may be enough. Indeed, in certain nontechnological cultures, it already makes sense to consider these children as young adults.

In literate and technologically oriented cultures, however, children are still remote from the concerns and capacities of competent adults. They must become able to read and to master the various notational systems of the culture: mathematical ones, scientific ones, graphing techniques (like maps and charts), and perhaps other specialized notations such as those used in music, dance, or specific vocations. It is the job—and the genius—of schooling to transmit this notational knowledge in the succeeding decade or so.

Children of this age differ in other ways from their younger counterparts. Preschoolers enjoy free exploration, fantasy, and experimenting with boundaries; their speech favors metaphors, and they readily embrace synesthetic connections. By the age of eight or nine, however, most children have become quite different creatures. During this middle childhood phase, they want to master the rules of their cultures and of its specific vocations and avocations. They want to use language precisely, not allusively; they want to draw pictures that are photographically realistic, not fanciful or abstract; and they expect a strict adherence to rules in dress, behavior, games, moral situations, and other cultural activities, brooking little deviation.

These shifts in mood and focus offer pedagogical opportunities. Certainly the first years of school are a time when it is important to master the notational systems of the culture. By and large, children cannot master these notations on their own; that is why school begins the world over at around the age of seven. It is now realized that this is a more difficult task than previously thought, because notational systems are not mastered in a knowledge vacuum. Rather, they must build upon and relate to the "commonsensical" understanding of domains that has been achieved in the preschool years. Thus, written language must be related to oral language skills; musical notational skills to the child's intuitive or "figural" perception of music; scientific concepts to common-sense understanding of the physical world. Effecting this connection is a crucial challenge. Otherwise, the child may be burdened with two disembodied systems of knowledge, neither adequate on its own, rather than one integrated understanding.

Also, at this age, children are both ready and eager to master skills in specific areas. They want to be able to draw in perspective, to compose in rhyme, to perform chemical experiments, to write a computer program. It would be desirable, in the best of all possible worlds, if all children could be exposed to each of these activities. Human finitude, however, guarantees that such a goal is utopian. An attempt to train children in all art forms, all athletic forms, and all scholastic activities would be certain to achieve superficial knowledge at best and a breakdown in less happy circumstances.

It is for these reasons that I recommend some degree of specialization during middle childhood—roughly from the ages of eight to fourteen. While children are mastering the crucial literacies, they should also have the opportunity to attain significant levels of skill in a small number of domains: perhaps, on the average, in one art form, one area of physical training, and one or two scholastic subjects. Thus a ten-year-old might take music or art lessons, engage in one after-school sport, gymnastic, or dance activity, and have regular cumulative lessons in a subject like history, biology, or mathematics.

I favor this early specialization for two reasons. First of all, I think it is important that youngsters early on receive some demonstrations of what it means, on a day-to-day basis, to master a subject matter or a cluster of skills—to drill, practice, monitor one's own progress, reflect upon it, compare it to that of peers at work in the same domain. Bereft of this opportunity, children may be at a severe disadvantage later on, when it becomes essential to achieve mastery in a vocational area. The need to experience mastery firsthand is nowhere more acute than in contemporary America, where so many of the cultural signals favor the quick fix rather than the lengthy apprenticeship.

The second reason relates more directly to subsequent careers. In my own view, an individual is most likely to achieve a satisfactory life—to make a contribution to society and gain self-esteem—if he or she finds vocational and avocational niches that complement his or her own aptitudes. If a child has had plenty of exposure to the range of domains and intelligences in early life, it seems reasonable that he or she should begin to narrow the focus to some extent in the years of middle childhood. At best, the child will then have already begun to gain needed expertise for later life. At the very least, he or she will at least have had the experience of gaining some competence and monitoring that process.

How should one go about choosing these areas? In a pluralistic and democratic society, the choice must be that of the child and the family, making use of whatever evidence and advice they care to secure from other sources. I believe that reasonable assessments of a child's strengths can already be made in middle childhood and that, therefore, the matching of child and discipline can be informed. It is possible, however, that even when these couplings are made at random, the results need not be unhappy. My observation in China, where such early matching is made in a relatively unsystematic manner, is that children become quite attached to those areas to which their attention has been directed and in which their skills have been assiduously cultivated.

Talk of the need to find some areas of specialization and the desirability of attaining clear skills through apprenticeships in these areas runs the risk of suggesting that this need be a serious and even painful experience. However, specialization need not resemble a diet of castor oil at all. An inspired teacher, a lively curriculum, a sympathetic mentor, a congenial group of peers can make the early stages of mastery a wonderful and enjoyable experience. In fact, I would urge that at the beginning of any specialization, there needs to be a period of relatively unstructured exploration, during which the possibilities of the medium or symbol system are widely sampled. More constrained training thereafter can build upon this initial survey and can be united with it as the incipient master begins to handle the medium in a more personal and more assured way.

There is never a need to suggest a single right answer or a prescribed way to do things. Indeed, just because children at this age are likely to make these erroneous assumptions, it is important for their elders to stress a plurality of approaches and responses.

In contrast to the realm of the "middle-aged" child, the world of the adolescent bursts open in at least three directions. It becomes *wider*—the youth's arena is now the larger society, even the world, and not merely the family or the local community. It becomes *higher*—the youth is capable of more abstract forms of reasoning, of speculation, and of dealing with the hypothetical and the theoretical. It also becomes *deeper*—the youth probes more insistently into his or her own life, dealing with personal feelings, fears, and aspirations in a much fuller way than a few years before.

While Piaget's characterization of "formal operational" thought is no longer accepted in its original form, it is still useful to think of the adolescent as one who can deal comfortably with whole systems of thought. The preadolescent is interested in facts, rules, and "sheer" skills, whereas the adolescent in our culture becomes more involved with values, with wide-reaching principles, with pregnant exceptions, and with the legitimacy of uses to which skills are put. The adolescent becomes newly concerned with the relations among different bodies of knowledge, different points of view, and different fields in which individuals can become productive. He or she tries to relate these issues to personal concerns—the emerging sense of identity and decisions about career, schooling, and personal relationships, including those with individuals of the other sex and of quite different backgrounds.

In our culture, adolescence is a time of "higher school"—high school and college. In many pockets of the world, developed as well as underdeveloped, this period is thought of as a time for increased specialization. In my view, this trend is ill-timed and unfortunate from a developmental perspective. Since people of this age are defining themselves with reference to a wider arena, I think it is particularly important that they remain (or become) exposed to a broad range of topics, themes, subject matter, value systems, and the like, and that they be encouraged to engage in thinking that spans these topics.

Thus, in contrast to the years of middle childhood, and also in opposition to educational practices in many places, there should be a shift of emphasis toward more comprehensive knowledge during the ages fourteen to twenty-one. In old-fashioned terms, this would be viewed as a call for the liberal arts, but defined in such a way as to include scientific and technological subjects as well as the classics and the humanities. It is also a call for the inclusion within the curriculum of a consideration of ethical issues, current events, and communal and global problems. It recommends student involvement in rich and multifaceted projects, which encourages them to sample widely and to make diverse connections.

Of course, whatever constraints applied to middle childhood do not mysteriously disappear in adolescence. If it is not possible in the years from seven to fourteen to survey the universe, it is obviously equally impossible to do so in the succeeding seven-year period. Nonetheless, I still call for a more catholic emphasis at this time, for three reasons: (1) such a broadening of curricula and concerns is consistent with the youth's own information-processing propensities at this life stage; (2) it is desirable that every growing individual in the world have at least a modicum of exposure to the principal disciplines and concerns of our planet; and (3) youths in this phase are far more willing to transcend boundaries and to risk interdisciplinary thinking.

Nearly all educators are wrestling with the problem of just how to ensure such exposure. They search for shortcuts: core curricula, major and minor subjects, courses that convey concepts or ways of thinking rather than attempting to provide all information from the ground up. Some go so far as to recommend a definite list of facts and terms that everyone who would be educated needs to know.

Even if I had arrived at one, there would be no room here to introduce the universal curriculum for adolescence. Nor do I feel that every student needs to study every subject or the same set of subjects as a matter of course. Rather, what I want to urge is that the third seven-year period of life, like the first years of life, be a time when relatively wide-ranging exploration is encouraged and narrow specialization is put aside or suspended, at least for most students, and that activities that synthesize, draw connections, or link school knowledge to extrascholastic concerns be encouraged and even mandated.

To this point, I have introduced understanding as the proper goal for education, outlined the kinds of performances of understanding for which one might strive, and indicated certain curricular options that one might adopt. It should be clear that most classrooms in the United States and abroad are not currently set up so as to encourage, let alone achieve, such an education. If anything, the insistence on having twenty to fifty students in a classroom, seated at desks while the teacher lectures, and moving arbitrarily from one subject to another at preordained timed intervals, makes the achievement of an education for understanding virtually impossible.

There is, alas, no formula for achieving understanding—though there may well be numerous formulas for thwarting it! However, important clues for a more effective education do exist in two institutions about which something is known: one the very ancient institution of the apprenticeship, the other the very modern one of the children's museum.

Imagine an educational environment in which youngsters at the age of seven or eight, in addition to—or perhaps instead of—attending a formal school, have the opportunity to enroll in a children's museum, a science museum, or some kind of discovery center or exploratorium. As part of this educational scene, adults are present who actually practice the disciplines or crafts represented by the various exhibitions. Computer programmers are working in the technology center, zookeepers and zoologists are tending the animals, workers from a bicycle factory assemble bicycles in front of the children's eyes, and a Japanese mother prepares a meal and carries out a tea ceremony in the Japanese house. Even the designers and the mounters of the exhibitions ply their trade directly in front of the observing students.

During the course of their schooling, youngsters enter into separate apprenticeships with a number of these adults. Each apprentice group consists of students of different ages and varying degrees of expertise in the domain or discipline. As part of the apprenticeship, the child is drawn into the use of various literacies—numerical and computer languages when enrolled with the computer programmer, the Japanese language in interacting with the Japanese family, the reading of manuals with the bicycle workers, the preparation of wall labels with the designers of the exhibition. The student's apprenticeships deliberately encompass a range of pursuits, including artistic activities, activities requiring exercise and dexterity, and activities of a more scholarly bent. In the aggregate, these activities incorporate the basic literacies required in the culture—reading and writing in the dominant language or languages, mathematical and computational operations, and skill in the notations drawn on in the various vocational or avocational pursuits.

Most of the learning and most of the assessment are done cooperatively; that is, students work together on projects that typically require a team of people having different degrees of and complementary kinds of skills. Thus, the team assembling the bicycle might consist of half a dozen youngsters, whose tasks range from locating and fitting together parts to inspecting the newly assembled systems to revising a manual or preparing advertising copy. The assessment of learning also assumes a variety of forms, ranging from the student's monitoring her own learning by keeping a journal to the "test of the street"—does the bicycle actually operate satisfactorily, and does it find any buyers? Because the older people on the team, or "coaches," are skilled professionals who see themselves as training future members of their trade, the reasons for activities are clear, the standards are high, and satisfaction flows from a job well done. And because the students are enrolled from the first in a meaningful and challenging activity, they come to feel a genuine stake in the outcome of their (and their peers') efforts.

A reader's first thought on the possibility of youngsters' attending such an intensive museum program rather than or in addition to the public school may be disbelief. The connotations of the two types of institution could scarcely be more different. "Museum" means an occasional, casual, entertaining, enjoyable outing; as Frank Oppenheimer, founder of San Francisco's Exploratorium, was fond of commenting, "No one flunks museum." "School," in contrast, connotes a serious, regular, formal, deliberately decontextualized institution. Would we not be consigning students to ruination if we enrolled them in museums instead of schools?

I believe we would be doing precisely the opposite. Attendance in most schools today does risk ruining the children. Whatever significance schooling might once have held for the majority of youngsters in our society, it no longer holds significance for many of them. Most students (and, for that matter, many parents and teachers) cannot provide compelling reasons for attending school. The reasons cannot be discerned within the school experience, nor is there faith that what is acquired in school will actually be utilized in the future. Try to justify the quadratic equation or the Napoleonic wars to an inner-city high-school student— or his parents! The real world appears elsewhere: in the media, in the marketplace, and all too frequently in the demimonde of drugs, violence, and crime. Much if not most of what happens in schools happens because that is the way it was done in earlier generations, not because we have a convincing rationale for maintaining it today. The often-heard statement that school is basically custodial rather than educational harbors more than a grain of truth.

Certainly there are exemplary schools, and just as certainly there are poorly designed and poorly run museums. Yet as institutions, schools have become increasingly anachronistic, while museums have retained the potential to engage students, to teach them, to stimulate their understanding, and, most important, to help them assume responsibility for their own future learning.

Such a dramatic reversal of institutional significance has come about for two complementary sets of reasons. On the one hand, youngsters live in a time of unparalleled excitement, where even the less privileged are exposed daily to attractive media and technologies, ranging from video games to space exploration, from high-speed transportation to direct and immediate means of communication. In many cases, these media can be used to create compelling products. Activities that might once have engaged youngsters—reading in classrooms or hearing teachers lecture about remote subjects—seem hopelessly tepid and unmotivating to most of them. On the other hand, science museums and children's museums have become the loci for exhibitions, activities, and role models drawn precisely from those domains that do engage youngsters; their customary wares represent the kinds of vocations, skills, and aspirations that legitimately animate and motivate students.

I have documented some of the difficulties exhibited by youngsters in coming to understand the topics of school. It is of course possible that, even if one cannot flunk museum, one might fail to appreciate the meanings and implications of exhibitions encountered there. Indeed, I suspect such non- or miscomprehension often happens on "one-shot" visits to museums. An active and sustained participation in an apprenticeship, however, offers a far greater opportunity for understanding. In such long-term relationships, novices have the opportunity to witness on a daily basis the reasons for various skills, procedures, concepts, and symbolic and notational systems. They observe competent adults moving readily and naturally from one external or internal way of representing knowledge to another. They experience firsthand the consequences of a misguided or misconceived analysis, even as they gain pleasure when a well-thought-out procedure works properly. They undergo a transition from a situation in which much of what they do is based on adult models to one in which they are trying out their own approaches, perhaps with some support or criticism from the master. They can discuss alternatives with more accomplished peers, just as they can provide assistance to peers who have recently joined the team. All these options, it seems to me, guide the student toward that state of enablement—exhibiting the capacity to use skills and concepts in an appropriate way—that is the hallmark of an emerging understanding.

If we are to configure an education for understanding, suited for the students of today and for the world of tomorrow, we need to take the lessons of the museum and the relationship of the apprenticeship extremely seriously. Not, perhaps, to convert each school into a museum, nor each teacher into a master, but rather to think of the ways in which the strengths of a museum atmosphere, of apprenticeship learning, and of engaging projects can pervade all educational environments from home to school to workplace. The evocativeness and open-endedness of the children's museum needs to be wedded to the structure, rigor, and discipline of an apprenticeship. The basic features I have just listed may assume a central place in educational environments that span the gamut of ages from preschool through retirement and the full range of disciplines.

Making It Happen: Teachers and Students

The setting of standards, the delineation of credible curricula, and the creation of supportive environments, are all important components of an education for understanding. In the end, however, effective education depends upon the quality and commitment of the personnel who are involved on a daily basis.

To assent to an education dedicated to understanding is one thing, to be able to achieve it quite another. Such an undertaking would constitute an enormous challenge for American teachers, who for the most part have been forced to settle for "coverage" rather than for "uncoverage," and whose own teaching performances have been evaluated either on purely technical grounds (paperwork properly filled out) or on the scores attained by students on externally mandated measures of dubious quality.

Teachers must be encouraged—I almost wrote "freed"—to pursue an education that strives for depth of understanding, and to assess students in terms of relevant performances. But encouragement is not enough. Most teachers would not be able on their own to implement such curricula and assessments and, to my knowledge, only a handful of effective models are currently available. A major challenge in the United States in the years ahead is to create schools and school systems where education for understanding is in fact carried out, and where performances of understanding are sought and assessed. Only in such an altered milieu will it be possible for teachers and other members of the community to see what such a radically different education might be like.

This is not the place to list candidate sites that educate for understanding. But it is worth noting that several national organizations are currently dedicated to developing distinctly different kinds of school, resembling the model outlined here. Perhaps the foremost effort is the Coalition of Essential Schools, directed by Theodore Sizer of Brown University. Worthy of mention as well are James Comer's School Development Program, Henry Levin's Accelerated Learning Schools, and the "key schools" and "master teachers" identified by the National Education Association, the American Federation of Teachers, the Nabisco RJR model schools, and the "break-the-mold" design teams identified by the New American Schools Development Corporation.

To complement the further development of such schools, it makes sense to constitute a National Faculty of Master Teachers: individuals who have worked in such schools; who themselves embody the skills of educating for understanding and assessing student performances of understanding in an appropriate way; and who have the additional desire and ability to help teaching candidates who wish to become familiar with new approaches to education. Master teachers knowledgeable about individual differences and individual approaches to learning ought to become members of such a faculty as well.

Researchers, such as the members of our group at Project Zero, can be of distinct help in these processes of modeling. We have identified some of the steps through which schools customarily pass as they attempt to adopt a program directed at understanding; we have also monitored their progress as they seek to institute specific practices, such as the collection and evaluation of portfolios or processfolios and the design of curricula directed toward students with different learning approaches. Every school needs to pass through some such developmental process, but there is no need for every school to start from scratch. Familiarity with the map of change—its opportunities, its forks, its roadblocks—can be of signal help.

In a book devoted to educational implications of MI theory, it may seem odd to have paid so little heed in this chapter to the different human faculties and different intellectual strengths exhibited by students. This omission has in fact been deliberate. I believe that, in laying out educational goals and processes, we need to acknowledge the common links among students and the kinds of expectations that we may properly hold with respect to their collective accomplishments.

But it is now time to repair this omission. The preceeding chapters have provided ample evidence of the fact that individuals learn in different ways and display different intellectual configurations and proclivities. Certainly, we would dismantle the entire edifice of MI theory if we were to bypass these differences and to insist on teaching all students the same contents in the same way.

At first consideration, it may seem that the fact of multiple intelligences renders the already formidable task of education even more difficult. After all, it would be highly desirable if all individuals did in fact exhibit pretty much the same faculties and learn in pretty much the same way. And, indeed, for a teacher faced with perhaps thirty students a class, and four or five classes a day, the prospect of individualizing education may appear daunting indeed. Since such individual differences do exist, however, and since a person's own particular intellectual configuration will necessarily color her trajectory and accomplishments throughout her life, it is a disservice to ignore these conditions.

So long as one tries to cover a huge amount of material in school, an education nuanced in the light of multiple intelligences becomes virtually impossible. But once one determines to teach for understanding, to probe topics in depth over a significant period of time, then the existence of individual differences can actually be an ally.

My research has suggested that any rich, nourishing topic—any concept worth teaching—can be approached in at least five different ways that, roughly speaking, map onto the multiple intelligences. We might think of the topic as a room with at least five doors or entry points into it. Students vary as to which entry point is most appropriate for them and which routes are most comfortable to follow once they have gained initial access to the room. Awareness of these entry points can help the teacher introduce new materials in ways in which they can be easily grasped by a range of students; then, as students explore other entry points, they have the chance to develop those multiple perspectives that are the best antidote to stereotypical thinking.

Let us look at these five entry points one by one, considering how each one might be used in approaching topics or concepts, one in the natural sciences (evolution) and one in the social sciences (democracy).

In using a *narrational entry point,* one presents a story or narrative about the concept in question. In the case of evolution, one might trace the course of a single branch of the evolutionary tree, or perhaps even the generations of a specific organism. In the case of democracy, one would tell the story of its beginnings in ancient Greece or, perhaps, of the origins of constitutional government in the United States.

In using a *logical-quantitative entry point,* one approaches the concept by invoking numerical considerations or deductive reasoning processes. Evolution could be approached by studying the incidence of different species in different parts of the world or in different geophysical epochs; or one might review the arguments for and against a particular claim about evolutionary processes. In the case of democracy, one could look at congressional voting patterns over time or the arguments used for and against democracy by the Founding Fathers.

A *foundational entry point* examines the philosophical and terminological facets of the concept. This tack proves appropriate for people who like to pose fundamental questions, of the sort that one associates with young children and with philosophers rather than with more practical (or more "middle-aged") spirits. A foundational approach to evolution might consider the difference between evolution and revolution, the reasons that we look for origins and changes, the epistemological status of teleology and finality. A foundational approach to democracy would ponder the root meaning of the word, the relationship of democracy to other forms of decision making and government, and the reasons that one might adopt a democratic rather than an oligarchic approach. The philosopher Matthew Lipman has developed engaging materials for introducing such a foundational approach to youngsters in middle childhood.

We shift gears quite sharply in considering an *esthetic approach*. Here the emphasis falls on sensory or surface features that will appeal to—or at least capture the attention of—students who favor an artistic stance to the experiences of living. In the case of evolution the examination of the structure of different evolutionary trees, or the study of the shifting morphology of organisms over time, might activate the esthetic sensitivity. With reference to democracy, one intriguing approach would be to listen to musical ensembles that are characterized either by group playing or by playing under the control of a single individual—the string quartet versus the orchestra. Another, less exotic tack might be to consider various forms of balance or imbalance as they are epitomized in different voting blocs.

The final entry point is an *experiential approach*. Some students—old as well as young—learn best with a hands-on approach, dealing directly with the materials that embody or convey the concept. Those bent on mastering concepts of evolution might breed numerous generations of Drosophila and observe the mutations that take place. Those in the social studies class might actually constitute groups that have to make decisions in accordance with various governmental processes, observing the pros and cons of democracy as compared with other, more "top-down" forms of government.

In one definition, a skilled teacher is a person who can open a number of different windows on the same concept. In our example, rather than presenting evolution and democracy only by definition, or only by example, or only in terms of quantitative considerations, such a teacher would make available several entry points over time. An effective teacher functions as a "student-curriculum broker," ever vigilant for educational prosthetics—texts, films, software—that can help convey the relevant contents, in as engaging and effective a way as possible, to students who exhibit a characteristic learning mode.

It should be evident that use of multiple entry points can be a powerful means of dealing with student misconceptions, biases, and stereotypes. So long as one takes only a single perspective or tack on a concept or problem, it is virtually certain that students will understand that concept in only the most limited and rigid fashion. Conversely, the adoption of a family of stances toward a phenomenon encourages the student to come to know that phenomenon in more than one way, to develop multiple representations and seek to relate these representations to one another.

This review suggests that, even in cases where one wishes to have a core curriculum mastered by all students, it is possible to craft an educational regimen that exploits the existence of multiple intelligences. Education needs to transcend common knowledge, however. Important as it is for all students to know about the history and literature of their land, or about the major biological and physical principles that govern the world, it is at least as important for students to identify their strengths, to pursue areas where they are comfortable and in which they can expect to achieve a great deal.

My own observations suggest that rarely in life are the fates of individuals determined by what they are unable to do. Their life trajectories are much more likely to be molded by the kinds of abilities and skills that they have developed, and these, in turn, are determined in significant measure by the profile of intelligences with which they have been endowed and/or that have been nurtured in early life. Many of the most creative individuals in human history have had significant learning problems: Thomas Edison, Winston Churchill, Pablo Picasso, even Albert Einstein come to mind. Far from being crippled by these difficulties, these individuals were able to build upon their strengths to make remarkable, and remarkably distinctive, contributions to their particular domain of achievement. Accordingly, those entrusted with education need to pay special attention to the strengths and the proclivities of youngsters under their charge.

It is probably no accident that my work came early to the attention of individuals involved with what one might call "special populations"—children who are gifted and talented, children who have learning difficulties, children who are exceptional or handicapped (or both) in one intellectual form or another. What characterizes these children is precisely the fact that they do *not* acquire the lessons of school in the ordinary way. And so those who teach these youngsters are faced with the choice of either writing them off or finding educational regimens and prosthetics that are effective. (Incidentally, this problem can be as acute with students who are highly gifted as with students who are considered disabled by current educational standards.)

MI theory can be of considerable help here. It not only supplies a categorical scheme and a set of definitions that are useful for diagnostic and training purposes, but may also actually suggest some steps that could be useful for students who exhibit one or another unusual learning pattern.

Take, for example, the case of children with dyslexia. In a significant number of cases, such children show enhanced facility with visual and/or spatial activities. These strengths can be mobilized to help students excel at vocations and avocations that exploit visual-spatial capacities; and at least sometimes, these strengths can be drawn on as ways of presenting linguistic materials. While I would scarcely recommend the imposition of a disability on any person, the experience of dealing with and over-coming a disability can itself become a great ally in dealing with subse-quent challenges. Perhaps this is another reason that many individuals of singular accomplishment turn out to have been dyslexic, ranging from the inventor Thomas Edison to the politician Nelson Rockefeller.

Or take the case of an individual whose native language is not English. While it is often thought that education simply involves sub-stituting one language for another, that view turns out to be an oversim-plification. Different cultures and subcultures not only use languages in different ways (for example, one group stresses story-telling and fan-tasy; another highlights exposition in a truthful fashion; a third is terse and indirect); but language may also interact in different ways with other modes of communication, such as gesturing, singing, or demonstrating what one means. Sensitivity to multiple intelligences may help a teacher not only determine which modalities are most effective for the presenta-tion of a new language but also how to make sure that the linguistic intelligence is interacting in optimal fashion with other intelligences that may participate in the communicative process.

Speaking more generally about students with learning problems, it is possible to use MI information in a number of ways. The most straightforward is simply to identify an area of strength—for example, through a Spectrum-style assessment instrument—and to give the child the opportunity to develop that strength. The child therefore can become skilled at endeavors that may have vocational or avocational linkages. Also, the feeling of self-esteem that accrues from a job well done may encourage the child to take up challenges that might previ-ously have been intimidating.

Identification of strengths, however, can have a more integral effect upon educational achievement. Sometimes it is possible to use an area of strength as an "entry point" to an area that has posed difficulties. For example, as suggested above, a child who is especially gifed with narratives may be introduced to difficult mathematical, musical, or scien-tific concepts through the comfortable vehicle of a story.

Most suggestively, structural affinities sometimes obtain between domains in which the child has talent and domains where the child appears to be impaired. For example, there are common numerical structures in mathematics and in music, and common spatial structures in geometry and in the arts. Provided that the "transfer" is attempted in a sensitive way, it may be possible for a child gifted in art or music to accomplish more in traditional subject matters, by exploiting those structural analogues that exist across domains customarily thought to be disparate.

Even when executed indifferently, education is a very complicated process; and when it is done well, it turns out to be amazingly complex, intricate, and subtle. Simply to list all of the interest groups and concerns is to threaten to overwhelm our information-processing capacities: the teachers, students, parents, union leaders, school board members, administrators, opinion leaders and the general public; the texts, tests, curricula, guidelines, schedules, teaching procedures, syllabi, building, grounds, and supplies. And both lists could be extended!

In part III of this book, I have made no effort to hide this complexity. Beginning with the focus that my own work has placed on assessment, I have gradually broadened the net to include most of the above considerations and have at least hinted at some others. I have sought to provide some degree of focus by insisting on four elements: (1) the goal of an education that is geared to understanding; (2) a stress on the cultivation of performances of understanding, which can be assessed primarily in context; (3) a recognition of the existence of different individual strengths; and (4) a commitment to mobilize these productively in the education of each child. To orchestrate these different elements into a seamless educational regimen is no mean task; but there are promising signs abroad that progress can be made, and that we can secure an education that celebrates our common heritage as human beings, the particular cultural backgrounds from which we come, and the ways in which each of us stands out as an individual.

It has been clear, I hope, that the theory of multiple intelligences is not a static entity, that it has evolved and continues to evolve each year. In the final part of this book, I look more directly at the place of the theory within the history of efforts to conceptualize intelligence, and cast a glance as well at where it might be headed in the future.

Part IV

THE FUTURE OF WORK ON MULTIPLE INTELLIGENCES

Introductory Note

The decade following publication of *Frames of mind* has been a busy and productive one for the group of researchers with whom I have been working. Most of our work, chronicled in the preceding pages, has centered around the consideration of specific educational issues and the devising of specific educational projects. This work continues with admirable energy and dedication: we hope that it might make a positive contribution to educational reform in the years ahead.

Aware of the general thrust of this work, I was momentarily thrown when a visitor recently asked "How has the theory of multiple intelligences changed in the past decade?" My first impulse was to say, "We have been working principally on educational applications of the theory, and so the theory itself has enjoyed benign neglect." But a moment's thought revealed the insufficiency—indeed, the inaccuracy—of that response. In fact there has been a good deal of theoretical work undertaken in the wake of *Frames;* but it has been initiated in significant measure by a number of gifted students and collaborators, among them Nira Granott, Thomas Hatch, Mara Krechevsky, and Mindy Kornhaber. I suspect that the future of MI theory lies more in their hands and in the hands of other capable colleagues than in my own.

In this final section, I offer two essays that suggest the future course of MI theory. In chapter 12 (which could serve as well as an Introduction

211

to this volume), I place MI theory within the broader context of theorizing about human intelligence. And in the concluding chapter 13, Mindy Kornhaber, Mara Krechevsky, and I view human intelligences as potentials that emerge from the contexts within which all human intellectual activities must unfold. The epilogue harbors some final thoughts on the course traversed so far and the distance yet to be trekked.

Chapter 12

Intelligences in
Seven Phases

S ome topics of scientific study are sufficiently esoteric that they elude public attention. Intelligence is not such a topic. Hardly a week goes by without some discussion in the media of the nature of intelligence, its source, its measurement, its uses. Nor are these discussions removed from the arena of policy. Consider the following two examples.

In the summer of 1988 the British newspaper the *Observer* ran an article under the title "Hunt is on to find the country's superkids: Controversy flares over new intelligence tests and the professor's intelligence measuring hat." The article describes new efforts to locate the brightest children in England—the ones with the highest intelligence— so that they can receive the most appropriate education. In years gone by, such children would be identified through administration of a standard intelligence test. Now, however, according to the article, such an exercise may no longer be necessary. Thanks to work of researchers like Hans Eysenck, England's most prominent psychologist, it is possible to place an electronic hat upon a person's head, activate various electrodes, measure brain wave patterns, and in that way determine "who is the smartest of us all." Some scholars even believe that such a determination can be made at birth or soon thereafter; thus the "streaming" at premium in an advanced industrial society need not wait until a child can talk, read, or grasp a number two pencil.

In the fall of 1989 the *Wall Street Journal* featured on its first page an article with the headline "Classroom Scandal: Cheaters in School May Not Be Students but Their Teachers." The article chronicles a remarkable series of events in South Carolina. Ms. Nancy Yeargin, a widely esteemed teacher, gave her students the answers to a standardized test. Of course, the students performed at an outstanding level. Unfortunately for Ms. Yeargin, her action was discovered by a colleague and reported to the authorities. Eventually Ms. Yeargin was dismissed from her position.

So far, the story is disconcerting, but falls under the familiar "Dog Bites Man" heading. What was irregular, however, was the community's reaction to this event. A majority of citizens supported Ms. Yeargin. The preponderant view held that important decisions were being made on the basis of test scores; Ms. Yeargin did not want her students to suffer because they did not do well; therefore she performed ethically—or at least justifiably—in giving them the correct answers. That the students were not truly knowledgeable—that their performances were sham—did not seem to bother many of the citizens in the community.

Two rather different stories, from diverse societies, but both conveying a common message: The assessment of intellectual powers has become very important; there is controversy about how best to accomplish this mission; and the community has a vital say in how such measurements are carried out, interpreted, and utilized for social and political purposes.

Presumably communal leaders, as well as ordinary citizens, have been making judgments about intellectual and cognitive traits for many centuries. At times, these decisions have had enormous consequence, as for example, in determining membership in philosophical schools in ancient Greece, or in the selection of the imperial bureaucracy in Confucian China. In this century interest in such matters has quickened, thanks to the scientific (or, possibly, pseudoscientific) efforts to study and measure intelligence and cognition, and to the adoption of these methods in selecting elites (Gould, 1981; Klitgaard, 1985).

In this essay, I review seven phases or steps that have characterized the study of intelligence, broadly construed, in our time. While the sequence is roughly chronological, there is nothing necessary about the order; moreover, the final phases are promissory notes for the future rather than established historical landmarks. At each phase, I consider both the views of the research community and the implications and applications within the world of educational practice.

The Seven Phases of Intelligence

LAY CONCEPTIONS OF INTELLIGENCE

Until this century, the word *intelligence* has been used by ordinary individuals in an effort to describe their own mental powers and those of other persons. Consistent with ordinary language usage more generally, "intelligence" was used in anything but a precise manner. Forgetting about meanings having to do with information gathering, secret services, or mere acquaintance, individuals living in the West were deemed "intelligent" if they were quick-witted or scientifically astute or wise. In many other cultures, there exists no term that translates easily into the Western notion of intelligence. However, some of the sheen associated with the honorific term *intelligent* has been applied to the individual who is obedient, or well behaved, or quiet, or adaptable, or equipped with magical powers (LeVine & White, 1986; Shweder & LeVine, 1984; Stigler, Shweder, & Herdt, 1990).

For the most part, the word *intelligent* has been used in a beneficent, if somewhat judgmental, way. Its imprecision can be readily displayed by a recognition that it has been applied to nearly all of the American presidents in this century, even though it is doubtful that any two of our presidents exhibited similar kinds of minds (Cannon, 1991). How, after all, to compare the silent Calvin Coolidge with the garrulous Theodore Roosevelt? The witty John Kennedy with the sober Woodrow Wilson? The devious Lyndon Johnson with the straightforward Harry Truman? Perhaps ironically, Herbert Hoover and Jimmy Carter, two of our least successful presidents, both of whom were engineers, probably came closest to the lay idea of "intelligence": it may be worth noting that they have become positively distinguished by their activities as *ex*-presidents.

In the absence of formal ways of measuring or assessing intelligence, both laypeople and leaders have had to make judgments of intellectual strength on the basis of informal criteria. So long as the sphere within which judgments were made was relatively restricted, it is probably the case that there was agreement about who is, or is not, "bright." When professors of history were judging future historians, or industrial magnates were hiring managers, or religious leaders were choosing ministerial candidates, consensus could be reached. When, however, individuals drawn from these diverse domains had to achieve a common judgment, far more disputation could be anticipated.

215

THE SCIENTIFIC TURN

In a sequence of events that is chronicled in earlier chapters, Alfred Binet, a gifted psychologist, responded to a pressing request from the educational authorities in his native Paris. At the turn of the last century some elementary school students were having great difficulties with their scholastic assignments; the authorities needed help in identifying these problematic children at an early point and deciding what to do with them.

Proceeding in an empirical manner, Binet and his colleagues administered hundreds of different items to young children. Among these items were definitions of words, mathematical problems, sensory discriminations, tests of memory, and the like (Binet & Simon, 1916; Boring, 1923). The psychological research team prized particularly those items that were *discriminating:* that is, items that tended to be passed by those students who did well in school, and failed by students with school problems. (Those items passed or failed by all students, or whose success did not correlate with school success, were dropped.) Necessarily, the school curriculum was that featured in Parisian schools shortly after the turn of the century. By and large, Binet and his associates administered these items on a one-on-one basis, and their interest lay in helping those students who experienced difficulty on the tests. But they had set into action a process that soon proceeded in a very different way (Block & Dworkin, 1976; Gould, 1981; Sternberg, 1985).

As word of the first intelligence tests and the concept of an intelligence quotient reached the shores of the United States, a number of psychologists and educators discerned the enormous potential of this Continental invention. Soon, such individuals had produced instruments that were more streamlined, that could be administered on a group basis, and that placed individuals precisely on a distribution in comparison with other individuals of the same age. Henry Goddard (1919) worked with institutionalized retarded individuals; Lewis Terman (1916) tested normal and "bright" students in California; Robert Yerkes (1921) designed a test that could be given to a million recruits in World War I. What had begun as a rough-and-ready index of scholastic preparedness became a conveniently administered instrument that could yield intellectual strength in an hour and place a precise numerical value on that strength (IQ of 115—one standard deviation above the norm).

By the 1920s and 1930s, intelligence tests had become deeply ensconced in American society and also had gained considerable notoriety elsewhere, particularly in the English-speaking world. (The different reactions to intelligence testing, in countries ranging from Nazi Germany to the Soviet Union, makes a fascinating study.) Though many of these uses were well motivated, and some of them were genuinely useful, the tests often came to be used in stigmatizing ways, to label and billet individuals, and to make judgments about their limitations. Perhaps surprisingly in a country that prided itself on the opportunities open to every individual, use of intelligence testing went hand-in-hand with a belief that intellectual strengths were largely inherited, and that IQ tapped a feature of an individual almost as inviolable as relative height or absolute hair color. As a consequence, there were few efforts to alter psychometric intelligence or to embrace Binet's original mission of using data about measured intelligence as a means of aiding students.

Work on the development of intelligence tests continued through mid-century and in fact persists until this day. There are dozens of competing tests, some geared toward all populations, others much more specialized. Tests differ in other ways as well: some pride themselves on the care and depth of administration, while other "quick tests" are advertised on the basis of efficient, group administration. Nearly all tests are validated by their correlation with already existing instruments and so, to a large extent, they are interchangeable with one another. Many other tests—perhaps most notably the Scholastic Aptitude Test—do not call themselves intelligence tests, and yet they closely resemble standard intelligence tests and correlate with them. While work on the measurement of intelligence and the selection and wording of items continues, there has until very recently been relatively little new theoretical work on the concept of intelligence; the theory-centered discussions of the 1920s and 1930s have reverberated in colloquies in much more recent times (*Educational Psychologist*, 1921; Sternberg & Detterman, 1986).

THE PLURALIZATION OF INTELLIGENCE

While Binet did not take a strong position on the ontological status of intelligence, most of his immediate successors chose to believe that intelligence was a unitary construct. Just as individuals differed in height and weight, or in introversion or integrity, so, too, they differed from one another in how smart they were. Probably these differences existed from early in life and they probably could not be altered very much. Lewis Terman (1916) in California and Charles Spearman (1927) in England led the cohort of investigators who claimed that intelligence was best conceptualized as a "general factor," one that may well have been rooted in an elementary property of the nervous system, such as speed, flexibility, or sensitivity. This perspective has had faithful adherents until this day, and in various forms is espoused by such authorities as Lloyd Humphreys (1986), Sandra Scarr (1985), Arthur Jensen (1980), and the aforementioned Hans Eysenck (1967).

Archilochus, the ancient Greek poet, noted the division of individuals into two primary groups: the foxes, who believed many little things, and the hedgehogs, who believed one big thing (Berlin, 1953). Echoes of this dichotomy reverberate in studies of intelligence. In reaction to the global claims of the unitarians, and as a result of their own empirical research, many students of intelligences have put forth alternative views, in which intellect is seen as composed of a number of different facets, factors, or even qualitatively different intelligences.

Probably the most strident controversies have raged concerning the application of a measurement technique termed *factor analysis*. Individuals are given a variety of test items and, through a correlational procedure, it is possible to determine whether certain of those items "hang together," thus reflecting the same underlying factor. At one extreme, all of the items are seen as reflecting the same general factor, for example, speed of response; were this the case, then the unitarians would be completely correct. At the opposite end of the spectrum, each item, or perhaps each small set of items, reflects a different underlying factor, and the notion of a unitary intellect emerges as entirely spurious. Most factor-analytic studies end up embracing some sort of intermediate position: that there are a small number of relatively independent factors (Thurstone, 1938); that there are both general and specific factors (Vernon, 1971); that there is some hierarchy of factors (Thomson, 1939).

Factor-analytic studies have helped to uncover the complexity of intelligence, but they are characterized by two recurring problems. First of all, they can be no better than the items used in the testing, and frequently these items are subjected to criticism. As some factor-analyzing pundit put it long ago, "Garbage in, garbage out." Second, the kinds of results one obtains from a factor analysis are a direct reflection of the mathematical assumptions made in defining and isolating (more technically, "rotating") factors. As Stephen Jay Gould (1981) has explained it, one can take exactly the same set of scores, and treat them as evidence for unitary or pluralistic views of intelligence, simply on the basis of the assumptions that happen to underly a particular factor-analytic investigation. For these reasons, factor-analytic studies cannot in themselves resolve discussions about the "true nature" of intelligence.

While most studies of intellectual plurality grow out of the testing and factor-analysis tradition, it is possible to proceed in quite a different investigative fashion. In my own work, I have spurned formal testing completely. Instead, I have sought to document the existence of different human intelligences by examining a wide variety of empirical sources, and by attempting to synthesize the picture of cognition that emerges therefrom (see part I).

Once MI theory had been enunciated and its educational interest had been demonstrated, my colleagues and I found ourselves drawn to issues of assessment. The attraction and urgency of assessment grew from two diverse sources. On the one hand, it was evident to us that the theory did not deserve to be taken seriously unless one had available methods by which the intelligences could be assessed. Yet just as clearly, standard paper-and-pencil tests could not be legitimately used across the range of intelligence; indeed, were one to use paper-and-pencil tests to investigate, say, personal or bodily-kinesthetic intelligence, one would in effect be converting these spheres into yet another occasion for logical or linguistic thinking. Thus, as alluded to above, it was necessary to develop intelligence-fair means of assessment—means that looked directly at an intelligence rather than indirectly, through the all-too-familiar lenses of linguistic and/or logical thinking (Gardner, 1991a).

There was another impetus for the development of means for assessing the range of intelligences. Like other American educators, I had become increasingly concerned by the problems that beset so many American classrooms. While admiring certain other educational systems (such as the Japanese), I also felt that they were narrow in what they taught, and even narrower in how they assessed the knowledge of their students. It was my hope that by devising means of assessing various intelligences, I would thereby be in a better position to affect what is being taught in classrooms, how it is taught, and how it is assessed. Indeed, it was—and still is—my conviction that assessment provides one of the most potent levers on education. If one can change the means of assessment, one can affect the contents of classrooms; yet all too often the assessment tail wags the curriculum dog in an unproductive way. My opening example of the teacher who taught to the test and then supplied the answers provides a poignant illustration of this human proclivity.

From the point of view of the standard psychometric community, particularly in its commercial facets, the theory of multiple intelligences had one inviting feature. Rather than having a single test of intelligence, it should now be possible to develop a handful of tests of intelligence. A number of testing companies approached me with precisely this request. Yet, as already indicated, the whole thrust of multiple intelligences theory proceeds in opposition to the notion that multiple intelligences can be assessed by the same methods as have been used in standard IQ tests. Just how different these modes of assessment might be has gradually become clear in recent years. At the same time, further changes in the way that intelligence has been conceptualized have had even more radical implications for the whole issue of teaching and assessment.

THE CONTEXTUALIZATION OF INTELLIGENCE

Nearly all theorists of intelligence have thought of intelligence as residing within the head of the individual. This practice has been sanctioned not only by language use (How smart is he? She was born smart), but also by the strictures of assessment. All of our armaments of assessment are predicated on the assumption that one can and should look at individuals in isolation as they solve problems or fashion products that are deemed important in their particular social context.

As originally stated, the theory of multiple intelligences did not challenge this viewpoint, though it was framed with greater sensitivity to varying social contexts than most other competing formulations. Recent trends throughout the behavioral sciences have combined to challenge the isolated view of intellect. Indeed, in my opinion, the two most important phases since the pluralization of intellect have been its contextualization and its distribution.

Let us consider first what it means to take a contextualized view of intelligence. Human beings are biological creatures but they are equally cultural creatures. Even before birth, the immature organism lies in the womb of a woman who has habits, styles, and practices that reflect her culture and subculture. And while it is possible to exaggerate the influence of these prenatal influences, there is no question that the life of the infant after birth is inextricably bound with the practices and assumptions of her culture.

Let me state two simple examples, each of which could be compounded in innumerable ways. Many cultures place different value on boys as compared to girls. If a boy is wanted, and girl is born, parents can telegraph their feelings in a variety of ways, ranging from infanticide in the most extreme cases, to efforts to compensate for the unwanted gender (for example, by treating the female child as a "tomboy" or giving her a masculine name). The goals that parents set for their children also come into play from the earliest times: the father who wants his son to be a doctor or scholar will behave in a very different way from the father who desires an athlete, or who places the greatest degree of occupational choice at a premium. The kinds of intelligence favored, and the models of intelligence provided, will differ from an early age, and it is highly unlikely that these differences will have no effect on the child (Cole & Cole, 1989; Rogoff & Lave, 1984; Vygotsky, 1978).

Consider, as a contrasting example, the ways in which language is treated in different cultures and subcultures. Shirley Brice Heath (1983) has documented contrasting practices in our own society: some parents read and talk to their children all the time, some encourage the use of imagination and fantasy, some use language for authority-establishing purposes, others demand literal truthfulness and actively discourage any fantasy use. Even before the advent of school, these differing emphases result in quite different skills and attitudes toward language. These strong within–United States differences are dwarfed by their even greater difference from practices exhibited by the Kaluli of Papua New Guinea. These people do not speak directly to their children at all. Rather, they hold the children up and speak as if they are speaking for the child. As is the case all over the world, Kaluli children end up speaking in perfectly normal fashion, but their linguistic assumptions and practices reflect the values and priorities of their culture (Ochs & Schieffelin, 1984).

What does such a contextualized view of development imply for our notion of intelligence? Quite simply, it does not make sense to think of intelligence, or intelligences, in the abstract, as biological entities, like the stomach, or even as a psychological entity, such as emotion or temperament. At most, intelligences are potentials or proclivities, which are realized or not realized, depending upon the cultural context in which they are found. Bobby Fischer might in some sense have had the potential to be a great chess player, but if he had happened to be born in a culture without chess, that potential might never have been manifest, let alone actualized. Perhaps he could have used his spatial or logical intelligence to become a scientist or a navigator, but just as possibly he would never have distinguished himself in any way. Intelligence, or intelligences, are always an interaction between biological proclivities and the opportunities for learning that exist in a culture (Kornhaber, Krechevsky, & Gardner, 1990).

This seemingly innocent formulation has profound implications for assessment. No longer does it make sense to think of intelligence as an entity, or a set of entities, that can be assessed in a pure form. In particular, the notion that one could assess intelligence by placing electrodes upon the skull emerges as bizarre. Instead, turning the notion on its head, one must first supply opportunities where intelligences, or sets of intelligences, can be activated (Bobby Fischer is introduced to the game of checkers or the game of chess; or he is given a chemistry set or a miniature sailboat). Only after ample opportunity for exploration or immersion has taken place does it make any sense to begin to assess intellectual strengths. And of course, by that time one is not assessing intellect in any pure sense. Rather, one is assessing a complex compound of initial proclivities and societal opportunities.

We have sought to build upon this new conception in Project Spectrum (see chapter 6; and Malkus, Feldman, & Gardner, 1988; Krechevsky & Gardner, 1990). Project Spectrum was originally designed collaboratively with David Feldman as a means of determining whether, as young as three or four years of age, children already exhibit distinctive profiles of intelligence. When we first began the project, having worked our way to the third "pluralistic" phase of the concept of intelligence, we had in mind seven separate instruments, each one geared to a different intelligence. Soon we realized, however, that it was not possible to measure an intelligence in the abstract; indeed, any effort that purported to accomplish this goal would in effect simply be assessing prior experiences. Thus, if we asked students to sing a song, or to create a new melody, we would not be assessing "sheer" musical intelligence; instead we would be ascertaining the nature and extent of previous experiences in the realm of music.

Gradually we evolved a quite different approach to assessment, one as close to curriculum as to classical notions of measurement. We devised a very rich classroom environment, replete with inviting materials designed to stimulate various intelligences and combinations of intelligences. Intrinsic to our new assessment method is the provision of these materials throughout the year. Students have ample opportunities to play with all of these materials, to gain familiarity with them, to explore their implications and applications. Teachers and researchers can observe the students throughout the year to see their profile of intelligences at work and play; there are also more punctate instruments, which allow, when appropriate, a more precise measurement of intellectual proclivities. At the end of the year in a Spectrum classroom, parents receive an essay in which their child's intellectual profile is described, together with informal suggestions about what might be done with the child, given his particular strengths and weaknesses at this moment in his development.

It should be evident that this assessment is dramatically different from most conventional measures of intelligence. It surveys a much broader set of competences; it provides plenty of opportunities for children to work with the materials with which they will be assessed; and it assesses them in a natural, comfortable, playful context, rather than in the decontextualized examination system associated with most standard testing. Indeed, it can be said that the classroom in which Spectrum is implemented and assessed more closely resembles a Children's Museum than it does a testing room. Not surprisingly, in the one sustained effort to evaluate Spectrum, we found that it yielded profiles of intelligence that were quite different from those documented by the Stanford-Binet, a widely used instrument for the evaluation of preschool "intelligence" (see chapter 6; Gardner & Hatch, 1989).

THE DISTRIBUTION OF INTELLIGENCE

Accompanying the growing realization that intelligence cannot be conceptualized apart from the context in which individuals live is a parallel realization that intelligence exists in significant measure outside of the physical body of the individual. Specifically, in a distributed notion of intelligence, it is recognized that rarely if ever do productive humans work alone, simply using their heads. Rather, it is the rule that individuals work with all kinds of human and inanimate objects and prosthetics; these entities become so integral to their activities that it is reasonable to think of them as part of the individual's intellectual armament (Hatch & Gardner, 1992; Pea, in press; Salomon, 1979).

Distributed intelligence is equally apparent in the simplest and in the most complex human environments (Fischer & Bullock, 1984; Fischer, Kenny, & Pipp, 1990). The newborn child's activities are integrally involved with the objects that she uses and with the older individuals with whom she interacts; part of the young child's intelligence inheres in the scaffolding provided by the mother, father, or older sibling; part of the intelligence inheres in the simple tools that are used to pull an object toward oneself, to gain a pleasurable sensation, or to remember where one has placed something. Much the same kind of statement can be made about an individual's operations in a complex professional setting; part of the intelligence inheres in the many other individuals on whom a person can draw for thinking out problems, making decisions, or recalling important facts, concepts, or procedures; part of the intelligence inheres in a variety of tools, ranging from a personal notebook in which notes relevant to current work are assembled to a personal or mainframe computer that has access to information from all over the world.

Obviously the decision to speak of intelligence as distributed in other persons, tools, techniques, and symbol systems, is a strategic one. Using the classical terminology, one could simply choose to restrict intelligence to the contents of the individual's mind, apart from any of these human or nonhuman prosthetics. Yet, the advocates of a distributed view, such as Lave (1988), claim that this traditional usage obscures rather than illuminates, because it creates the misleading view that intellectual work typically occurs in isolation. The most convincing demonstration of the weakness of this view comes from the thought experiment in which one removes an infant from the social and physical supports, or removes the professional from the environment of the office with colleagues, computers, and records. Bereft of these supports, the organism becomes "stupid" indeed. Moreover, even in those cases where the individual *appears* to be working largely alone, he or she is actually drawing on lessons and skills that were acquired in a distributed environment but that have, with time, become internalized and automated (Vygotsky, 1978).

In our own work in the schools, we have increasingly taken into account the distributed view of intelligence. Our chosen vehicles for doing so have been student projects and portfolios (Gardner, 1991a; Wolf et al., 1991). In our view, most productive human work takes place when individuals are engaged in meaningful and relatively complex projects, which take place over time, are engaging and motivational, and lead to the development of understanding and skill. Such projects can take place within specific disciplines or can range across a number of disciplines. It is paradoxical that most students take hundreds of tests within school but that, once they have left school, they are almost never tested again. Conversely, most of productive life consists of projects— projects that are mandated by others, projects that are initiated by the person herself, or, most commonly, projects that represent an amalgam of personal desire and communal need.

From our view projects are an excellent exemplar of distributed intelligence. In nearly all cases, work on a project involves the interaction with other persons: mentors or teachers who help one to conceptualize and begin the project; peers or experts who help one to pursue the project; teams of collaborators each of which can make a distinctive contribution to the project; and an audience (ranging from a single parent or teacher to the whole school) that ultimately views the project and, possibly, evaluates it in an informal or formal way.

When a project is a completely derivative exercise, it is possible to execute it simply by mimicking already completed models. Rarely are such projects at a premium in our society. Much more commonly, and more appropriately as well, projects provide occasions where an individual can engage in some planning, make sketches or drafts, receive interim cooperation and feedback, and ultimately reflect on the ways in which the project achieved success as well as the ways in which it might have been altered or improved. In such activities, individuals are greatly helped by a form of distributed intelligence that we call a *processfolio*.

In a standard portfolio, an individual collects his or her best work, preliminary to some kind of competition or exhibition. As a contrast, in a processfolio, the student deliberately attempts to document—for himself as well as for others—the rocky road of his involvement in a project: the initial plans, the interim sketches, the false starts, the pivotal turning points, objects from the domain that are relevant and that he likes or dislikes, various forms of interim and final evaluations, and plans for new and subsequent projects (Wolf et al., 1991). Such an exercise is useful at the time of project execution; it can also be used as a reflective device, either at the time or later, for a student to see where he has been and where he is headed. The collection of materials amplifies the student's awareness of his options, supplementing imperfect memory and countering the tendency to reconceptualize past work in terms of present understandings. The combination of human support and personal documentation in a physical or conceptual portfolio is a vivid illustration of the extent to which intelligence can be distributed within the school setting.

It should be evident that, like the Spectrum approach, this way of conceptualizing learning and assessment is dramatically different from that associated with standardized testing. Rather than being isolated for the purpose of testing, the individual is encouraged to work with, and to take advantage of, the contributions of others, ranging from domain experts to fellow novices or journeymen. Rather than reacting to an instrument created by someone else, the individual is deeply involved in a project of his or own design. And rather than being evaluated by an individual or a machine at some distance removed, the assessment occurs primarily within the familiar context, and can be used as feedback to improve one's performance and one's understanding.

Though the use of such contextualized assessments may seem unproblematic within the confines of the class, it clearly presents new problems if it is to be used for the purposes of accountability. Some critics claim that such activities as projects, and such instrumentalities as processfolios, are inherently inappropriate for student or school account-ability purposes; others respect them in principle but feel that they are too costly, unwieldy, or subjective ever to be used on a wide context; still others believe that they could be so used, but that they would then become undermined by the same factors that have made "high-stakes" testing so problematic.

At Harvard Project Zero, we have taken these reservations seriously but have sought to develop projects and processfolios in such a way that they can be used beyond the classroom. Our efforts have taken place around three major collaborations: Arts PROPEL, an assessment effort at the middle and secondary school level, in collaboration with Educa-tional Testing Service and the Pittsburgh Public Schools (Gardner, 1990a; Gardner, 1989a; Zessoules, Wolf, & Gardner, 1988); Key School Projects, work at the elementary school level, in conjunction with an Indianapolis public school that has sought to build its curriculum around MI theory (Olson, 1988; Winn, 1990); and Project Catalyst, a computer-based effort for elementary and secondary school, in which children create projects aided by simple software (Scripp & Meyaard, 1991). It should be noted that our original work centered in the arts, but that projects and processfolios can be used profitably across the curriculum (Wiggins, 1989). Details of these projects differ significantly, of course, and each one needs to be described and evaluated in terms of its own goals, as outlined in the aforementioned references (see also chapters 7 through 9). At the risk of some distortion, however, I can indicate a few properties of assessment that can be applied across diverse settings and used for accountability purposes.

First of all, such projects or processfolios ought to be conceptualized in terms of a manageable number of dimensions. For example, projects in the elementary school can be viewed in terms of how well they have been conceptualized; how well they have been presented; how accurate they are; how original they are; and how appropriate they are to both the assignment posed by student or teacher and the genre of which they are an instance. It is also appropriate to assess the projects on certain dimensions that are not themselves evaluative, such as how much they reveal about the person who carried out the project; to what extent they have been developed cooperatively; and how engaged the student has been in the project.

Similarly, processfolios can be assessed in terms of a manageable number of dimensions. Crucial here is how well the student has conceptualized his current project; how it relates to, builds upon, and represents progress beyond earlier projects; how well concepts and skills from class have been integrated; to what extent assessments have been solicited from self and others; and how well these assessments have been used.

My own view is that it is most profitable to conceptualize student progress in developmental terms. That is, on the various dimensions considered, it should be possible to delineate the features of a novice, the features of an expert, and a number (ranging from 3 to 6) of intervening levels. The more carefully the characteristics of these stages can be delineated, and the better the range of exemplifying instances that is provided to the assessor, the more readily agreement can be reached on how to assess a student project or processfolio.

Of course, local considerations and value judgments will affect the evaluations of student work, and this is not in itself a bad feature. Problems arise when such evaluations prove idiosyncratic and misleading from the point of view of a wider community (Gardner, 1990b). The best procedure for mediating such deviations is *moderation,* a technique used for many years in British school evaluation circles. In moderating assessments, teachers or examiners from different locales assemble, evaluate one another's students works, identify areas of significant disagreement, and then determine what causes these different evaluations. Such moderating activities reveal whether different evaluations reflect different but equally legitimate value schemes (for example, one teacher likes expository writing that is matter-of-fact and unadorned, while another values expository writing that is more literary and imaginative); or whether the evaluation of one teacher (or one group of teachers) is inconsistent, self-contradictory, or reflects inadequate discriminative powers.

It should be stressed that a distributed view of intelligence does not dictate a certain curriculum, teaching style, or mode of assessment; rather it is a way of thinking about what transpires in any intellectual activity. Still, the current examples should indicate that it is possible to sculpt an educational environment that takes seriously the distributed view of intellect and that can go some distance toward judicious and reliable evaluation of student work.

Until this point, I have described phases in the conceptualization of intelligence that have taken place, in roughly chronological order, over the course of this century; and, wherever possible, I have designated educational procedures and assessment techniques that reflect the disparate views of intellect. It would be misleading to indicate that we have heard the last word from any of the five schematizations mentioned in the preceding discussion; it would be equally misleading to suggest that conceptualization of intelligence cannot advance even further. In closing this essay, I will briefly describe two further phases in thinking about intelligence that I believe will eventually come to pass.

THE INDIVIDUALIZATION OF INTELLIGENCE

The further we move beyond a unitary view of intelligence, where all persons can be gauged using the same cognitive thermometer, the more evident it becomes that each person's mind is different from that of every other person. The pluralization of intelligence suggests that there may be anywhere from seven to several hundred dimensions of mind (see Guilford, 1967); and of course, the combinations and recombinations of these dimensions soon generate an indefinitely large number of minds. Once one adds to this the next two realizations—that each mind has its own peculiar social-cultural context and that each mind partakes of various human and nonhuman extensions—it is evident that every human being has a sharply distinctive mind. We look different from one another, we have different personalities, and we have uniquely distinctive minds.

Education may have paid lip service to these distinctive configurations, but for the most part these differences have been almost completely ignored in classrooms and ateliers. If anything, education has proceeded according to the opposite assumption—there is one way of teaching, one way of learning, and individuals can be arrayed in terms of their skill at this mandated form. Only in recent years have there been efforts to describe different teaching and learning styles and to begin to sculpt educational environments or milieus that are sensitive to these differences. Efforts like Spectrum represent initial attempts to develop an educational environment that takes seriously such differences; but clearly we have only begun to define the size and scope of a truly individual-centered education (Gardner, 1987, 1989c). Ultimately, in some distant but still imaginable future, it should be possible to develop the educational environment that is optimal for each student at a particular historical moment; we will be aided in this process by better measuring devices, better understanding of the role of cultural milieu and distributed artifacts, more sensitive behaviors on the part of teachers and parents, and, not least, by the individual's own increasing awareness of his or her own characteristic intellectual strengths and style.

THE EDUCATION OF INTELLIGENCES

Hand-in-glove with an accurate and accurately evolving description of each person's intelligence is the need for an educational regimen that helps every person achieve his or her maximal potential across the range of disciplines and crafts. It goes without saying that such an educational regimen represents a massive undertaking, one difficult even to conceptualize let alone to achieve. Arrayed at one end is all the information about the individual's characteristic strengths, styles, and desires, within a given historical moment and cultural context; on the contrasting end, there is the vast number of scholarly domains, artistic crafts, cultural practices, and idiosyncratic domains, where an individual may wish to learn, to develop, to master what is known and perhaps go on to create new forms of knowledge or skill.

From my point of view, even our best educational environments do only an indifferent job in educating individuals to their maximum potential (Gardner, 1990c). While the reasons have been widely documented, I wish to propose one that has rarely been considered: most schools are content to accept performances that are rote, ritualized, or conventionalized; that is, performances that in some way merely repeat or give back what the teacher has modeled. However, at least in our current cultural context, and with our current value systems, educators ought to embody a more ambitious goal: the production of education for understanding. In such education, individuals do not merely spew back what they have been taught; rather they use the concepts and skills acquired in school to illuminate new and unfamiliar problems or to carry out fresh projects, in the process revealing that they have *understood*, and not merely imitated, the teachings to which they have been exposed (see chapter 11; Gardner, 1991b).

The nature of understanding will differ significantly across domains; the understanding of the physicist differs from that of the historian, and both differ significantly from that of the painter or musician. Such understandings are likely to come to pass only if teachers embody these understandings and know how to convey them to their students in personally effective ways.

In insisting on the distinctiveness of domains, and the challenge of teaching for understanding, it may appear that I have made an already difficult task into a distinct impossibility. Yet, paradoxically, I think that a multiple-intelligences, individual-based perspective can actually make feasible the task of education for understanding. An important clue comes from the insight that nearly every concept worth understanding can be conceptualized in a number of ways, and represented and taught in several ways as well. Thus, the concepts of importance in each domain allow a number of "entry points," ranging from the aesthetic and the narrative at one extreme, to the logical, the philosophical, and the experiential at the other. Given a variety of entry points, it should be possible to find at least one that is appropriate for each student. Moreover, since understanding itself involves the ability to approach a concept or skill from a number of different angles, the offering of several points of introduction and several routes to mastery should increase the likelihood that every individual can attain at least some understanding across a variety of human domains (see chapter 11; Gardner, 1983, 1991b).

This concise treatise on intelligence has covered a wide expanse, from lay conceptions to scientific disputes, from research findings to applied efforts in the classroom, from a critique of current practices to a glimpse into one possibly utopian future. In this way, for better or for worse, it is characteristic of most current work in educational research, and perhaps disappointingly remote from the crystalline conditions of the physics laboratory or the unambiguous message of a profit-and-loss statement in the annual report of a corporation.

Many years ago, it was quipped that intelligence is what the tests test. I have argued here that intelligence is too important to be left to the test-makers; it should be possible to put forth views of intelligence that are better justified by scientific research on the one hand, and that show more promise of educational utility on the other. Quite clearly, the concepts and efforts outlined here are tentative and preliminary. My opening vignettes serve as a chilling reminder of the misuses to which presumably well-motivated research-and-development efforts can be put. Only time and careful reflective investigation will reveal whether the concepts and practices urged here turn out to be more effective, and less malignant, than earlier efforts to ascertain the nature of human intellect.

Chapter 13

Engaging Intelligence

Coauthored by
Mindy Kornhaber and
Mara Krechevsky

All definitions of intelligence are shaped by the time, place, and culture in which they evolve. Although these definitions may differ across societies, we believe that the dynamics behind them are influenced by the same matrix of forces: (a) the domains of knowledge necessary for survival of the culture, such as farming, literacy, or the arts; (b) the values embedded in the culture, such as respect for elders, scholarly traditions, or pragmatic leanings; and (c) the educational system that instructs and nurtures individuals' various competences. In this chapter, we construct a new theory of intelligence—one that considers not only the familiar territory of the human mind, but the societies in which all minds must operate.

Unlike some other intelligence theorists, we do not seek to reduce the concept of intelligence to a less complex form in order to devise a test that measures "it." Rather, we wish to explain the diverse manifestations of intelligence within and across cultures. We hope the theory will help us to see when and where we might expect to find manifestations of intelligence, and how these manifestations might be increased. We favor assessments that are aimed at building on the range of individuals' cognitive potentials or competences. These competences, in turn, enable individuals to participate in the variety of end states human beings have developed. We hope, too, that such assessments may help to create environments that foster individual as well as group potential.

We seek to establish a theory of intelligence that spans the range of cultures. To do so, we first look across this span at two types of societies—traditional and industrial—in terms of the domains of knowledge each requires to survive and thrive, and how individuals within each type of society are motivated to engage their competences in various domains of knowledge. After defining more precisely the contents of our current theory, we then examine from that perspective the recent trajectories of two contemporary postindustrial societies, Japan and the United States. Finally, we close with a discussion of the new types of assessment that we believe should be developed in accordance with our expanded notion of intelligence.

Two Sketches of Human Intelligence in Social Perspective

THE TRADITIONAL/AGRARIAN SOCIETY

By definition, a traditional society is one in which the majority of the population is engaged in ensuring an adequate supply of food (LeVine & White, 1986). Obtaining food in these societies is typically very labor-intensive. Thus, most people must pursue domains such as fishing, farming, hunting, or herding. But even in these societies, food is not the only source of sustenance. Although there are no formal schools, a kind of curriculum exists nonetheless. Domains of knowledge have evolved around religion, myth, music, dance, and visual art forms. Children must also be socialized into the value system of the society, its religion and ethics, and its social order; the latter is usually determined by age and gender (LeVine & White, 1986).

How are the elements of this crucial curriculum acquired? For the most part, children learn the values and skills of their culture by watching what adults do and then imitating them. The children's environment is rich with real-life opportunities for applying the skills they learn, and so these skills get regular practice. In fact, practice of these skills usually takes the form of labor on which the community relies. Whatever actual instruction children receive from adults is largely informal. Both instruction and assessment occur in the context of carrying out work within the society's domains, and take the form of encouragement, advice, criticism, or helpful techniques (Gardner, 1990).

In some traditional societies, the evolution of skilled occupations and prized crafts comes to require a more structured form of learning. These crafts are transmitted to youngsters primarily through an apprenticeship system. Frequently these apprenticeships are linked to a family's customary occupation and take place at the feet of one's parent. Other times, a youngster is assigned to a master who acts *in loco parentis* (Bailyn, 1960). In either case, much of the instruction and evaluation is informal (though not necessarily benign). A child carries out minor tasks related to the master's work and watches what the master does. Gradually, through practice, the apprentice becomes skilled in various, well-defined steps that comprise the making of the final product (Lave, 1977). Eventually, the individual becomes a journeyman, capable of fashioning the final product under supervision of a master. After some years' experience, the individual may create the requisite "masterpiece" and himself become a master (Gardner, 1989a).

In more complex traditional societies, political and religious organizations evolve and trade routes develop (LeVine & White, 1986). Human memory is no longer adequate to retain the knowledge and skills on which these societies rely. Marks or pictures, used in less complex societies, must become organized into systems (Csikszentmihalyi, 1990). The first literacy systems, beginning with the invention of writing, were used for financial record keeping, with the first extended texts detailing stark historical records. Later on, texts set down the prevalent social virtues of traditional societies, most notably, "fertility and respect for parents" (LeVine & White, 1986, p. 32).

Because texts ensure the survival of complex, traditional societies, and because they serve powerful institutions, those who are literate typically hold highly desirable places within the social hierarchy. However, only an extremely small group of people in these societies possess more than rudimentary literacy skills. Any given society has many roles to fill that do not require literacy. In fact, a society might not withstand the shortage of agricultural labor incurred by a population that spent undue time acquiring and using advanced literacy skills. Therefore, with few exceptions (for example, Kobayashi, 1976), formal education in literate skills is reserved for the sons of the hierarchy of boys who show great promise. Academies or schools develop primarily to prepare young men for leadership roles in political and religious life (and in many societies these frequently overlap).

Defining intelligence in remote cultures is neither a simple nor a straightforward matter. Though people in traditional societies may admire literacy, intelligence is not especially defined by skills associated with it. Rather, as LeVine and White (1986) noted:

If you are intelligent, you behave according to the moral norms of the community because to do otherwise would antagonize those with whom you are permanently connected—which no intelligent adult would want to do. . . . Those who behave in accordance with social convention are assumed to be intelligent in the way that counts the most, i.e., in their maintenance of the social linkages that mean long-term security, though this implies normal rather than exceptional intelligence. Those in the community who are most respected for their moral virtue are credited with being wisest and most intelligent. . . . (Pp. 39–40)

Thus, we see that in traditional societies, intelligence involves the ability to maintain the community's social ties. In a society that likely depends on the cooperation of many individuals for such basic needs as food and shelter, it makes eminent sense that those who can secure such cooperation would be deemed intelligent.

THE INDUSTRIAL SOCIETY

In contrast to traditional societies, the advances of industrial societies in science and technology free—and indeed compel—large portions of the population to engage in labor unrelated to the production of food. These societies develop a wide range of occupations that both stem from, and further the use of, technological knowledge. Thus, coal miners and steel workers help to support the infrastructure of new industry; factory employees are needed to churn out a great variety of mass-produced goods; and scientists and engineers are trained to develop new equipment and processes, as well as new forms of information and knowledge. The demand for new inventions, as well as the increased economic complexity of trade, banking, and distribution, requires literacy from a greater proportion of people. Literacy is necessary in order to draw from science, mathematics, and the other vast stores of knowledge generated in these societies.

Though children continue to learn much from their elders, parents in industrial societies rarely provide instruction for their children's future occupations. In traditional societies, occupations were largely passed on from one generation to another; in industrial societies, parents may work outside the home, or they may not want—or be in a position to have—their children following in their footsteps. Furthermore, those footsteps may be erased by technological advances. For these and other reasons, the young in industrial societies acquire literacy and learn domains of knowledge primarily through schooling. Governments reinforce this change in parental responsibility by legislating schooling, because widespread literacy is regarded as a social good (see Kobayashi, 1976).

As in traditional societies, the activities of schooling in industrial societies do not resemble the daily routines of the surrounding adult community. In schools, skills and knowledge are assessed with little recourse to other persons, and evaluation is more formal and less frequent. In addition, schoolwork often does not engage the experiences a youngster has had outside the school setting (Brembeck, 1978; Brown, Collins, & Duguid, 1989; Gardner, 1991; Resnick, 1987; Sarason, 1983).

Schooling in industrialized societies differs in important ways from schooling in traditional societies. In the latter, the texts that are emphasized form the core values and often the political guidelines of the surrounding community. Therefore, what youths study in schools carries status in the larger community, even if their activity is removed from the community's daily routine of trade and agriculture (Gardner, 1991). Unlike schools in traditional societies, the decontextualized tasks of schooling in industrialized societies may or may not bear a meaningful connection to the values held by the surrounding community. This depends in part on the relationship of a school's population to the larger society and also on the values of the society.

A change in the conception of intelligence appears to attend the increased demand for literacy and the legislation of schooling. Whereas initially, honorifics like "intelligent" or "wise" were applied to the virtuous or moral individual—regardless of that person's level of education—in industrialized societies, those who are illiterate are unlikely to attain positions of social power or influence. And because community ties become lessened, so does the importance of intelligence associated with maintaining social cohesion, at least in some societies. For example, among the Gusii tribe in Kenya, after the introduction of Western schooling, the label of intelligent changed from being identified with morality and virtue to describing successful performance in school (LeVine, 1989).

A New Theory of Intelligence

The social contexts described previously suggest two different ways in which intelligence has been defined. In traditional societies, intelligence is linked to skill in interpersonal relations, whereas in many industrial societies intelligence centers more on advanced abilities in the three Rs. Yet despite these differences, the two definitions are derived in a similar way. Both definitions are intertwined with issues of cultural survival—in traditional societies, maintaining the necessary social cohesion, and in industrial societies, providing the means to shape technology and advance industry.

We believe that these disparate definitions make sense in their societies of origin. As Keating (1984) argued, our notions of intelligence have been profoundly distorted by our continued failure to consider the social, historical, and political contexts from which such ideas arise. If intelligence is conceptualized as representing a dynamic between individual proclivities and a society's needs and values (as opposed to a characteristic of an individual), then it appears that the realization of individual potentials and the needs of the aforementioned cultures were organized in a way that proved effective for the society's particular social and economic structures. It is our claim that the capacity of individuals to acquire and advance knowledge in a cultural domain, and apply it in some purposeful fashion toward a goal—key features of some definitions of intelligence—has equally to do with the competences inside one's head and with the values and opportunities afforded by society to engage these competences.

Hence, we might define intelligence primarily as the manifestation of engagements between two components: (a) individuals, who are capable of using their array of competences in various domains of knowledge; and (b) the societies that foster individual development through the opportunities they provide, the institutions they support, and the value systems they promote. Individual competences represent only one aspect of intelligence; intelligence also requires social structures and institutions that enable the development of these competences. In this framework, intelligence becomes a flexible, culturally dependent construct. Either the individual or the societal agent may play a dominant role, but both must take part if intelligence is to be achieved. In so-called field societies such as Japan, the action takes place much more on the society's part; in our own "particle" society, the human agent plays a more significant role.

For roughly a century, Western industrialized societies and the schools within them could afford to mobilize the competences of only a minority of their populations. However, with the rise of postindustrial economies, it is no longer feasible to enable only those who are adept at decontextualized learning to develop their competences. We need to broaden our notion of what can be considered intelligence, in terms of both individual and cultural components. Along with new attitudes about intelligence, new forms of schooling and assessment are needed to foster the competences of the majority.

INDIVIDUALS: THE CASE FOR MULTIPLE INTELLIGENCES

In postindustrial societies, the notion that intelligence is a trait of individuals may be tied to the innovations in psychological testing that took place at the beginning of this century. Binet's (1905) intelligence scales were developed to identify children who were performing poorly in school and who might benefit from special education. Though Binet never intended to reify intelligence, and though he did not maintain intelligence was a unitary trait (Gould, 1981), the fact that his test results could be summarized by a single score fostered visions of intelligence as a unitary attribute situated in the heads of individuals.

However, several contemporary views (Ceci, 1990; Feldman, 1980; Gardner, 1983) suggest a more pluralistic notion of intelligence, in order to account for individuals' diverse abilities both to pursue various domains of knowledge and to create new ones. Gardner (1983) proposed his theory of multiple intelligences, which suggests that individuals are capable of cognitive functioning in at least seven relatively autonomous areas (see part I of this volume). The different profiles, trajectories, and rates of development that emerge across intelligences enable a person to grasp, more or less readily, the symbol systems in which the domains of his or her culture are transmitted (Gardner, 1983).

Although individuals are capable of developing a range of competences toward various end states, they do not do so in isolation. Even in the case of a universally developing competence like language, it is only in the interaction of adult and child that such a faculty develops. Not only does learning generally take place in the context of social interaction, but the great majority of what is learned after the age of two is socially constructed (Snow & Ferguson, 1977). Societies teach their children those bodies of facts, theories, skills, and methods that comprise its various domains of knowledge, ranging from fishing to physics (Csikszentmihalyi & Robinson, 1986). We maintain that human cognition is best developed and nurtured through tasks within the bounds of such *authentic domains*—that is, in socially valued disciplines, where an individual can acquire skills and knowledge through effort over time, typically with feedback from people knowledgeable in the discipline.

Multiple intelligences theory seems to provide a useful framework within which to consider the broad range of individual competences, the first component of our proposed theory. However, to flesh out our theory more fully, we need to consider the dynamic between individuals and the societies in which they operate, and turn to a discussion of two contemporary societies from the perspective of the theory's cultural component. The first society illustrates a case where intelligence seems to be abundantly manifested, whereas such manifestations are far less conspicuous in the other.

Contemporary Postindustrial Society: Two Examples

THE CASE OF JAPAN

Given our definition of intelligence as representing effective engagements between individuals and the societies in which they live, we might expect Japan to serve as a particularly instructive example. In Japan, the development of intelligence is fostered by widely shared values, which in turn are supported by the institutions of the society. Among these values are school achievement and diligent study. Parents demand high-quality schools and have high expectations for their children. They believe children can fulfill these expectations through hard work and commitment rather than through innate capacity. Thus, mothers actively tutor their children, and teachers are held in high regard. Maximizing the Japanese child's potential is adopted as a social responsibility, not only on the rhetorical level but in actual practice (White, 1987).

The concern with developing children's potential is reinforced in part by the structure of the Japanese educational system and its connection to job security and success. In the United States, there are scores of colleges whose reputations could ultimately enable students to secure professional careers. However, there are very few such institutions in Japan, and most employers look only to these few when they hire for top positions. The competition to attend these universities calls for a seriousness of purpose (and a level of stress) that is world renowned.

In Japan, performing to one's highest level is not simply promoted as a way to make it through the narrow pipeline to professional success. The motivation to realize individuals' competences stems from the fact that such realization helps to secure one's place in a society that emphasizes and values interpersonal bonds. Failure to study hard and contribute within the larger society threatens these bonds (Shimizu, 1988).

The stimulus of social connection upon achievement is also evident in Japanese employment. In the work world, employees identify strongly with their firms, in part because they often expect to have lifelong careers within them. Furthermore, employees do not feel especially competitive with their fellow workers, and no particular premium is placed on a single individual's possessing all of the requisite competences himself or herself. Indeed, the Japanese corporation seems to recognize the profile of human competences and accepts the notion that individuals with different profiles can make their own distinctive contributions to the success of the firm (Gardner, 1983).

Japan, then, seems to exemplify some of the elements of our normative—as opposed to descriptive—theory. The engagements between individuals and society are evident at many levels: between individual and family, family and school, school and work, and employee and employer. Furthermore, societal values support both schooling and an emphasis on effort and motivation, rather than innate ability. Individual competences are nurtured by institutions that encourage their development in a supportive context. When all of these forces align, according to our theory, intelligence is likely to be manifested.

THE CASE OF THE UNITED STATES

The United States provides a useful counterexample to Japan. By now, we are all too familiar with the reports showing that American schoolchildren score lower on standardized tests than nearly any other Western or industrialized nation (Stevenson, 1987; Stevenson et al., 1985). We see national studies that indicate that large proportions of American youngsters do not master basic school subjects. At age seventeen, 80 percent of our students appear unable to write a persuasive letter (Applebee, Langer, & Mullis, 1986). Half of our students do not give reasonable estimates, let alone precise answers, to basic numerical problems (Dossey, Mullis, Lindquist, & Chambers, 1988). Although neurologically based learning disabilities certainly exist, it is unlikely that these statistics are reflective of such problems. There is no reason to believe that our affluent country contains disproportionate numbers of people who are inherently limited. To determine how our society might better elicit intelligence, it may prove edifying to examine the course that led us to this point.

The social connections afforded by widely shared values between parent and child were threatened in America from the first colonial days. Although the Puritans had every intention of educating their own children, maintaining traditional apprenticeships, and schooling boys to become ministers, the environment undermined these plans. Unlike other industrial societies, the solder of traditional society—respect for one's elders and dependency upon them—disintegrated in America long before industrialization had prevailed. The Puritan leaders, fearing that the next generation was becoming barbarians, decided to build schools to perpetuate their unraveling culture (Bailyn, 1960). However, it was quite clear to the Puritan young that the tradition-bound knowledge possessed by their elders was not especially useful for surviving in the wilderness. Labor was at a premium, land was abundant, and households broke up (Bailyn, 1960).

As the United States became an industrial society a century ago, the dubious regard for school-based knowledge remained in effect. Literacy, numeracy, and an acquaintance with texts that captured our cultural legacy were accepted to a certain extent, but competent, active engagement in practical affairs was generally more valued. As Andrew Carnegie put it, "In my own experience I can say that I have known few young men intended for business who were not injured by a collegiate education" (cited in Callahan, 1962, p. 9). The popular view was that intelligent people applied themselves in practical domains and that a traditional school curriculum was of little utility (Bailyn, 1960; see also Hofstadter, 1963). Thus, the close alignments existing in Japan between individual and family, family and school, and school and work never took hold in this country.

America's break with tradition-bound learning (Bailyn, 1960), coincident with its love for new technology, may have rendered it especially vulnerable to explanations of intelligence that claimed to be scientific. In any event, it was easy for a variety of hereditarian views and the eugenics movement to take hold here, especially in light of the influence of Darwin's (1859) *On the origin of species* and the social Darwinism that followed (Gould, 1981). The adaptation of intelligence tests in America for mass administration to World War I recruits increased the shift from social to scientific designations. Science, with its paper-and-pencil tests, formulae, and factor analysis—rather than just social judgments about performance in different domains of knowledge—supported views that white, Christian, northern Europeans possessed the most intelligence. In the minds of many, these people came from the best genetic stock. Thus, in America, we came to believe that intelligence was born and not made.

As Gould (1981) noted, the rendering of the concept of intelligence into a reified, inherited trait was "an American invention" (p. 147).

At the same time that IQ tests were being developed, American schools were subjected to the forces of another science-related trend, the efficiency movement. In business and commerce, people were turning to science and technology to solve the problems of manufacturing. Jobs were broken down into discrete tasks that could be performed on assembly lines. In education, public schools were increasingly pressured to operate efficiently, to minimize retention, and to provide a disciplined workforce (Callahan, 1962). The introduction of principles of scientific management and mass production into the schools dampened educators' efforts to provide remediation for those with scholastic difficulties. Attempts were made to determine children's competences early on and to provide them with education that was fitting for their presumed adult end state. Although the development of competences among immigrant groups was especially threatened, all children were affected by the schools' adoption of business values and practices (Oakes, 1986a, 1986b; Powell, Farrar, & Cohen, 1985).

Excessive reliance on psychometric instruments tended not only to divorce individuals from teachers or others who evaluated their performance in a social context, but also tended to divorce people from the domains of knowledge valued by the society. The determination of intelligence by intelligence tests is made outside of what we consider the legitimate boundaries of human cognition. One reason for this is that intelligence tests do not operate within the bounds of an authentic domain of human endeavor. In creating the contents of the *Mental measurements yearbook* (Buros, 1941) psychometricians and psychologists established a domain of sorts. Yet, although this domain is also subject to the interpretation of experts in the field, it is largely devoid of features that mark authentic domains. Missing from mental testing are opportunities for practicing domain-relevant tasks and using them in meaningful contexts. Also absent is the possibility of progressing through a series of stages—often with feedback from those more skilled in the domain—toward proficiency in a socially valued end state. Except perhaps in the domain of television game shows (another American invention), one is rarely expected to repeat series of numbers, to solve analogies, or to identify well-known figures within a time period of a few seconds in order to achieve a social reward.

The absence of an authentic domain threatens the grounds on which intelligence experts make their judgments. Their situation is akin to that of other experts who must make judgments in domains in which criteria are not agreed on. The case of creativity offers a useful model for comparison. According to Csikszentmihalyi (1988b), three dynamic systems are at play in determining creativity: (a) the individuals who create works; (b) the domains of knowledge in which they work; and (c) the field of experts in the domains who judge the works of individuals. In this framework, attributions of creativity rely on the recognition of individual efforts by the field of judges. Such attributions are widely accepted in disciplines where criteria are well established and agreed upon (such as mathematics). In other disciplines, where criteria are not widely shared (such as modern painting), the attribution of creativity is less likely to depend on an individual's work within the domain than upon the extent to which the individual possesses social traits that are synchronous with the members of the field (Getzels & Csikszentmihalyi, 1976).

Attributions of intelligence share similar judgment calls. We believe that, lacking an authentic domain, the attribution of intelligence is even more dependent on the degree to which the experts and the judged share social characteristics. The history of intelligence testing, prior to the restriction of its uses by legal and political efforts, bears witness to the importance of social synchrony in the attribution of intelligence (Gould, 1981; see Heubert, 1982).

Given the previous analysis, a focus on testing for an allegedly general ability is no longer tenable. We must look instead at meaningful performances within a culture. Whereas intelligence tests look only at the individual, intelligence must take into account both individuals and societies. Even when intelligence tests have attempted to measure what we are calling individual competences, they have been narrow in scope. Rather than examining the range of human cognition, they have focused on a thin band of human cognitive competences—in the terms given in *Frames of mind* (1983), on certain aspects of linguistic and logical intelligence. Intelligence tests are limited not only in the competences that they examine, but in the way they examine them. They require people to deal with atypical, decontextualized tasks, rather than probing how people function when they are able to draw upon their experience, feedback, and knowledge as they typically do. And they may well "tease out" individuals who excel at taking short-answer tests, but who do not function well in organizations that demand other skills.

It is not even clear that the thinking called upon in these tests bears a significant relation to the usual reasoning employed in learning (Keating, 1984). As Resnick and Neches noted,

The extensive attention given to the cognitive components of test performance is based on an implicit assumption that the processes required for *performance* on the tests are also directly involved in *learning*. We believe that this is a risky assumption. . . . (1984, p. 276)

Test items such as abstract analogies may tell us something about how people attempt to solve extremely decontextualized problems—and which people are more practiced at solving such test items—but they do not tell us much about intelligence in our expanded view (Johnson-Laird, 1983). Unless assessment is placed in the context of authentic domains and social environments, we doubt it can adequately represent human intellectual performance.

Some contemporary approaches to assessment recommend using standardized tests as only one component of a broad-based evaluation. Although more comprehensive assessments—including observations of the child in his or her setting and interviews with the child's parents—provide a needed improvement, the world is an imperfect place, and scientific measurements hold disproportionate sway. When funds and staffing are stretched, test scores serve as cutoff points. Hard-looking data are used to fend off parents hoping to get their children into programs for the gifted and talented; test measurements often furnish the fallback position for deciding who gets remediation. In a society that has advanced far on technology and scientific data, numbers act as the primary basis for triage (Neill & Medina, 1989).

THE NEED FOR A SOCIAL FRAMEWORK

Just as America overly emphasized the technocratic aspects of education—with its heavy focus on testing and measurement—it also neglected the social glue that had always been an important part of education, whether in the schools (as in Japan) or in the wider community (as in traditional apprenticeships). Yet, as mentioned earlier, individual competences need to be encouraged within a social framework. Motivation is not simply a function of competence alone; it also depends on interactions with the social world (Fordham & Ogbu, 1986; Ogbu, 1978; see also Scarr, 1981). Such interactions eventually become internalized over time and serve as a guide to individual behavior (Vygotsky, 1978). Our society has tended to ignore the impact of interpersonal experiences in part because it is not readily abstracted and measured when analyzing differences in competences and achievements. Hence, the educationally disadvantaged have typically been defined in terms of demographic and educational variables (Bereiter, 1985).

Nonetheless, the creation of cooperative, supportive environments in homes, schools, and communities has been shown to have a positive effect on students' social and psychological well-being, which eventually leads to higher academic achievement (Cochran, 1987; Comer, 1980, 1988a; Damon, 1990; Henderson, 1987; Leler, 1983; Zigler & Weiss, 1985). The intervention projects designed by Comer (1980) and his colleagues to help low-income children stress the importance of relationships: "[W]hen relationships improve in the schools, the children themselves become the carriers of desirable values" (Comer, 1988a, p. 29). Effective schools seem to be determined not so much by the students themselves or their aptitudes as by parental and teacher support, involvement, and the transmission of their high expectations (Ascher, 1988; Brookover, 1985; Chubb, 1988; Comer, 1980; Edmonds, undated).

In America, there has always been a lack of continuity among (a) the range of individual competences; (b) what is learned in school; and (c) what our society values. In our postindustrial society, where these discontinuities remain, the derivation of intelligence via decontextualized, scientific instruments is no longer serviceable; the education that flows from them no longer supports the adult end states that have evolved in our culture. Advances in communication, transportation, and automatization, and the exportation of manufacturing to other countries, mean that many people sorted and educated under the old system cannot take up meaningful roles. We need to develop alternative assessments that will take into account our expanded notion of intelligence. Ideally, such a development will lead to the creation of assessment environments where the engagement of individuals in meaningful tasks in society can be looked at more directly.

Enabling Intelligences by Contextualized Assessment

Tests of intelligence serve as traps not only for theorists, but for educators and students as well. Rather than constructing tests that do not measure intelligence, but instead tend to sort individuals and potentially limit their growth, we prefer to design vehicles that simultaneously help to uncover and foster an individual's competences. Our proposed model considers assessment in terms of meaningful adult end states that are valued by the community. The concept of adult end states is helpful for focusing assessment on abilities that are relevant to achieving significant and rewarding adult roles in our society. Thus, if we value the roles of novelist and lawyer, a more valid assessment of language skills might examine a young child's ability to tell a story or provide a descriptive account of an experience, rather than examine her ability to repeat a series of sentences, define words, or solve antonymic or syllogistic tasks. The latter tasks bear no discernible relationship to a domain or adult end state. The implications of highly contextualized assessments for instruction and remediation are more immediate and direct than decontextualized items. For example, mentoring experiences in a domain of knowledge such as the visual arts or mechanical science might be one way to work closely with the central issues and materials of a field.

Apprenticeships also embed learning in a social and purposeful context. They are valuable not only because they build on student interests and strengths, but because they foster critical thinking through regular, informal assessment in the context of an authentic domain. In this respect, they are much more similar to the robust learning that goes on outside of school (Brown, Collins, & Duguid, 1989; Resnick, 1987). Apprenticeships also serve as a means of providing greater community involvement with schools. As mentioned earlier, the cooperative involvement of parents and others in the surrounding community strengthens the cognitive outcomes of the community's schoolchildren (Chubb, 1988; Comer, 1988b; Heath, 1983; Henderson, 1987). Every child should have the opportunity to work closely with an adult who serves as a "model of serious study, reflection, and application in the world that is meaningful to [him] . . ." (Gardner, 1990, p. 106). Although the domains of knowledge have shifted over time, it is in human relationships that societies have managed to develop individual competences from their very beginning (see Comer, 1984).

In addition to advocating apprentice-type learning environments where possible, we believe that education should be firmly grounded in the institutions and practices of society—art and science museums, ateliers, scouting, and so on. Science, discovery, and children's museums offer a rich and powerful opportunity for children to draw upon the different forms of knowledge that are generally left unintegrated, treated in isolation from each other, or perhaps ignored in school. The materials in museums are in a sense already pretested for their appeal to children. Many of these materials are quite educational for children, and can be utilized in a variety of ways over significant periods of time. A number of current interactive technologies such as video discs and HyperCard allow children to combine intuitive and school-based knowledge in various endeavors, from understanding the principles of physics to appreciating a foreign culture (Bransford, Franks, Vye, & Sherwood, 1989; Wilson, 1988).

Assessment environments should follow a number of desiderata. They should integrate curriculum and assessment and invite individuals to deploy their various competences in the context of carrying out meaningful projects or activities. Such assessments should also make available a range of intrinsically interesting and motivating materials that would be used over time and that would be sensitive to individual differences. They should also be intelligence-fair, that is, capable of engaging specific competences without the need to rely on linguistic or logical means or abilities as an intermediary. Ideally, these assessments would also meet Fredericksen and Collins's criteria for "systemically valid tests": tests that induce "in the education system curricular and instructional changes that foster the development of the cognitive traits that the test[s] [are] designed to measure" (1989, p. 1).

In chapters 6 through 9 we examined educational interventions framed in this spirit. Both Spectrum and Arts PROPEL represent attempts to identify a wider range of competences in a context that is both embedded in the culture and meaningful to the child. By building on a child's interest and motivation, schools might have more success in carrying out what may be their most crucial task: empowering children to engage meaningfully in their own learning. As we have seen, one way to develop meaningful engagement is through apprenticeships. These might be arranged for students through school specialists, with some apprenticeships being conducted by teachers, and others with individuals from the surrounding community. Although discovering the rewards of learning in a domain as an end in itself is important (Amabile, 1983; Csikszentmihalyi, 1990), Comer's (1980, 1984) works, among others, show that an interpersonal relationship is critical in motivating students to learn.

The Key School reflects an environment where school, children, and the community come together in a productive way. The school encourages children to develop competence in the various domains through an interdisciplinary curriculum. Equal time is devoted to English, math, music, art, computers, movement, and other subjects. In addition, children are allowed to develop in their areas of strength in an apprentice-like situation, known as a *pod*. Pods are small classes conducted by teachers along their special lines of interest that children from any grade are free to join. Children can also develop their interests in an after-school program, led by the principal and teachers.

As a "magnet" school, this institution draws children from all neighborhoods of the city. An advisory board made up of representatives from local businesses, cultural institutions, and universities helps the school take advantage of local resources. Parents are also involved in the school, through teacher conferences, parent-advisory committees, and occasional presentations in their areas of expertise. Thus, the Key School attempts to bridge the individual, the school, and the community. In this way, the Key School may be thought of as a contemporary American effort to develop intelligences to the fullest.

Enhancing the development of individual competences is a many-sided effort. We see prospects for it in new forms of assessment, like Arts PROPEL and Spectrum, in closer working relationships between young people and mentors, and in increased cooperation between schools and communities. We also believe that significantly different ideas about intelligence have a large part to play.

Most theories of intelligence have attempted to answer the question "what?" To the extent that tests have been based on such theories, they have served more to label individuals than to promote their development. Instead, we have focused our search for a new theory around the questions "when? where? and how?" We believe the theory generated by these inquiries provides a constructive framework to advance both analysis and practical interventions.

We hope that our theory will act as an impetus for the study of intelligence to change from a focus on individuals to a focus on interactions between individuals and societies. To the greatest extent possible, psychological and cognitive factors must be considered in conjunction with the social contexts in which they operate.

Therefore, the study of intelligence requires a meeting of the minds. Research based on individual cognition—studies involving information processing approaches, means-ends models, factor analysis, and the like—will continue to be useful. But although these domains may provide insights into the kinds of strategies people use in specific kinds of problem solving, these peculiarly decontextualized problems are not the crux of human intelligence (Neisser, 1983). In life, most problems are not presented ready-made to the solver, but must be shaped out of events and information existing in the surrounding environment (Csikszentmihalyi, 1988a). We need a deeper understanding of how social settings motivate individuals to delve into these kinds of problems, of the policies that have spurned people from engaging their competences and the policies that encourage engagement, of the effect of parents and peer groups and how this effect might be enhanced, and of the effects of school organization and curriculum on a variety of students and teachers. In short, because we believe that the great majority of people are capable of using their competences in a skillful way, we need to explore how such use can be encouraged within a social framework. Once we recognize that intelligence evolves through a dynamic of individuals' competences and society's values and institutions, we are more likely to devise policies and to support initiatives that effectively engage more people's minds.

Epilogue

Multiple Intelligences
Theory in 2013

Having begun this volume with an imaginary voyage back to 1900, I'd like to conclude by taking a speculative voyage forward to the year 2013. That year will mark the thirtieth anniversary of the publication of *Frames of mind*, and, as it happens, the time when I am scheduled to retire. Should work continue on the theory and the practices of multiple intelligences, what might one expect to observe on that occasion?

Without question, neuroscientists will have established far more firm knowledge about the organization and development of the nervous system. After years of observing mental processes as they actually occur in the living brain, they will be able to describe the neural structures that are entailed in the conduct of various intellectual activities; they will be able to indicate the extent to which these activities are actually independent of one another; and they will know to what extent individuals who are exceptional performers in one or another intellectual realm actually exhibit neural processes that differ from those exhibited by less extraordinary individuals. Genetic studies are likely to reveal whether specific intellectual strengths (such as musical or spatial intelligence) are under the control of individual genes or gene complexes; and studies of identical and fraternal twins reared together and apart will enhance our knowledge of the extent to which different intellectual profiles are heritable.

Progress in the cognitive sciences is more difficult to predict, and we do not know to what extent various forms of artificial intelligence will prove to be close simulations of human intelligence. Without doubt, however, there will exist far more detailed and convincing models of various kinds of human intellectual activity; and it should be clearer to which extent the "same" processes are at work in different activities, and to which extent one must posit the existence of different information-processing capacities across human intellectual competences.

Twenty years from now, it will surely be a worthwhile exercise to conduct the kind of review and synthesis that my colleagues and I undertook around 1980 in preparing *Frames of mind*. Such a review will indicate the reasonableness of the original list of seven intelligences, as well as the ways in which the mental landscape might be reconfigured in light of accumulated knowledge. I have every reason to believe that the map would be drawn in a somewhat different way; I hope that the *idea* of multiple intelligences will seem even more reasonable in 2013 than it does in 1993.

Even as the scientific underpinning of the theory of multiple intelligences is likely to alter in the coming years, so, too, the educational practices undertaken in its spirit will also change. So far, the focus has fallen largely on the devising of alternative means of assessment. I expect that this emphasis will continue. I hope that educators and designers will rise to the challenge of creating environments in which intelligences can be assessed in as naturalistic and intelligence-fair a way as possible. The more that we can accrue firm information in such realistic settings, the less need there will be for the construction of standardized and decontextualized instruments that sample so meager a proportion of human talents.

At present, the notion of schools devoted to multiple intelligences is still in its infancy, and there are as many plausible recipes as there are educational chefs. I hope that in the next twenty years, a number of efforts will be made to craft an education that takes multiple intelligences seriously; should this be done, we will be in a position to know which of these "thought" and "action experiments" make sense and which prove to be impractical or ill-advised. Perhaps, if careful studies are done, we will even know *why* some educational approaches work and why some do not.

One area poised for progress entails the development of curricular approaches that prove effective for individuals with different intellectual profiles. With every year we have available a greater store of promising and inexpensive educational technologies, ranging from videodisc libraries of artistic images to interactive simulations of political processes to transmission of newly assembled scientific data by electronic mail. These technologies can be crafted so as to maximize the chances that each student can learn—and can display her learnings—in ways that are comfortable to her. Of course, there are also many powerful curricular options that do not depend on any of the new technologies. I will be extremely disappointed if education in 2013 has not become significantly more individually nuanced than it is today.

I hope that the idea of multiple intelligences will become part of teacher training. While lip service is paid to the existence of differences among students (and among teachers!), there have been few systematic attempts to elaborate the educational implications of these differences. Should a sensitivity to different intelligences or learning styles become part of the "mental models" constructed by new teachers, the next generation of instructors are far more likely to be able to reach each of their students in the most direct and effective way.

I have mentioned the possibility of additional work on the scientific underpinnings of MI theory, as well as the pursuit of a number of educational pathways. For me, the most exciting area within multiple intelligences work today is one that cuts directly across the science/practice dichotomy. That entails an investigation of the different contexts in which intelligences are nourished and deployed.

As I have argued at length in this book, nearly all of the previous work on intelligence has presupposed a particular (and, in my view, a particularly narrow) context: the secular school of today. We know an enormous amount about what it takes to be a success in the schools of today, especially when those schools stress standardized short-answer instruments as the means for assessing aptitude and achievement.

MI theory illuminates the fact that humans exist in a multitude of contexts and that these contexts both call for and nourish different arrays and assemblies of intelligence. A formidable challenge and opportunity exists in a closer study of these contrasting contexts. Different contexts exist at several levels of analysis: at the level of the country (see chapter 13); at the level of the community (see interlude I); at the level of the individual classroom (see work by Tom Hatch, reported in Hatch & Gardner, 1992); and even in the individual family. We need to understand far more about these contexts—which kinds of values they embody, which kinds of signals they give, how they interact with and shape the proclivities of the young individuals raised in their midst.

Of particular interest to me are the contexts that exist at a level somewhere in between the overarching unit of the country or culture, and the intimate unit of the family or the classroom. The numerous workplaces in any industrialized country each exhibit characteristic kinds of needs, demands, options, and opportunities; and there may well be some features that span a variety of workplaces of the near future (Zuboff, 1988). We very much need careful studies about how intelligences are deployed within the workplaces of today and tomorrow. Also at a premium will be the study of other kinds of contemporary organizations and institutions, ranging from corporations and hospitals to museums and universities. Finally, the assumptions about the intelligences that are relevant (or at peril) in a society drenched in consumerism, the mass media, and mass culture all want sensitive study.

In this "fast forward" to 2013, I have mentioned a number of possible scientific, educational, and institutional sequelae of MI theory. To do so is perhaps to attribute to a psychologically based theory an importance that it does not merit. I happen to believe that social science cannot aspire to the same kinds of "permanent truths" that are the lodestone of the physical and biological sciences. Social or behavioral science is a much more tentative affair, which may yield powerful insights and understandings, but which may not sum up to an edifice of permanent knowledge. Nonetheless, human society is the richer because social scientists have helped us to understand a range of phenomena, ranging from the Oedipal complex to the identity crisis, from the culture of poverty to the affluent society. To this point, the concept of intelligence as IQ has been psychology's most successful contribution to the conversation of our society. If, by 2013, there is a wider acceptance of the notion that intelligence deserves to be pluralized, I will be pleased indeed.

APPENDICES

Appendix A
Acknowledgments,
References,
Collaborators,
and Funders

Chapter 1. In a Nutshell

Article reprinted in its entirety: Gardner, H. (1987, May). Developing the spectrum of human intelligences. *Harvard Educational Review, 57* (2), 187–93.

Acknowledgments

This chapter is based on an informal talk given at the 350th anniversary of Harvard University on 5 September 1986. The work reported in this article was supported by the Rockefeller Foundation, the Spencer Foundation, and the Bernard Van Leer Foundation.

Chapter 2. A Rounded Version

Article reprinted in its entirety: Walters, J., & Gardner, H. (1985). The development and education of intelligences. In F. Link (Ed.), *Essays on the intellect* (pp. 1–21). Washington, D.C.: Curriculum Development Associates.

Appendix A

Acknowledgments

The research reported in this chapter was supported by grants from the Bernard Van Leer Foundation of The Hague, the Spencer Foundation of Chicago, and the Carnegie Corporation of New York. We are grateful to Mara Krechevsky, who gave many helpful comments on earlier drafts.

References

Connor, A. (1982). *Voices from Cooperstown.* New York: Collier. (Based on a quotation taken from *The Babe Ruth story,* Babe Ruth & Bob Considine. New York: Dutton, 1948.)

Gallwey, T. (1976). *Inner tennis.* New York: Random House.

Gardner, H. (1983). *Frames of mind: The theory of multiple intelligences.* New York: Basic Books.

Jencks, C. (1972). *Inequality.* New York: Basic Books.

Keller, E. (1983). *A feeling for the organism.* Salt Lake City: W. H. Freeman.

Lash, J. (1980). *Helen and teacher: The story of Helen Keller and Anne Sullivan Macy.* New York: Delacorte.

Menuhin, Y. (1977). *Unfinished journey.* New York: Knopf.

Selfe, L. (1977). *Nadia: A case of extraordinary drawing ability in an autistic child.* New York: Academic Press.

Soldo, J. (1982). Jovial juvenilia: T. S. Eliot's first magazine. *Biography, 5,* 25–37.

Walters, J., & Gardner, H. (1986). The crystallizing experience: Discovering an intellectual gift. In R. Sternberg & J. Davidson (Eds.), *Conceptions of giftedness* (pp. 306–31). New York: Cambridge University Press.

Woolf, V. (1976). *Moments of being.* Sussex: The University Press.

Chapter 3. Questions and Answers About Multiple Intelligences Theory

Article reprinted in part: Walters, J., & Gardner, H. (1986). The theory of multiple intelligences: Some issues and answers. In R. Sternberg & R. Wagner (Eds.), *Practical intelligences* (pp. 163–81). New York: Cambridge University Press.

References

Bloom, B. (1985). *Developing talent in young people.* New York: Ballantine Books.

Connor, A. (1982). *Voices from Cooperstown.* New York: Collier. (Based on a quotation taken from *The Babe Ruth story*, Babe Ruth & Bob Considine. New York: Dutton, 1948.)

Eimas, P., Siqueland, E., Jusczyk, P., & Vigorito, J. (1971). Speech perception in infants. *Science, 171*, 303–6.

Ericsson, K. (1984, December). Presented at the Workshop on Expertise, sponsored by the Social Science Research Council, New York City.

Fodor, J. (1983). *Modularity of mind.* Cambridge, Mass.: MIT Bradford Press.

Gallwey, T. (1976). *Inner tennis.* New York: Random House.

Gardner, H. (1975). *The shattered mind.* New York: Vintage.

Gardner, H. (1983). *Frames of mind: The theory of multiple intelligences.* New York: Basic Books.

Gardner, H. (1984, June). Assessing intelligences: A comment on "Testing intelligence without IQ tests" by R.J. Sternberg. *Phi Delta Kappan, 65* (10), 699–700.

Gardner, H., & Feldman, H. (1985). *First annual report on Project Spectrum.*

Keller, E. (1983). *A feeling for the organism.* San Francisco: Freeman.

Lash, J. (1980). *Helen and teacher: The story of Helen Keller and Anne Sullivan Macy.* New York: Delacorte.

Menuhin, Y. (1977). *Unfinished journey.* New York: Knopf.

Selfe, L. (1977). *Nadia: A case of extraordinary drawing ability in an autistic child.* New York: Academic Press.

Soldo, J. (1982). Jovial juvenilia: T. S. Eliot's first magazine. *Biography, 5*, 25–37.

Sternberg, R. (1983). How much gall is too much gall? A review of *Frames of mind: The theory of multiple intelligences. Contemporary Education Review, 2*, 215–24.

Sternberg, R. (1984). Toward a triarchic theory of human intelligence. *Behavioral and Brain Sciences, 7*, 269–315.

Trehub, S., Bull, D., & Thorpe, L. (1984). Infants' perception of melodies: The role of melodic contour. *Child Development, 55*, 821–30.

Walters, J., & Gardner, H. (1986). The crystallizing experience: Discovering an intellectual gift. In R. Sternberg & J. Davidson (Eds.), *Conceptions of giftedness.* New York: Cambridge University Press.

Weinreich-Haste, H. (1985). The varieties of intelligences: An interview with Howard Gardner. *New Ideas in Psychology, 3*, 47–65.

Woolf, V. (1976). *Moments of being.* Sussex: The University Press.

Chapter 4. The Relation of Intelligence to Other Valued Human Capacities

Article reprinted in part: Gardner, H. (in press). The "giftedness matrix" from a multiple intelligences perspective. *Developmental approaches to identifying exceptional ability.*

References

Albert, R., & Runco, M. (1986). The achievement of eminence: A model based on a longitudinal study of exceptionally gifted boys and their families. In R. Sternberg & J. Davidson (Eds.), *Conceptions of giftedness* (pp. 332–57). New York: Cambridge University Press.

Bamberger, J. (1982). Growing up prodigies: The midlife crisis. In D. Feldman (Ed.), *Developmental approaches to giftedness and creativity. New Directions for Child Development* (Vol. 17, pp. 61–78). San Francisco: Jossey-Bass.

Barron, F. (1969). *Creative person and creative process.* New York: Holt, Rinehart and Winston.

Bloom, B. (1985). *Developing talent in young people.* New York: Ballantine.

Csikszentmihalyi, M. (1988). Society, culture, and person: A systems view of creativity. In R. J. Sternberg (Ed.), *The nature of creativity* (pp. 325–39). New York: Cambridge University Press.

Csikszentmihalyi, M. (in press). *Talented teens.*

Feldman, D. H. (with L. Goldsmith). (1986). *Nature's gambit.* New York: Basic Books.

Gardner, H. (1982). *Art, mind, and brain.* New York: Basic Books.

Gardner, H. (1983). *Frames of mind: The theory of multiple intelligences.* New York: Basic Books.

Gardner, H. (1988a). Creative lives, creative works. In R. Sternberg (Ed.), *The nature of creativity* (pp. 298–321). New York: Cambridge University Press.

Gardner, H. (1988b). Creativity: An interdisciplinary perspective. *Creativity Research Journal, 1,* 8–26.

Gardner, H. (1989). *To open minds: Chinese clues to the dilemma of contemporary education.* New York: Basic Books.

Gardner, H. (1991). Intelligence in seven phases. Paper delivered at the Centennial of the Harvard Graduate School of Education, September 1991. Reprinted in part as chapter 12 of this book.

Gardner, H. (in press). *The creators of the modern era.*

MacKinnon, D. (1961). Creativity in architects. In D. W. MacKinnon (Ed.), *The creative person* (pp. 291–320). Berkeley: Institute of Personality Assessment Research.

Perkins, D. N. (1981). *The mind's best work.* Cambridge, Mass.: Harvard University Press.

Sternberg, R. (1988). A three-facet model of creativity. In R. J. Sternberg (Ed.), *The nature of creativity* (pp. 125–47). New York: Cambridge University Press.

Walters, J., & Gardner, H. (1986). The crystallizing experience: Discovering an intellectual gift. In R. Sternberg & J. Davidson (Eds.), *Conceptions of giftedness* (pp. 306–31). New York: Cambridge University Press.

Other Material Drawn Upon in Part I

Gardner, H. (1983, March). Artistic intelligences. *Art Education,* 47–49.

Gardner, H. (1990). Multiple intelligences: Implications for art and creativity. In W. J. Moody (Ed.), *Artistic intelligences: Implications for education* (pp. 11–27). New York: Teachers College Press.

Kornhaber, M., & Gardner, H. (1991). Critical thinking across multiple intelligences. In S. Maclure & P. Davies (Eds.), *Learning to think: Thinking to learn* (pp. 147–68). Oxford: Pergamon Press.

Symposium on the theory of multiple intelligences (1987). In D. N. Perkins & J. C. Bishop (Eds.), *Thinking: The second international conference* (pp. 77–101). Hillsdale, N.J.: Lawrence Erlbaum.

Walters, J., and Gardner, H. (1986). The crystallizing experience: Discovering an intellectual gift. In R. Sternberg and J. Davidson (Eds.), *Conceptions of giftedness* (pp. 306–31). New York: Cambridge University Press.

Weinreich-Haste, H. (1985). The varieties of intelligence: An interview with Howard Gardner. *New Ideas in Psychology,* 3 (1), 47–65.

Chapter 5. A School of the Future

Acknowledgments

The research described in this article has been generously supported by the Grant Foundation, the Lilly Endowment, the McDonnell Foundation, the Rockefeller Brothers Fund, the Rockefeller Foundation, the Spencer Foundation, and the Bernard Van Leer Foundation.

References

Gardner, H. (1983). *Frames of mind: The theory of multiple intelligences.* New York: Basic Books.

Gardner, H. (1987a). An individual-centered curriculum. In *The schools we've got, the schools we need.* Washington, D.C.: Council of Chief State School Officers and the American Association of Teacher Education.

Gardner, H. (1987b). Developing the spectrum of human intelligences. *Harvard Educational Review, 57,* 187–93.

Gardner, H. (1989a). Zero-based arts education: An introduction to Arts PRO-PEL. *Studies in Art Education: A Journal of Issues and Research, 30* (2), 71–83.

Gardner, H. (1989b, November 8). The academic community must not shun the debate on how to set national educational goals. *The Chronicle of Higher Education,* A52.

Gardner, H. (1990). Four factors in educational reform. In *In Context, 27,* 15.

Gardner, H. (1991a). Assessment in context: The alternative to standardized testing. In B. R. Gifford & M. C. O'Connor (Eds.), *Changing assessments: Alternative views of aptitude, achievement, and instruction.* Boston: Kluwer.

Gardner, H. (1991b). The school of the future. In John Brockman (Ed.), *Ways of knowing: The reality club #3* (pp. 199–218). Englewood Cliffs, N.J.: Prentice Hall.

Krechevsky, M., & H. Gardner. (1990a). Approaching school intelligently: An infusion approach. In D. Kuhn (Ed.), *Developmental perspectives on teaching and learning thinking skills* (pp. 79–94). Basel: S. Karger.

Krechevsky, M., & H. Gardner. (1990b). The emergence and nurturance of multiple intelligences: The Project Spectrum approach. In M. J. A. Howe (Ed.), *Encouraging the development of exceptional skills and talents* (pp. 221–44). Leicester, England: The British Psychological Society.

Olson, L. (1988, January 27). Children flourish here: Eight teachers and a theory changed a school world. *Education Week, 7* (18), 1, 18–19.

Interlude. The Two Rhetorics of School Reform: Complex Theories versus the Quick Fix

Article reprinted in its entirety: Gardner, H. (1992, May 6). The two rhetorics of school reform: Complex theories vs. the quick fix. *Chronicle of Higher Education, 38* (35), B1–2.

Chapter 6. The Emergence and Nurturance of Multiple Intelligences in Early Childhood: The Project Spectrum Approach

Article reprinted in large part: Krechevsky, M., & Gardner, H. (1990). The emergence and nurturance of multiple intelligences: The Project Spectrum approach. In M. J. A. Howe (Ed.), *Encouraging the development of exceptional skills and talents* (pp. 221–44). Leicester, England: The British Psychological Society.

Appendix A

Acknowledgments

The work described in this chapter was supported in part by grants from the Spencer Foundation, the William T. Grant Foundation, and the Rockefeller Brothers Fund.

References

Ceci, S. J. (1990). *On intelligence . . . more or less: A bio-ecological treatise on intellectual development.* Englewood Cliffs, N.J.: Prentice Hall.

Csikszentmihalyi, M., & Robinson, R. (1986). Culture, time and the development of talent. In R. Sternberg and J. Davidson (Eds.), *Conceptions of giftedness.* New York: Cambridge University Press.

Feldman, D. H. (1980). *Beyond universals in cognitive development.* Norwood, N.J.: Ablex.

Feldman, D. H. (with Goldsmith, L.). (1986). *Nature's gambit.* New York: Basic Books.

Feldman, D. H., & Gardner, H. (1989). *Project Spectrum: July 1987–June 1989* (Final Annual Report to the Spencer Foundation).

Fodor, J. (1983). *Modularity of mind.* Cambridge, Mass.: MIT Bradford Press.

Gardner, H. (1983). *Frames of mind: The theory of multiple intelligences.* New York: Basic Books.

Gardner, H. (1991) Assessment in context: The alternative to standardized testing. In B. R. Gifford, & M. C. O'Connor (Eds.), *Changing assessments: Alternative views of aptitude, achievement, and instruction.* Boston: Kluwer.

Gardner, H., & Hatch, T. (1989). Multiple intelligences go to school: The educational implications of the theory of multiple intelligences. *Educational Researcher, 18,* 4–10.

Jencks, C. (1972). *Inequality.* New York: Basic Books.

Jenkins, J. J., & Patterson, D. G. (Eds.), (1961). *Studies in individual differences.* New York: Appleton-Century-Crofts.

Keil, F. C. (1984). Mechanics in cognitive development and the structure of knowledge. In R. Sternberg (Ed.), *Mechanics of cognitive development.* San Francisco: W. H. Freeman.

Keil, F. C. (1986). On the structure-dependent nature of stages in cognitive development. In I. Levin (Ed.), *Stage and structure.* Norwood, N.J.: Ablex.

Lewis, M. (Ed.) (1976). *Origins of intelligence.* New York: Plenum Press.

Malkus, U., Feldman, D. H., and Gardner, H. (1988). Dimensions of mind in early childhood. In A. Pelligrini (Ed.), *The psychological bases of early education.* Chichester, England: Wiley.

Olson, D. (1977). From utterance to text: The basis of language in speech and writing. *Harvard Educational Review, 47,* 257–82.

Ramos-Ford, V., Feldman, D. H., & Gardner, H. (1988). A new look at intelligence through Project Spectrum. *New Horizons for Learning, 8* (3), 6–7, 15.

Renninger, A. K. (1988). Do individual interests make a difference? In *Essays by the Spencer Fellows 1987–1988.* Cambridge, Mass.: National Academy of Education.

Sattler, J. M. (1988). *Assessment of children* (3rd ed.). San Diego: Sattler.

Sternberg, R. J., & Davidson, J. E. (1985). Cognitive development of the gifted and talented. In F. D. Horowitz & M. O'Brien (Eds.), *The gifted and talented: Developmental perspectives.* Washington, D.C.: American Psychological Association.

Chapter 7. The Elementary Years: The Project Approach in the Key School Setting

Passage reprinted in part: Gardner, H. (1991). *The unschooled mind: How children learn, and how schools should teach* (pp. 214–19). New York: Basic Books.

References

Csikszentmihalyi, M. (1990). *Flow.* New York: HarperCollins.

Olson, L. (1988, January 27). Children flourish here: eight teachers and a theory changed a school world. *Education Week, 7* (18), 1, 18–19.

Seidel, S., & Walters, J. (1991). *Five dimensions of portfolio assessment.* Cambridge, Mass.: Project Zero.

Winn, M. (1990, April 29). New views of human intelligence. In The Good Health Magazine, *New York Times.*

Chapter 8. Approaching School Intelligently: Practical Intelligence at the Middle School Level

Article reprinted in large part: Krechevsky, M., & Gardner, H. (1990). Approaching school intelligently: An infusion approach. In D. Kuhn (Ed.), *Developmental perspectives on teaching and learning thinking skills. Series of Contributions to Human Development* (Vol. 21, pp. 79–94). Basel: Karger.

Acknowledgments

The work described in this chapter was supported by a grant from the James S. McDonnell Foundation. We are grateful to Tina Blythe and Noel White, who gave many helpful comments on earlier drafts.

References

Boole, G. (1984/1952). *The laws of thought*. Lasalle: Open Court.

Brown, A. L., & Campione, J. C. (1984). Three faces of transfer: Implications for early competence, individual differences, and instruction. In M. Lamb, A. Brown, & B. Rogoff (Eds.), *Advances in developmental psychology* (Vol. 3). Hillsdale, N.J.: Lawrence Erlbaum.

Bruner, J., Olver, R., & Greenfield, P. (1966). *Studies in cognitive growth*. New York: Wiley.

Csikszentmihalyi, M., & Robinson, R. (1986). Culture, time and the development of talent. In R. Sternberg & J. Davidson (Eds.), *Conceptions of giftedness*. New York: Cambridge University Press.

Dweck, C. S., & Elliott, E. S. (1983). Achievement motivation. In P. H. Mussen (Ed.), *Handbook of child psychology* (pp. 643–91). New York: Wiley.

Edwards, B. (1979). *Drawing on the right side of the brain: A course in enhancing creativity and artistic confidence*. Los Angeles: J. P. Tarcher, Boston: Houghton Mifflin.

Feldman, D. H. (1980). *Beyond universals in cognitive development*. Norwood, N.J.: Ablex.

Feldman, D. H. (1986). *Nature's gambit*. New York: Basic Books.

Fodor, J. (1983). *The modularity of mind*. Cambridge, Mass.: MIT Press.

Gardner, H. (1983). *Frames of mind: The theory of multiple intelligences*. New York: Basic Books.

Gardner, H. (1990). The difficulties of school: Probable causes, possible cures. *Daedalus, 119*, 85–113.

Gardner, H. (1991). Assessment in context: The alternative to standardized testing. In B. R. Gifford, & M. C. O'Connor (Eds.), *Changing assessments: Alternative views of aptitude, achievement, and instruction* Boston: Kluwer.

Gardner, H., Krechevsky, M., Sternberg, R. J., & Okagaki, L. (in press). Intelligence in context: Enhancing students' practical intelligence for school. In K. McGilly (Ed.), *Classroom lessons*. Cambridge: Bradford Books/MIT Press.

Goldman, J., Krechevsky, M., Meyaard, J., & Gardner, H. (1988). A developmental study of children's practical intelligence for school. Harvard Project Zero Technical Report.

Hyde, A., & Bizar, M. (1989). *Thinking in context: Teaching cognitive processes across the elementary school curriculum*. New York: Longman.

Nisbet, J. (1989). The curriculum redefined: Learning to think—Thinking to learn. Background paper presented at the International Conference of the Centre for Educational Research and Innovation, Paris, France.

Palincsar, A. S., & Brown, A. L. (1984). Reciprocal teaching of comprehension-fostering and monitoring activities. *Cognition and Instruction, 1*, 117–75.

Perkins, D. N., & Salomon, G. (1989). Are cognitive skills context-bound? *Educational Researcher, 18*, 16–25.

Resnick, L. (1987). Learning in school and out. *Educational Researcher, 16*, 13–20.

Rogoff, B., & Lave, J. (Eds.). (1984). *Everyday cognition: Its development in social context.* Cambridge: Harvard University Press.

Schoenfeld, A. H. (1988). Problem solving in context(s). In R. I. Charles & E. A. Silver (Eds.), *The teaching and assessing of mathematical problem solving.* Reston, Va.: National Council of Teachers of Mathematics.

Scribner, S., & Cole, M. (1973). Cognitive consequences of formal and informal education. *Science, 182,* 553–59.

Sternberg, R. J. (1985). *Beyond IQ: A triarchic theory of human intelligence.* New York: Cambridge University Press.

Sternberg, R. J. (1988). *The triarchic mind.* New York: Viking.

Strauss, C. (1988). Culture, discourse, and cognition: Forms of beliefs in some Rhode Island working men's talk about success. Unpublished doctoral dissertation, Harvard University.

Strauss, S. (Ed.). (1982). *U-Shaped behavioral growth.* New York: Academic Press.

Wagner, D. A., & Stevenson, H. W. (Eds.). (1982). *Cultural perspectives on child development.* San Francisco: Freeman.

Wiggins, G. (1989). A true test: Toward more authentic and equitable assessment. *Phi Delta Kappan, 70,* 703–13.

Chapter 9. Disciplined Inquiry in the High School: An Introduction to Arts PROPEL

Articles reprinted in part: Gardner, H. (in press). The assessment of student learning in the arts. In D. Boughton, E. Eisner, & J. Ligtvoet (Eds.), *International perspectives on assessment and evaluation in art education;* and Gardner, H. (1989). Zero-based arts education: An introduction to Arts PROPEL. *Studies in Art Education, 30* (2), 71–83.

Acknowledgments

Preparation of this paper was supported by the Rockefeller Foundation. Earlier versions of the paper were presented at the Canadian Art Education Association, Halifax, Nova Scotia (November 1987) and the Philosophy of Education Research Center, Harvard University (December 1987). For their help in the execution of this complex project, I want to express thanks to my many valued colleagues at the Educational Testing Service, the Pittsburgh Public School System, Harvard Project Zero, and the Rockefeller Foundation. For comments on an earlier draft of this essay I am indebted to Drew Gitomer, Jonathan Levy, Kenneth Marantz, and Dennie Wolf.

References

Arnheim, R. (1969). *Visual thinking*. Berkeley: University of California Press.

Arts, Education, and the Americans. (1977). *Coming to our senses*. New York: McGraw-Hill.

Bamberger, J. (1982). Revisiting children's drawings of simple rhythms: A function reflection-in-action. In S. Strauss (Ed.), *U-shaped behavioral growth*. New York: Academic Press.

Berger, R. (1991). Building a school culture of high standards: A teacher's perspective. In V. Perrone (Ed.), *Expanding student assessment* (pp. 32–39). Alexandria, Va.: Association for Supervision and Curriculum Development.

Brown, N. (1987, August). Pivotal points in artistic growth. Presentation at the 1987 Arts PROPEL summer workshop, Pittsburgh, Pa.

Burton, J., Lederman, A., & London, P. (Eds.). (1988). *Beyond dbae: The case for multiple visions of art education*. University Council on Art Education.

Cassirer, E. (1953–57). *The philosophy of symbolic forms*. New Haven: Yale University Press.

Chideya, F. (1991, December 2). Surely for the spirit, but also for the mind. *Newsweek*, p. 61.

Collins, A., & Brown, J. S. (1988, April). *Cognitive apprenticeship and social interaction*. Paper presented at the American Educational Research Association, New Orleans.

Dewey, J. (1959). *Art as experience*. New York: Capricorn.

Dobbs, S. (Ed.). (1983). Art and the mind [special issue]. *Art Education, 36* (2).

Dobbs, S. (Ed.). (1988). *Research readings for discipline-based art education: A journey beyond creating*. Reston, Va.: National Art Education Association.

Eisner, E. (1987). *The role of discipline-based art education in America's schools*. Los Angeles: The Getty Center for Education in the Arts.

Ewens, T. (1988). Flawed understandings: On Getty, Eisner, and DBAE. In J. Burton, A. Lederman, & P. London (Eds.), *Beyond dbae: The case for multiple visions of art education* (pp. 5–25). North Dartmouth, Mass.: University Council on Art Education.

Gardner, H. (1973). *The arts and human development*. New York: Wiley.

Gardner, H. (1975). *The shattered mind*. New York: Knopf.

Gardner, H. (1980). *Artful scribbles*. New York: Basic Books.

Gardner, H. (1982). *Art, mind, and brain*. New York: Basic Books.

Gardner, H. (1983a). *Frames of mind: The theory of multiple intelligences*. New York: Basic Books.

Gardner, H. (1983b). Artistic intelligences. In S. Dobbs (Ed.), Art and the mind [special issue]. *Art Education, 36* (2), 47–49.

Gardner, H. (1985). *The mind's new science*. New York: Basic Books.

Gardner, H. (1986). Notes on cognitive development: Recent trends, future prospects. In S. Friedman, K. Klivington, & R. Peterson (Eds.), *The brain, cognition and education*. New York: Academic Press.

Gardner, H. (1989). Balancing specialized and comprehensive knowledge: The growing education challenge. In Thomas Sergiovanni (Ed.), *Schooling for tomorrow: Directing reforms to issues that count.* Boston: Allyn & Bacon.

Gardner, H. (1991a). Assessment in context: The alternative to standardized testing. In B. R. Gifford & M. C. O'Connor (Eds.), *Changing assessments: Alternative views of aptitude, achievement, and instruction* (pp. 77–120). Boston: Kluwer.

Gardner, H. (1991b). The school of the future. In John Brockman (Ed.), *Ways of knowing: The reality club #3* (pp. 199–218). Englewood Cliffs, N.J.: Prentice Hall.

Gardner, H. & Perkins, D. (Eds.). (1988). Art, mind, and education. *Journal of Aesthetic Education* [special issue on Harvard Project Zero], *22* (1).

Gardner, H., & Winner, E. (1982). First intimations of artistry. In S. Strauss (Ed.), *U-shaped behavioral growth.* New York: Wiley.

The Getty Center for Education in the Arts. (1986). *Beyond creating: The place for art in American schools.*

Goodman, N. (1976). *Languages of art.* Indianapolis: Hackett.

Goodman, N. (1978). *Ways of worldmaking.* Indianapolis: Hackett.

Goodman, N., Perkins, D., & Gardner, H. (1972). *Summary report, Harvard Project Zero.* Available as Technical Report from Harvard Project Zero.

Jackson, P. (1987). Mainstreaming art: An essay on discipline based arts education. *Educational Researcher, 16,* 39–43.

Kaplan, J. A., & Gardner, H. (1989). Artistry after unilateral brain disease. In F. Boller & J. Graffman (Eds.), *Handbook of neuropsychology* (Vol. 2). Elsevier Science Publishers B.V.

Langer, S. K. (1942). *Philosophy in a new key.* Cambridge: Harvard University Press.

Lowenfeld, V. (1947). *Creative and mental growth.* New York: Macmillan.

National Endowment for the Arts. (1988). *Towards civilization.*

Peirce, C. S. (1940). *Philosophical writings of Peirce.* (J. Buchler, Ed.) London: Routledge and Kegan Paul.

Perkins, D., & Leondar, B. (Eds.). (1977). *The arts and cognition.* Baltimore: Johns Hopkins University Press.

Piaget, J. (1970). Piaget's theory. In P. Mussen (Ed.), *Carmichael's manual of child psychology.* New York: Wiley.

Resnick, L. (1987, December). Learning in school and out. *Educational Researcher, 16,* 13–19.

Schon, D. (1984). *The reflective practitioner.* New York: Basic Books.

Sizer, T. (1984). *Horace's compromise.* Boston: Houghton Mifflin.

Winner, E. (1982). *Invented worlds.* Cambridge: Harvard University Press.

Winner, E., Blank, P., Massey, C., & Gardner, H. (1983). Children's sensitivity to aesthetic properties of line drawings. In D. R. Rogers and J. A. Sloboda (Eds.), *The acquisition of symbolic skills.* London: Plenum Press.

Winner, E., Rosenblatt, E., Windmueller, G., Davidson, L., & Gardner, H. (1986).

Children's perceptions of "aesthetic" properties of the arts: Domain specific or pan artistic? *British Journal of Developmental Psychology, 4,* 149–60.

Wolf, D. (1988a). Opening up assessment. *Educational Leadership, 45* (4), 24–29.

Wolf, D. (1988b). Artistic learning: What and where is it? *Journal of Aesthetic Education, 22* (1), 144–55.

Wolf, D. (1989). Artistic learning as conversation. In D. Hargreaves (Ed.), *Children and the arts.* Philadelphia: Open University Press.

Wolf, D., Davidson, L., Davis, M., Walters, J., Hodges, M., & Scripp, L. (1988). Beyond A, B, and C: A broader and deeper view of literacy. In A. Pelligrini (Ed.), *Psychological bases of early education.* Chichester, England: Wiley.

Wolf, D., & Gardner, H. (1980). Beyond playing or polishing: The development of artistry. In J. Hausman (Ed.), *The arts and the schools.* New York: McGraw-Hill.

Wolf, D., & Gardner, H. (1981). On the structure of early symbolization. In R. Schiefelbusch and D. Bricker (Eds.), *Early language: Acquisition and intervention.* Baltimore: University Park Press.

Wolf, D., & Gardner, H. (Eds.). (1988). *The making of meanings.* Available as Harvard Project Zero Technical Report.

Zessoules, R., Wolf, D. P., & Gardner, H. (1988). A better balance. In J. Burton, A. Lederman, & P. London (Eds.), *Beyond dbae: The case for multiple visions of art education.* North Dartmouth, Mass.: University Council on Art Education.

Other Material Drawn Upon in Part II

Gardner, H. (1991, Winter). Four factors in educational reform. *In Context,* 15.

Gardner, H. (1991). *The unschooled mind: How children think and how schools should teach.* New York: Basic Books.

Chapter 10. Assessment in Context: The Alternative to Standardized Testing

Article reprinted in part: Gardner, H. (1991). Assessment in context: The alternative to standardized testing. In B. R. Gifford and M. C. O'Connor (Eds.), *Changing assessments: Alternative views of aptitude, achievement, and instruction* (pp. 77–120). Boston: Kluwer.

References

Aiken, W. (1942). *The story of the eight year study.* New York: Harper and Brothers.

Anderson, M. (1987). Inspection time and the development of intelligence. Paper delivered to British Psychological Society Conference, Sussex University.

Bamberger, J. (1982). Revisiting children's drawings of simple rhythms: A function for reflection-in-action. In S. Strauss (Ed.), *U-shaped behavioral growth.* New York: Academic Press.

Bijou, S., & Baer, D. (1965). *Child development.* New York: Appleton-Century-Crofts.

Binet, A., & Simon, T. (1905). Méthodes nouvelles pour le diagnostique du niveau intellectuel des anormaux. *L'année psychologique, 11,* 236–45.

Block, N., & Dworkin, G. (1976). *The IQ controversy.* New York: Pantheon.

Bloom, A. (1987). *The closing of the American mind.* New York: Simon & Schuster.

Brainerd, C. (1978). The stage question in cognitive-developmental theory. *The Behavioral and Brain Sciences, 2,* 173–213.

Brown, R., & Herrnstein, R. (1975). *Psychology.* Boston: Little, Brown.

Buros, O. (1978). *The eighth mental measurements yearbook.* Highland Park, N. J.: Gryphon Press.

Carini, P. (1987, October). Another way of looking. Paper presented at the Cambridge School Conference, Weston, Massachusetts.

Case, R. (1985). *Intellectual development: Birth to adolescence.* New York: Academic Press.

Collins, A., Brown, J. S., & Newman, S. E. (1989). Cognitive apprenticeship: Teaching the craft of reading, writing, and mathematics. In L. Resnick (Ed.), *Cognition and instruction: Issues and agendas.* Hillsdale, N.J.: Lawrence Erlbaum.

Cronbach, L. (1984). *Essentials of psychological testing.* New York: Harper and Row.

Cronbach, L., & Snow, R., (1977). *Aptitudes and instructional methods.* New York: Irvington.

Cross, K. P., & Angelo, T. (1988). *Classroom assessment techniques: A handbook for faculty.* Ann Arbor: National Center for Research to Improve Postsecondary Teaching and Learning (NCRIPTL).

Csikszentmihalyi, M. (1988). Society, culture, and persons: A systems view of creativity. In R. Sternberg (Ed.), *The nature of creativity.* New York: Cambridge University Press.

Csikszentmihalyi, M., & Robinson, R. (1986). Culture, time, and the development of talent. In R. Sternberg & J. Davidson (Eds.), *Conceptions of giftedness.* New York: Cambridge University Press.

Dewey, J. (1938). *Experience and education.* New York: Collier.

Eisner, E. (1987). Structure and magic in discipline-based arts education. In *Proceedings of a National Invitational Conference.* Los Angeles: The Getty Center for Education in the Arts.

Eysenck, H. J. (1967). Intelligence assessment: A theoretical and experimental approach. *British Journal of Educational Psychology, 37,* 81–98.

Eysenck, H. J. (1979). *The nature and measurement of intelligence.* New York: Springer-Verlag.

Feldman, D. (1980). *Beyond universals in cognitive development.* Norwood, N.J.: Ablex.

Fischer, K. W. (1980). A theory of cognitive development. *Psychological Review,* 87, 477–531.

Fodor, J. (1983). *The modularity of mind.* Cambridge: MIT Press.

Gardner, H. (1975). *The shattered mind.* New York: Knopf.

Gardner, H. (1982). *Art, mind, and brain.* New York: Basic Books.

Gardner, H. (1983). *Frames of mind: The theory of multiple intelligences.* New York: Basic Books.

Gardner, H. (1985). *The mind's new science.* New York: Basic Books.

Gardner, H. (1986). The development of symbolic literacy. In M. Wrolstad & D. Fisher (Eds.), *Toward a greater understanding of literacy.* New York: Praeger.

Gardner, H. (1987a). Developing the spectrum of human intelligence. *Harvard Education Review,* 57, 187–93.

Gardner, H. (1987b). An individual-centered curriculum. In *The schools we've got, the schools we need.* Washington, D.C.: Council of Chief State School Officers and the American Association of Colleges of Teacher Education.

Gardner, H. (1988a). Creative lives and creative works: A synthetic scientific approach. In R. J. Sternberg (Ed.), *The nature of creativity.* New York: Cambridge University Press.

Gardner, H. (1988b). Mobilizing resources for individual-centered education. In R. Nickerson (Ed.), *Technology in education: Looking toward 2020.* Hillsdale, N.J.: Lawrence Erlbaum.

Gardner, H. (1989a). Balancing specialized and comprehensive knowledge. In T. Sergiovanni (Ed.), *Schooling for tomorrow: Directing reforms to issues that count.* Boston: Allyn & Bacon.

Gardner, H. (1989b). The school of the future. In J. Brockman (Ed.), *Ways of knowing: The reality club #3.* Englewood Cliffs, N.J.: Prentice Hall.

Gardner, H. (1989c). Zero-based arts education: An introduction to Arts PROPEL. *Studies in Art Education,* 30 (2), 71–83.

Gardner, H., & Wolf, C. (1988). The fruits of asynchrony: Creativity from a psychological point of view. *Adolescent Psychiatry 15,* 106–23.

Gardner, H., Howard, V. & Perkins, D. (1974). Symbol systems: A philosophical, psychological and educational investigation. In D. Olson (Ed.), *Media and symbols.* Chicago: University of Chicago Press.

Gelman, R. (1978). Cognitive development. *Annual Review of Psychology, 29,* 297–332.

Getty Center for Education in the Arts. (1985). *Beyond creating: The Place for art in American schools.* Los Angeles: J. Paul Getty Trust.

Goodman, N. (1976). *Languages of art.* Indianapolis: Hackett.

Gould, S. J. (1981). *The mismeasure of man.* New York: Norton.

Grant, G., (Ed.). (1978). *On competence.* San Francisco: Jossey-Bass.

Grant, G. (1988). *The world we created at Hamilton High.* Cambridge: Harvard University Press.

Gruber, H. (1981). *Darwin on man.* 2d ed. Chicago: University of Chicago Press.

Gruber, H. (1985). Giftedness and moral responsibility: Creative thinking and human survival. In F. Horowitz & M. O'Brien (Eds.), *The gifted and talented: developmental perspectives.* Washington: American Psychological Association.

Guilford, J. P. (1950). Creativity. *American Psychologist, 5,* 444–54.

Guilford, J. P. (1967). *The nature of human intelligence.* New York: McGraw-Hill.

Hatch, T., & Gardner, H. (1986). From testing intelligence to assessing competences: A pluralistic view of intellect. *The Roeper Review, 8,* 147–50.

Hirsch, E. D. (1987). *Cultural literacy.* Boston: Houghton Mifflin.

Hoffmann, B. (1962). *The tyranny of testing.* New York: Crowel-Collier Press.

Jencks, C. (1972). *Inequality.* New York: Basic Books.

Jensen, A. R. (1980). *Bias in mental testing.* New York: Free Press.

Jensen, A. R. (1987). Individual differences in the Hick paradigm. In P. Vernon (Ed.), *Speed of information processing and intelligence.* Norwood, N.J.: Ablex.

Kagan, J., & Kogan, N. (1970). Individual variation in cognitive processing. In P. Mussen (Ed.), *Handbook of child psychology.* New York: Wiley.

Kaplan, E. (1983). Process and achievement revisited. In S. Wapner & B. Kaplan (Eds.), *Toward a holistic developmental psychology.* Hillsdale, N.J.: Lawrence Erlbaum.

Laboratory of Comparative Human Cognition. (1982). Culture and intelligence. In R. J. Sternberg (Ed.), *Handbook of human intelligence.* New York: Cambridge University Press.

Langer, S. K. (1942). *Philosophy in a new key.* Cambridge: Harvard University Press.

Lave, J. (1980). What's special about experiments as contexts for thinking? *Quarterly Newsletter of the Laboratory of Comparative Human Cognition, 2,* 86–91.

Malkus, U., Feldman, D. & Gardner, H. (1988). Dimensions of mind in early childhood. In A. D. Pelligrini (Ed.), *The psychological bases of early childhood.* Chichester, England: Wiley.

Messick, S. (1988). Validity. In R. Linn (Ed.), *Educational measurement.* 3d ed. New York: Macmillan.

Newell, A., & Simon, H. A. (1972). *Human problem-solving.* Englewood Cliffs, N.J.: Prentice Hall.

Olson, L. (1988, January 27). Children flourish here: Eight teachers and a theory changed a school world. *Education Week, 7* (18), 1, 18–19.

Perkins, D. (1981). *The mind's best work.* Cambridge: Harvard University Press.

Piaget, J. (1983). Piaget's theory. In P. Mussen (Ed.), *Manual of child psychology.* New York: Wiley.

Polanyi, M. (1958). *Personal knowledge.* Chicago: University of Chicago Press.

Ravitch, D., & Finn, C. (1987). *What do our seventeen-year-olds know?* New York: Harper and Row.

Resnick, L. (1987). The 1987 presidential address: Learning in school and out. *Educational Researcher, 16* (9), 13–20.

Rogoff, B. (1982). Integrating context and cognitive development. In M. Lamb & A. Brown (Eds.), *Advances in developmental psychology* (Vol. 2). Hillsdale, N.J.: Lawrence Erlbaum.

Scribner, S. (1986). Thinking in action: Some characteristics of practical thought. In R. Sternberg & R. K. Wagner (Eds.), *Practical intelligence: Nature and origins of competence in the everyday world.* New York: Cambridge University Press.

Sizer, T. (1984). *Horace's compromise.* Boston: Houghton Mifflin.

Squire, L. (1986). Mechanisms of memory. *Science, 232,* 1612–19.

Sternberg, R. (1977). *Intelligence, information processing, and analogical reasoning.* Hillsdale, N.J.: Lawrence Erlbaum.

Sternberg, R. (1985). *Beyond IQ.* New York: Cambridge University Press.

Sternberg, R. (Ed.). (1988). *The nature of creativity.* New York: Cambridge University Press.

Strauss, S. (1982). *U-shaped behavioral growth.* New York: Academic Press.

Thurstone, L. (1938). *Primary mental abilities.* Chicago: University of Chicago Press.

Uzgiris, I., & Hunt, J. McV. (1966). *An instrument for assessing infant intellectual development.* Urbana, Ill.: University of Illinois Press.

Wallach, M. (1971). *The intelligence/creativity distinction.* Morristown, N.J.: General Learning Press.

Wallach, M. (1985). Creativity testing and giftedness. In F. Horowitz & M. O'Brien (Eds.), *The gifted and talented: Developmental perspectives.* Washington, D.C.: American Psychological Association.

Walters, J., & Gardner, H. (1986). The crystallizing experience: Discovering an intellectual gift. In R. Sternberg & J. Davidson (Eds.), *Conceptions of giftedness.* New York: Cambridge University Press.

Wexler-Sherman, C., Gardner, H., & Feldman, D. H. (1988). A pluralistic view of early assessment: The Project Spectrum approach. *Theory into Practice, 27* (1), 77–83.

Willingham, W. (1985). *Success in college.* New York: College Entrance Examination Board (CEEB).

Zessoules, R., Wolf, D., & Gardner, H. (1988). A better balance: Arts PROPEL as an alternative to discipline-based art education. In J. Burton, A. Lederman, & P. London (Eds.), *Beyond discipline-based art education.* North Dartmouth, Mass.: University Council on Art Education.

Chapter 11. Beyond Assessment: The Aims and Means of Education

Most of this material has been prepared especially for this chapter.

References

Gardner, H. (1989). *To open minds: Chinese clues to the dilemma of contemporary education.* New York: Basic Books.

Gardner, H. (1991). *The unschooled mind: How children learn, and how schools should teach.* New York: Basic Books.

Lipman, M., Sharp, A. M., & Oscanyan, F. (1990). *Philosophy in the classroom.* Philadelphia: Temple University Press.

Other Material Drawn Upon in Part III

Gardner, H. (1986). The waning of intelligence tests. In R. Sternberg and D. Detterman (Eds.), *What is intelligence?* (pp. 73–76). Hillsdale, N.J.: Lawrence Erlbaum.

Gardner, H. (1986). Notes on the educational implications of the theory of multiple intelligences. In *College Board Colloquium on Measures in the College Admissions Process.*

Gardner, H. (1989). Balancing specialized and comprehensive knowledge: The growing educational challenge. In T. J. Sergiovanni and J. H. Moore (Eds.), *Schooling for tomorrow: Directing reforms to issues that count* (pp. 148–65). Boston: Allyn & Bacon.

Chapter 12. Intelligences in Seven Phases

Most of this material has been prepared especially for this book.

Acknowledgments

Portions of this paper were presented at the 1990 University of Louisville Grawemeyer Awards convocation and at the 1991 symposium marking 100 years of Education at Harvard University. The research described in this paper has been supported by generous grants from the Grant Foundation, the Lilly Endowment, the Markle Foundation, the McDonnell Foundation, the Rockefeller Brothers Fund, the Rockefeller Foundation, and the Spencer Foundation. I would like to thank Patricia Graham, Tom Hatch, Mindy Kornhaber, and Joseph Walters for their helpful comments on an earlier version of the paper.

References

Berlin, I. (1953). *The hedgehog and the fox: An essay on Tolstoy's view of history.* London: Weidenfeld & Nicholson.

Binet, A., & Simon, T. (1916). *The development of intelligence in children.* Baltimore: Williams & Wilkins.

Block, N., & Dworkin, G. (1976). *The IQ controversy.* New York: Pantheon.

Boring, E. G. (1923, June 6). Intelligence as the tests test it. *New Republic,* pp. 35–37.

Cannon, L. (1991). *President Reagan: The role of a life-time.* New York: Simon & Schuster.

Cole, M., & Cole, S. (1989). *The development of children.* New York: Freeman.

Educational Psychologist (1921). *Intelligence and its measurement: A symposium.*

Eysenck, H. (1967). Intelligence assessment: A theoretical and experimental approach. *British Journal of Educational Psychology, 37,* 81–98.

Fischer, K., & Bullock, D. (1984). Cognitive development in school age children: Conclusions and new directions. In W. A. Collins (Ed.), *The years from six to twelve: Cognitive development during middle childhood* (pp. 70–146). Washington, D.C.: National Academy Press.

Fischer, K., Kenny, S., & Pipp, S. (1990). How cognitive processes and environmental conditions organize discontinuities in the development of abstractions. In C. Alexander & E. Langer (Eds.), *Higher stages of human development* (pp. 162–87). New York: Oxford University Press.

Gardner, H. (1983). *Frames of mind: The theory of multiple intelligences.* New York: Basic Books.

Gardner, H. (1987). An individual-centered curriculum. In *The schools we've got, the schools we need.* Washington D.C.: Council of Chief State School Officers and the American Association of Colleges of Teacher Education.

Gardner, H. (1989a). Zero-based arts education: An introduction to Arts PROPEL. *Studies in Art Education, 30* (2), 71–83.

Gardner, H. (1989b). *To open minds: Chinese clues to the dilemma of contemporary education.* New York: Basic Books.

Gardner, H. (1989c). Balancing specialized and comprehensive knowledge: The growing educational challenge. In T. Sergiovanni (Ed.), *Schooling for tomorrow: Directing reforms to issues that count.* Boston: Allyn & Bacon.

Gardner, H. (1990a). *Arts education and human development.* Los Angeles: Getty Center for Education in the Arts.

Gardner, H. (1990b). The assessment of student learning in the arts. Paper presented at the conference on assessment in arts education, Holland, December 1990. To be published.

Gardner, H, (1990c). The difficulties of school: Probable causes, possible cures. *Daedalus, 119* (2), 85–113.

Gardner, H. (1991a). Assessment in context: The alternative to standardized testing. In B. Gifford and M. C. O'Connor (Eds.), *Future assessments: Changing views of aptitude, achievement, and instruction.* Boston: Kluwer.

Gardner, H. (1991b). *The unschooled mind: How children learn, and how schools should teach.* New York: Basic Books.

Gardner, H., & Hatch, T. (1989). Multiple intelligences go to school. *Educational Researcher, 18,* 4–10.

Goddard, H. H. (1919). *Psychology of the normal and subnormal.* New York: Dodd, Mead.

Gould, S. J. (1981). *The mismeasure of man.* New York: Norton.

Guilford, J. P. (1967). *The nature of human intelligence.* New York: McGraw-Hill.

Hatch, T., & Gardner, H. (1992). Finding cognition in the classroom:. An expanded view of human intelligence. In G. Salomon (Ed.), *Distributed cognitions.* New York: Cambridge University Press.

Heath, S. B. (1983). *Ways with words.* New York: Cambridge University Press.

Humphreys, L. G. (1986). Describing the elephant. In R. J. Sternberg & D. K. Detterman (Eds.), *What is intelligence?* Norwood, N.J.: Ablex.

Jensen, A. (1980). *Bias in mental testing.* New York: Free Press.

Klitgaard, R. (1985). *Choosing elites.* New York: Basic Books.

Kornhaber, M., Krechevsky, M., & Gardner, H. (1990). Engaging intelligences. *Educational Psychologist, 25* (384), 177–99.

Krechevsky, M., & Gardner, H. (1990). The emergence and nurturance of multiple intelligences. In M. J. A. Howe (Ed.), *Encouraging the development of exceptional abilities and talents* (pp. 221–44). Leicester, England: British Psychological Society.

Lave, J. (1988). *Cognition in practice: Mind, mathematics, and culture in everyday life.* New York: Cambridge University Press.

LeVine, R. A., & White, M. I. (1986). *Human conditions.* New York: Routledge & Kegan Paul.

Malkus, U., Feldman, D., & Gardner, H. (1988). Dimensions of mind in early childhood. In A. D. Pelligrini (Ed.), *The psychological bases of early childhood* (pp. 25–38). Chichester, England: Wiley.

Ochs, E., & Schieffelin, B. (1984). Language acquisition and socialization: Three developmental stories. In R. Shweder and R. LeVine (Eds.), *Culture theory: Essays in mind, self, and emotion* (pp. 276–320). New York: Cambridge University Press.

Olson, L. (1988, January 27). Children flourish here: Eight teachers and a theory changed a school world. *Education Week, 7* (18), 1, 18–19.

Pea, R. (in press). Distributed cognitions and education. In G. Salomon (Ed.), *Distributed cognitions.* New York: Cambridge University Press.

Perkins, D. N., Lochhead, J., & Bishop, J. (1987). *Thinking: The second international conference* (pp. 77–101). Hillsdale, N.J.: Lawrence Erlbaum.

Piaget, J. (1983). Piaget's theory. In P. Mussen (Ed.), *Manual of child psychology* (Vol. 1). New York: Wiley.

Rogoff, B., & Lave, J. (1984). *Everyday cognition: Its development in social context.* Cambridge: Harvard University Press.

Salomon, G. (1979). *Interaction of media, cognition, and learning.* San Francisco: Jossey-Bass.

Scarr, S. (1985). Review of *Frames of mind. New Ideas in Psychology, 3* (1), 95–100.

Scarr, S. (1986). Intelligence revisited. In R. J. Sternberg & D. K. Detterman (Eds.), *What is intelligence?* Norwood, N.J.: Ablex.

Scripp, L., & Meyaard, J. (1991, November). Encouraging musical risks for learning success. *Music Educators Journal.*

Shweder, R., & LeVine, R. A. (1984). *Culture theory.* New York: Cambridge University Press.

Spearman, C. (1927). *The abilities of man: Their nature and measurement.* New York: Macmillan.

Sternberg, R. J. (1985). *Beyond IQ.* New York: Cambridge University Press.

Sternberg, R. J. (1988). *The triarchic mind.* New York: Viking.

Sternberg, R. J., & Detterman, D. K. (Eds.). (1986). *What is intelligence?* Norwood, N.J.: Ablex.

Stigler, J., Shweder, R., & Herdt, G. (1990). *Cultural psychology.* New York: Cambridge University Press.

Terman, L. (1916). *The measurement of intelligence.* Boston: Houghton Mifflin.

Thomson G. (1939). *The factorial analysis of human ability.* London: University of London Press.

Thurstone, L. L. (1938). *Primary mental abilities.* Chicago: University of Chicago Press.

Vernon, P. E. (1971). *The structure of human abilities.* London: Methuen.

Vygotsky, L. S. (1978). *Mind in society.* Cambridge: Harvard University Press.

Wiggins, G. (1989). A true test: Toward more authentic and equitable assessment. *Phi Delta Kappan, 70* (9), 703–13.

Winn, M. (1990, April 29). New views of human intelligence. The Good Health Magazine, *New York Times.*

Wolf, D. (1989, April). What's in it? Portfolio assessment. *Educational Leadership.*

Wolf, D. P., Bixby, J., Glenn, J., and Gardner, H. (1991). To use their minds well: Investigating new forms of student assessment. In G. Grant, (Ed.), *Review of Research in Education* (Vol. 17, pp. 31–74). Washington, D.C.: American Educational Research Association.

Yerkes, R. M. (1921). *Psychological examining in the United States Army* (Vol. 15) *Memoirs of the National Academy of Sciences.* Washington, D.C.

Zessoules, R., Wolf, D. P., & Gardner, H. (1988). A better balance: Arts PROPEL as an alternative to discipline-based art education. In J. Burton, A. Lederman, & P. London (Eds.), *Beyond dbae: The case for multiple visions of art education.* North Dartmouth, Mass.: University Council on Art Education.

Chapter 13. Engaging Intelligence

Article reprinted in part: Kornhaber, M., Krechevsky, M., & Gardner, H. (1990). Engaging Intelligence. *Educational Psychologist, 25* (3–4), 177–99.

Appendix A

Acknowledgments

Research described in this article was supported in part by the William T. Grant Foundation, Lilly Endowment, James S. McDonnell Foundation, Rockefeller Foundation, Rockefeller Brothers Fund, Spencer Foundation, and Bernard Van Leer Foundation.

References

Amabile, T. (1983). *The social psychology of creativity.* New York: Springer-Verlag.

Applebee, A. N., Langer, J. A., & Mullis, I. V. S. (1986). *The writing report card: Writing achievement in American schools.* Princeton, N.J.: Educational Testing Service.

Ascher, C. (1988). Improving the school-home connection for poor and minority urban students. *The Urban Review, 20,* 109–23.

Bailyn, B. (1960). *Education in the forming of American society.* Chapel Hill: University of North Carolina Press.

Bereiter, C. (1985). The changing face of educational disadvantagement. *Phi Delta Kappan, 66,* 538–41.

Binet, A., & Simon, T. (1905). Méthodes nouvelles pour le diagnostique du niveaux intellectuel des anormaux [New methods for the diagnosis of the intellectual level of the abnormal]. *L'année psychologique, 11,* 236–45.

Bransford, J. D., Franks, J. J., Vye, N. J., & Sherwood, R. D. (1989). New approaches to instruction: Because wisdom can't be told. In S. Vosniadou & A. Ortony (Eds.), *Similarity and analogical reasoning* (pp. 470–97). New York: Cambridge University Press.

Brembeck, C. (1978). *Formal education, non-formal education, and expanded conceptions of development: Occasional paper #1.* East Lansing, Mich.: Non-formal Education Information Center, Institute for International Studies in Education, Michigan State University.

Brookover, W. B. (1985). Can we make schools effective for minority students? *Journal of Negro Education, 54,* 257–68.

Brown, J. S., Collins, A., & Duguid, P. (1989). Situated cognition and the culture of learning. *Educational Researcher, 18* (1), 32–42.

Buros, O. K. (Ed.). (1941). *The nineteen forty mental measurements yearbook.* Highland Park, N.J.: The Mental Measurements Yearbook.

Callahan, R. (1962). *Education and the cult of efficiency.* Chicago: University of Chicago Press.

Ceci, S. J. (1990). *On intelligence . . . more or less: A bio-ecological theory of intellectual development.* Englewood Cliffs, N.J.: Prentice Hall.

Chubb, J. E. (1988). Why the current wave of school reform will fail. *Public Interest, 90,* 29–49.

Cochran, M. (1987). The parental empowerment process: Building on family strengths. *Equity and Choice, 4* (1), 9–23.

Comer, J. (1980). *School power.* New York: Free Press.

Comer, J. (1984). Home-school relationships as they affect the academic success of children. *Education and Urban Society, 16,* 323–37.

Comer, J. (1988a, August). The social factor. *New York Times,* Education Life, pp. 27–31.

Comer, J. (1988b). Educating poor minority children. *Scientific American, 259* (5), 42–48.

Csikszentmihalyi, M. (1988a). Motivation and creativity: Towards a synthesis of structural and energistic approaches to cognition. *New Ideas in Psychology, 6* (2), 159–76.

Csikszentmihalyi, M. (1988b). Society, culture and person: A systems view of creativity. In R. Sternberg (Ed.), *The nature of creativity* (pp. 325–39). New York: Cambridge University Press.

Csikszentmihalyi, M. (1990). Literacy and intrinsic motivation. *Daedalus, 119* (2), 115–40.

Csikszentmihalyi, M., & Robinson, R. (1986). Culture, time, and the development of talent. In R. Sternberg (Ed.), *Conceptions of giftedness* (pp. 264–84). Cambridge, England: Cambridge University Press.

Damon, W. (1990). Reconciling the literacies of generations. *Daedalus, 119* (2), 33–53.

Darwin, C. (1859). *On the origin of species.* London: John Murray.

Dossey, J. A., Mullis, I. V. S., Lindquist, M. M., & Chambers, D. L. (1988). *The mathematics report card.* Princeton, N.J.: Educational Testing Service.

Edmonds, R. (n.d.). *A discussion of the literature and issues related to effective schooling.* Harvard University, unpublished manuscript.

Feldman, D. H. (1980). *Beyond universals in cognitive development.* Norwood, N.J.: Ablex.

Feldman, D. (1986). *Nature's gambit.* New York: Basic Books.

Fordham, S., & Ogbu, J. (1986). Black students' school success: Coping with the "burden of acting white." *The Urban Review, 18,* 176–206.

Fredericksen, J. R., & Collins, A. (1989). A systems theory of educational testing. *Educational Researcher, 18* (9), 27–32.

Gardner, H. (1983). *Frames of mind: The theory of multiple intelligences.* New York: Basic Books.

Gardner, H. (1989a). *To open minds: Chinese clues to the dilemma of contemporary education.* New York: Basic Books.

Gardner, H. (1989b). Zero-based arts education: An introduction to Arts PROPEL. *Studies in Art Education, 30,* 71–83.

Gardner, H. (1990). The difficulties of school: Probable causes, possible cures. *Daedalus, 119* (2), 85–113.

Gardner, H. (1991). Assessment in context: The alternative to standardized testing. In B. R. Gifford & M. C. O'Connor (Eds.), *Future assessments: Changing views of aptitude, achievement, and instruction.* Boston: Kluwer.

Getzels, J., & Csikszentmihalyi, M. (1976). *The creative vision.* New York: Wiley.

Gould, S. J. (1981). *The mismeasure of man.* New York: Norton.

Heath, S. B. (1983). *Ways with words.* New York: Cambridge University Press.

Henderson, A. (1987). *The evidence continues to grow: Parent involvement improves student achievement.* Columbia, Md.: National Committee for Citizens in Education.

Heubert, J. (1982). *Minimum competency testing and racial discrimination: A legal analysis, policy summary and program review for education lawyers.* Harvard Graduate School of Education, unpublished manuscript.

Hofstadter, R. (1963). *Anti-intellectualism in American life.* New York: Knopf.

Johnson-Laird, P. N. (1983). *Mental models.* Cambridge: Harvard University Press.

Keating, D. (1984). The emperor's new clothes: The "new look" in intelligence research. In R. Sternberg (Ed.), *Advances in the psychology of human intelligence* (Vol. 2, pp. 1–45). Hillsdale, N.J.: Lawrence Erlbaum.

Kobayashi, T. (1976). *Society, schools, and progress in Japan.* Oxford, England: Pergamon.

Krechevsky, M., & Gardner, H. (1990). The emergence and nurturance of multiple intelligences: The Project Spectrum approach. In M. J. A. Howe (Ed.), *Encouraging the development of exceptional skills and talents* (pp. 222–45). Leicester, England: The British Psychological Society.

Laboratory of Comparative Human Cognition. (1982). Culture and intelligence. In R. Sternberg (Ed.), *Handbook of human intelligence* (pp. 642–719). Cambridge, England: Cambridge University Press.

Lave, J. (1977). Tailor-made experiments and evaluating the intellectual consequences of apprenticeship training. *Quarterly Newsletter of the Institute for Comparative Human Development, 1,* 1–3.

Leler, H. (1983). Parent education and involvement in relation to the schools and to parents of school-aged children. In R. Haskins & D. Adams (Eds.), *Parent education and public policy* (pp. 141–80). Norwood, N.J.: Ablex.

LeVine, R. A., & White, M. I. (1986). *Human conditions: The cultural basis of educational development.* New York and London: Routledge & Kegan Paul.

LeVine, R. A. (1989, December 7). Personal communication.

Malkus, U., Gardner, H., & Feldman, D. (1988). Dimensions of mind in early childhood. In A. D. Pelligrini (Ed.), *The psychological bases of early childhood* (pp. 25–38). Chichester, England: Wiley.

Neill, D. M., & Medina, N.J. (1989). Standardized testing: Harmful to educational health. *Phi Delta Kappan, 70,* 688–97.

Neisser, U. (1983). Components of intelligence or steps in routine procedures? *Cognition, 15,* 189–97.

Oakes, J. (1986a). Keeping track, part 1: The policy and practice of curriculum inequality. *Phi Delta Kappan, 68,* 12–17.

Oakes, J. (1986b). Keeping track, part 2: Curriculum inequality and school reform. *Phi Delta Kappan, 68,* 148–54.

Ogbu, J. (1978). *Minority education and caste: The American system in cross-cultural perspective.* New York: Academic Press.

Olson, D., & Bruner, J. (1974). Learning through experience and learning through media. In D. Olson (Ed.), *Media and symbols: The forms of expression, communication and education* (pp. 125–50). Chicago: University of Chicago Press.

Powell, A. G., Farrar, E., & Cohen, D. K. (1985). *The shopping mall high school: Winners and losers in the educational marketplace.* Boston: Houghton Mifflin.

Resnick, L. (1987). Learning in school and out. *Educational Researcher, 16* (9), 13–20.

Resnick, L., & Neches, R. (1984). Factors affecting individual differences in learning ability. In R. Sternberg (Ed.), *Advances in the psychology of human intelligence* (Vol. 2, pp. 275–323). Hillsdale, N.J.: Lawrence Erlbaum.

Sarason, S. (1983). *Schooling in America: Scapegoat or salvation.* New York: Free Press.

Scarr, S. (1981). Testing for children. *American Psychologist, 36,* 1159–66.

Shimizu, H. (1988). *Hito no tsunagari* ["Interpersonal continuity"] *as a Japanese children's cultural context for learning and achievement motivation: A literature review.* Harvard Graduate School of Education, unpublished manuscript.

Snow, C. E., & Ferguson, C. A. (1977). *Talking to children: Language input and acquisition.* Cambridge, England: Cambridge University Press.

Sternberg, R. J. (1985). *Beyond IQ.* Cambridge, England: Cambridge University Press.

Stevenson, H. W. (1987). The Asian advantage: The case of mathematics. *American Educator, 11* (2), 26–31, 47.

Stevenson, H. W., Stigler, J. W., Lee, S., Lucker, G. W., Kitamura, S., & Chen-Chin, H. (1985). Cognitive performance and academic achievement of Japanese, Chinese and American children. *Child Development, 56,* 718–34.

Vygotsky, L. S. (1978). *Mind in society: The development of higher psychological processes.* Cambridge, Mass.: Harvard University Press.

White, M. (1987). *The Japanese educational challenge: A commitment to children.* New York: Free Press.

Wilson, K. S. (1988). *The Palenque Design: Children's discovery learning experiences in an interactive multimedia environment.* Unpublished doctoral dissertation, Harvard Graduate School of Education, Cambridge, Mass.

Zessoules, R., Wolf, D. P., & Gardner, H. (1988). A better balance: Arts PROPEL as an alternative to discipline-based arts education. In J. Burton, A. Lederman, & P. London (Eds.), *Beyond dbae: The case for multiple visions of art education* (pp. 117–29). Dartmouth, Mass.: University Council on Art Education.

Zigler, E., & Weiss, H. (1985). Family support systems: An ecological approach to child development. In R. Rapoport (Ed.), *Children, youth, and families* (pp. 166–205). Cambridge, England: Cambridge University Press.

Epilogue. Multiple Intelligences Theory in 2013

References

Hatch, T., & Gardner, H. (1992). Finding cognition in the classroom: An expanded view of human intelligence. In G. Salomon (Ed.), *Distributed cognitions.* New York: Cambridge University Press.

Zuboff, S. (1988). *In the age of the smart machine.* New York: Basic Books.

Collaborators

Tina Blythe
Mindy Kornhaber
Mara Krechevsky
Joseph Walters

Funders

Carnegie Corporation
J. Paul Getty Trust
William T. Grant Foundation
Lilly Endowment
John D. and Catherine T. MacArthur Foundation
Markle Foundation
James S. McDonnell Foundation
Pew Charitable Trusts
Rockefeller Brothers Fund
Rockefeller Foundation
Spencer Foundation
Bernard Van Leer Foundation
Veterans Administration

Appendix B
Related Articles Authored or Coauthored by Howard Gardner

Gardner, H. (1984, June). Assessing intelligences. A comment on "Testing intelligence without IQ tests" by R. J. Sternberg. *Phi Delta Kappan, 65* (10), 699–700.

Gardner, H. (1984). The development of competence in culturally defined domains. In R. Shweder & R. LeVine (Eds.), *Culture theory: Essays of mind, self and emotion.* New York: Cambridge University Press.

Gardner, H. (1985). On discerning new ideas in psychology. *New Ideas in Psychology, 3,* 101–4.

Gardner, H. (1985). Towards a theory of dramatic intelligence. In J. Kase-Polisini (Ed.), *Creative drama in a developmental context.* University Press of America.

Gardner, H. (1986). An individual-centered curriculum. In *The schools we've got, the schools we need* (pp. 93–115). Washington D.C.: Council of Chief State School Officers and the American Association of Colleges of Teacher Education.

Gardner, H. (1987). The assessment of intelligences: A neuropsychological perspective. In M. Meier, A. Benton, & L. Diller (Eds.), *Neuropsychological rehabilitation* (pp. 59–69). London: Churchill.

Gardner, H. (1987, December–1988, January). On assessment in the arts: A conversation with Ron Brandt. *Educational Leadership, 45* (4), 30–34.

Gardner, H. (1987). The theory of multiple intelligences. *Annals of Dyslexia, 37,* 19–35.

Gardner, H. (1988). Beyond a modular view of mind. In W. Damon (Ed.), *Child development today and tomorrow* (pp. 222–39). San Francisco: Jossey-Bass.

Gardner, H. (1988, Fall). Challenges for museums: Howard Gardner's theory of multiple intelligences. *Hand to hand: Children's museum network.*

Gardner, H. (1988). Intelligences. In K. Jervis & A. Tobier (Eds.), *Education for democracy: Proceedings from the Cambridge School on progressive education* (pp. 86–102). Weston, Mass.: The Cambridge School.

Gardner, H. (1988). Mobilizing resources of individual centered education. In R. Nickerson & P. Zhodiates (Eds.), *Technology in education: Looking toward 2020.* Hillsdale, N.J.: L. Erlbaum.

Gardner, H. (1988, Summer). Multiple intelligences in today's schools. *Human Intelligence Newsletter, 9* (2), 1–2.

Gardner, H. (1988). The theory of multiple intelligences: Educational implications. In *Language and the world of work in the 21st century.* Massachusetts Bureau of Transitional Bilingual Education.

Gardner, H. (1990, Spring). Building on the range of human strengths. *The Churchill Forum, 12* (1), 1–2, 7.

Gardner, H. (1990). The difficulties of school: Probable causes, possible cures. *Daedalus, 119* (2), 85–113.

Gardner, H. (1991). Concepts of mind and intelligence. In D. Goleman & R. A. F. Thurman (Eds.), *MindScience: An East-West dialogue* (pp. 75–87). Boston: Wisdom Publications.

Gardner, H. (1991). Intelligence in seven steps. *New Horizons for Learning* (newsletter). Also in *Intelligence Connections, 1* (1), 1, 3, 7, 8.

Gardner, H. (1991). The nature of intelligence. In A. Lewin (Ed.), *How we think and learn: A lecture series* (pp. 41–46). Washington D.C.: The National Learning Center.

Gardner, H. (1992, January). The "intelligence-giftedness" complex. Paper delivered at Edythe Bush Symposium on Giftedness, Tampa, Florida. To be published in the *Proceedings,* ed. by Hilde Rosselli.

Gardner, H. (1992, March). The unschooled mind. Presentation to the Cambridge Forum.

Gardner, H. (in press). Entry on multiple intelligences. In R. Sternberg (Ed.), *Encyclopedia of intelligence.* New York: Macmillan.

Gardner, H. (in press). Perennial antinomies and perpetual redrawings: Is there progress in the study of mind? In R. Solso and D. Massaro (Eds.), *Science of mind: 2001 and beyond.* New York: Oxford University Press.

Coauthored by Howard Gardner

Gardner, H., & Viens, J. (1990, Winter). Multiple intelligence and styles: Partners in effective education. *The Clearinghouse Bulletin, 4* (2), 4–5.

Granott, N., & Gardner, H. (in press). When minds meet: Interactions, coincidence, and development in domains of ability. In R. J. Sternberg & R. K. Wagner (Eds.), *Mind in context: Interactionist perspectives on human intelligence.* New York: Cambridge University Press.

Goldman, J., & Gardner, H. (1988). Multiple paths to educational effectiveness. In D. K. Lipsky & A. Gartner (Eds.), *Beyond separate education: Quality education for all children* (pp. 121–40). Baltimore: Brookes.

Goldman, J., Krechevsky, M., Meyaard, J., & Gardner, H. (1988). A developmental study of children's practical intelligence for school. (Tech. Rep.). Cambridge: Harvard University, Project Zero.

Hatch, T., & Gardner, H. (1986). From testing intelligence to assessing competences: A pluralistic view of intellect. *The Roeper Review, 8,* 147–50.

Hatch, T., & Gardner, H. (1988, December). New research on intelligence. *Learning, 17* (4), 36–39.

Hatch, T., & Gardner, H. (1989). Multiple intelligences go to school. *Educational Researcher, 9,* 4–10.

Hatch, T., & Gardner, H. (1990). If Binet had looked beyond the classroom: The assessment of multiple intelligences. *International Journal of Educational Research, 14* (5), 415–29.

Hatch, T., & Gardner, H. (in press). Finding cognition in the classroom: An expanded view of human intelligence. In G. Salomon (Ed.), *Distributed cognitions.* New York: Cambridge University Press.

Kornhaber, M., & Gardner, H. (1991). Varieties of excellence and conditions for their achievement. In S. Maclure & P. Davies (Eds.), *Learning to think: Thinking to learn* (pp. 147–68). The Proceedings of the 1989 OECD Conference. Oxford: Pergamon Press.

Krechevsky, M., & Gardner, H. (1990). Multiple intelligences, multiple chances. In D. Inbar (Ed.), *Second chance in education: An interdisciplinary and international perspective* (pp. 69–88). London: The Falmer Press.

Krechevsky, M., & Gardner, H. (in press). Multiple intelligences in multiple contexts. In D. Detterman (Ed.), *Current topics in human intelligence: Vol. 4. Theories of Intelligence.*

Malkus, U., Feldman, D. H., & Gardner, H. (1988). Dimensions of mind in early childhood. In A. D. Pelligrini (Ed.), *The psychological bases of early education* (pp. 25–38). Chichester, England: Wiley.

Ramos-Ford, V., Feldman, D. H., & Gardner, H. (1988, Spring). A new look at intelligence through Project Spectrum. *New Horizons in Learning, 6, 7,* 15.

Ramos-Ford, V., & Gardner, H. (1991). Giftedness from a multiple intelligences perspective. In N. Colangelo & G. Davis (Eds.), *The handbook of gifted education* (pp. 55–64). Boston: Allyn & Bacon.

Walters, J., & Gardner, H. (1988, April). Managing intelligences (Tech. Rep. No. 33). Cambridge: Harvard University, Project Zero.

Walters, J., Krechevsky, M., & Gardner, H. (1987). Development of musical, mathematical, and scientific talents in normal and gifted children (Tech. Rep. No. 31). Cambridge: Harvard University, Project Zero.

Wexler-Sherman, C., Gardner, H., & Feldman, D. (1988). A pluralistic view of early assessment: The Project Spectrum approach. *Theory into Practice, 27,* 77–83.

White, N., Blythe, T., & Gardner, H. (in press). Multiple intelligences theory: Creating the thoughtful classroom. In A. Costa, J. Bellanca, and R. Fogarty (Eds.), *If mind matters: A foreword to the future* (Vol. 2, pp. 127–34). Palatine, Ill.: Skylight Publishers.

Wolf, D., Bixby, J., Glenn, J., & Gardner, H. (1991). To use their minds well: Investigating new forms of student assessment. In G. Grant (Ed.), *Review of research in education* (Vol. 17, pp. 31–74). Washington, D.C.: American Educational Research Association.

Zessoules, R., & Gardner, H. (1991). Authentic assessment: Beyond the buzzword and into the classroom. In V. Perrone (Ed.), *Expanding student assessment* (pp. 47–71). Washington, D.C.: Association for Supervision and Curriculum Development.

Zessoules, R., Wolf, D., & Gardner, H. (1988). A better balance: Arts PROPEL as an alternative to discipline-based art education. In J. Burton, A. Lederman, & P. London (Eds.), *Beyond dbae: The case for multiple visions of art education* (pp. 117–29). North Dartmouth, Mass.: University Council on Art Education.

Appendix C
Other
Works About
the Theory of
Multiple Intelligences*

Selected Books and
Monographs

Armstrong, T. (1987). *In their own way: Discovering and encouraging your child's personal learning style.* Los Angeles: J. P. Tarcher; New York: St. Martin's Press.

Campbell, B., Campbell, L., & Dickinson, D. (1992). *Teaching and learning multiple intelligences.* Seattle: New Horizons for Learning.

Dee Dickinson
New Horizons for Learning
4649 Sunnyside North
Seattle, WA 98103

Haggerty, B. (in press). *Introduction to the theory of multiple intelligences.*

Brian Haggerty
Editor Instructional Materials Development
San Diego Public Schools
4100 Normal Street
San Diego, CA 92103-2682

Haggerty, B. (in press). *Multiple intelligence theory and instructional design: Creating literature units for teaching across the curriculum.*

*Names and addresses of contacts have been provided when works are not yet published or are most readily available from the author.

Brian Haggerty
Editor Instructional Materials Development
San Diego Public Schools
4100 Normal Street
San Diego, CA 92103-2682

Healy, J. (1987). *Your child's growing mind: A parent's guide to learning from birth.* Garden City, N.Y.: Doubleday.
Lazear, D. G. (1991). *Seven ways of knowing: Teaching for multiple intelligence: Handbook of techniques for expanding intelligence.* With a foreword by Howard Gardner, Ph.D. Palantine, Ill.: Skylight Publishers.
Lazear, D. (1991). *Seven ways of teaching.* Palantine, Ill.: Skylight Publishers.
Lazear, D. G. (in press). *Seven pathways of learning.* Palantine, Ill.: Skylight Publishers.
Marks, T. (in press). *Creativity inside out: Multiple intelligences across the curriculum.* With a preface by Howard Gardner. Reading, Mass.: Addison-Wesley.
Miller, L. (in press). *The smart profile: A qualitative approach for describing learners and designing instruction.*

Lynda Miller
Smart Alternatives, Inc.
P.O. Box 5849
Austin, TX 78763

Miller, L. (in press). *Your personal smart profile.*

Lynda Miller
Smart Alternatives, Inc.
P.O. Box 5849
Austin, TX 78763

Mollan-Masters, R. *You are smarter than you think.*

Renee Mollan-Masters
Reality Productions
6245 Old Highway 99 South
P.O. Box 943
Ashland, OR 97520

Moody, W. (Ed.). (1990). *Artistic intelligences: Implications for education.* New York: Teacher's College Press.
Peterson, D. (in press). *Seven ways to success—Aptitude and interest measure for high school students.*

David Peterson
Watchung Hills Regional High School
108 Stirling Road
Warren, NJ 07060

Rainey, F. (1991). *Multiple intelligences: Seven ways of knowing.* Denver, Colo: Colorado Dept. of Education Gifted and Talented Education.

Robinson, E. W. (in press). *Care givers's annual 1991—A guide to multiple intelligences for the elderly.*

Ellen W. Robinson
Life Enhancement Research
P.O. Box 3756
Salem, OR 97302

Shearer, B. (in press). *Hillside assessment of pro-trauma intelligence (HAPI).*

Dr. Branton Shearer
Comprehensive Physical and Substance Dependency Rehabilitation
Hillside Hospital
8747 Squires Lane, NE
Warren, OH 44484

Shelton, L. (1991). *Honoring diversity.* California State Library.

Leslie Shelton, Director
Project Read
South San Francisco Public Library
840 W. Orange Avenue
South San Francisco, CA 94080

Smagorinsky, P. (1991). *Expressions: Multiple intelligences in the English class.* Theory and Research in Practice, NCTE.

Dr. Peter Smagorinsky
College of Education
820 Van Vleet Oval—Room 114
University of Oklahoma
Norman, OK 73019

Tubb, L. G. *Gifted deaf students: Case studies describing profiles of domains of intelligence.*

Dr. Linda G. Tubb
Teacher Education
Louisiana Tech University
P.O. Box 3161
Ruston, LA 71272-0001

Vail, P. L. (1987). *Smart kids with school problems: Things to know and ways to help.* New York: Dutton.

Wass, L. L. (1991). *Imagine that: Getting smarter through imagery practice.* Rolling Hills Estate, Calif.: Jalmar Press.

Lane Longino Wass
P.O. Box 443
Glenville, NC 28736

Selected Articles and Reviews

Altman, L. K. (1991, September 24). Can the brain provide clues to intelligence? Medical Science, *New York Times.*

Aschettino, E. M. (1986, March). Children aren't always traditionally smart. *Massachusetts Elementary Educator.*

Atchity, K. (1984, February 26). Profound thoughts on the thinking process. *Los Angeles Times.*

Barko, N. (1989, September). Discover your child's hidden IQ. *Working Mother.*

Bornstein, M. H. (1986). Review of *Frames of mind. Journal of Aesthetic Education,* 20 (1).

Bouchard, T. J., Jr. (1984, July 20). Review of *Frames of mind. American Journal of Orthopsychiatry.*

Bruner, J. (1983, October 27). State of the child. Review of *Frames of mind. New York Review of Books.*

Bryant, P.E. (1984, June 8). A battery of tests. Review of *Frames of mind. The Times Higher Education Supplement.*

Buescher, T. M. (1985). Seeking the roots of talent: An interview with Howard Gardner. *Journal for the Education of the Gifted,* 8 (3), 179–87.

Campbell, B. Multiple intelligences in the classroom. *Cooperative Learning,* 12 (1), 24–25 (reprinted from *In Context,* 27 [Winter 1991]).

Carroll, J. B. (1984). An artful perspective on talents. Review of *Frames of mind. Contemporary Psychology,* 29 (11).

Carroll, J. B. (1985). Like minds, like sympathies: Comments on the interview with Howard Gardner. *New Ideas in Psychology,* 3 (1).

Chideya, F. (1991, December 2). Surely for the spirit but also for the mind: Arts PROPEL as one of the outstanding educational programs in the world. *Newsweek.*

Clinchy, B. M. (1984). Review of *Frames of mind. Boston University Journal of Education,* 166 (2).

Cohen, M. (1990, December 12). Test questions: A subject for the '90s. Learning Section, *Boston Globe.*

Deitel, B. (1990, May 20). The key to education. *Courier Journal* (Louisville, Ky.).

Eisenman, L. (1984, July). Neuropsychology sheds new light on intelligence. Review of *Frames of mind. American School Board Journal.*

Fanelli, L. (in press). Theater in motion—Educational Theater—Participatory educational theater (Creative Drama) and the Seven Intelligences—A set of exercises for teachers and artists/Multicultural Education.

Leslie Fanelli
Theater in Motion
121-25 6th Avenue
Queens, NY 11356

Gold, D. L. (1988, March 30). Early testing said to have "long-term negative effects." *Education Week.*

Goleman, D. (1986, February 18). Influencing others: Skills are identified. *New York Times.*

Goleman, D. (1986, March 11). Psychologists study sources of influence and power. *New York Times.*

Goleman, D. (1986, November 9). Rethinking the value of intelligence tests. *New York Times.*

Goleman, D. (1988, April 5). New scales of intelligence rank talent for living. Science Times, *New York Times.*

Goleman, D. (1990, October 2). The study of play yields clues to success. Science Times, *New York Times.*

Grimm, M. (1986, October). Mind benders. *Creativity.*

Grow, G. (in press). Writing and the seven intelligences.

Gerald Grow, Ph.D.
Division of Journalism
Florida A&M University
Tallahassee, FL 32307

Gursky, D. (1991, November–December) The unschooled mind. *Teacher Magazine,* pp. 40–44.

Hall, B. (1986, August). "Portfolio" proposed as adjunct to SAT score. *Christian Science Monitor.*

Hammer, S. Stalking intelligence: IQ isn't the end of the line; you can be smarter. *Science Digest.*

Hoerr, T. R. (in press). Implementing the theory of multiple intelligences: One school's experience (MID).

Thomas R. Hoerr
The New City School
5209 Waterman Avenue
St. Louis, MO 63108

Jacobson, R. L. (1986, July). As SAT endures, new testing methods are sought. *Chronicle of Higher Education.*

Johnson-Laird, P. (1984, May 11). More faculties than one. Review of *Frames of mind. Times Literary Supplement.*

Kendel, R. (in press). Intelligence—Dr. Howard Gardner's multiple intelligences. *Effective Classrooms: The In-Service Newsletter.*

Ruth Kendel
1810 Park Avenue
Richmond, Virginia 23220

Kolata, Gina. (1989, April 9). Project Spectrum explores many sided minds. *New York Times.*

Leonard, L. S. (1990, August). Storytelling as experiential education. *Journal of Experiential Education,* 13 (2), 12–17.

Levenson, T. (1984, January). Review of *Frames of mind*. *Discover*, p. 79.

Marshall, M. (1981, July 26). Musical wunderkinds. *Boston Globe Magazine*.

McKean, K. (1985, October). Intelligence: New ways to measure the wisdom of man. *Discover*.

Miller, L. (1988, Summer/Fall). Multiple intelligences offer multiple ways to become literate. *Update*.

Miller, G. A. (1983, December 25). Varieties of intelligence. Review of *Frames of mind*. Book Review, *New York Times*.

Miller, N. (1986, March 18). Changing your mind. *Boston Phoenix*.

Moorman, M. (1989, Summer). The great art education debate. *ARTnews*.

Mumme, R. (in press). Figurative frames and tacit tropes: from Giambattista Vico to Howard Gardner: Toward the possibility of a tropological-logical intelligence.

Roy Mumme
University of Southern Florida at Fort Myers
8111 College Parkway SW
Fort Myers, FL 33919

Obler, L. (1984, May). Plus ça change. Review of *Frames of mind*. *Women's Review of Books*, 1 (8).

Olson, L. (1988, January 27). Children flourish here: Eight teachers and a theory changed a school world. *Education Week*, 7 (18), 1, 18–19.

Olson, L. (1988, November 16). In Pittsburgh: New approaches to testing track arts "footprints." *Education Week*, 8 (11).

Olson, L. (1989, September–October). A revolution of rising expectations. *Teacher Magazine*.

Page, J. (1986, December). From bright to dull: The different kinds of intelligence. *Minneapolis Star and Tribune*.

Page, J. (1987, January 22). Your brain is not a computer. *San Francisco Chronicle*.

Price, S. (1985, October). An I.Q. to live by: Developing personal intelligence. *Human Potential*.

Rawson, D. (1990, Spring). A lot to learn. *Life*.

Roberts, F. (1985, March). The trouble with back to basics. *Parents*.

Rothman, S., & Snyderman, M. (1987, February). Survey of expert opinion on intelligence and aptitude testing. *American Psychologist*.

Rubin, J. (1992, February). Multiple intelligence: From theory to practice: The Javits 7 plus gifted and talented program. Paper delivered at the Esther Katz Rosen Symposium on the Psychological Development of Gifted Children, Lawrence, Kansas.

Joyce Rubin
Director, Gifted Program
Javits 7 + Gifted and Talented Program
Community School District 18

755 E. 100th Street
Brooklyn, NY 11236

Scarr, S. (1985). An author's frame of mind. Review of *Frames of mind. New Ideas in Psychology, 3* (1).

Scialabba, G. (1984, March–April). Mindplay. Review of *Frames of mind. Harvard Magazine.*

Scherer, M. (1985, January). How many ways is a child intelligent? *Instructor and Teacher.*

Schwager, I. (1986, Summer). Different children, different gifts. *Sesame Street Parent's Guide.*

Seven styles of learning—based on Howard Gardner's theory of multiple intelligences (1990, September). *Instructor, 52* (table).

Shaughnessy, M. F. (1985). What's new in IQ: Contemporary analysis with implications for gifted/talented/creative. *Creative Child and Adult Quarterly, 10* (2).

Simon, N. (1985, August). Your child's imagination. *Parents.*

Sloane, B. (1990, January 7). Flouting tradition, some educators begin to change A-to-F grading system. *Chicago Tribune School Guide.*

Snow, R. E. (1985, November). Review of *Frames of mind. American Journal of Psychiatry.*

Starnes, W. T., Barton, J., & Leibowitz, D. G. (1992, February). Using multiple intelligences to identify and nurture young potentially gifted children. Paper delivered at the Esther Katz Rosen Symposium on the Psychological Development of Gifted Children, Lawrence, Kansas.

Dr. Waveline Starnes
Program Director
Early Childhood Gifted Model Program
850 Hungerford Drive
Rockville, MD 20850

Sternberg, R. J. (1993, Winter). How much gall is too much gall? A review of *Frames of mind: The theory of multiple intelligences. Contemporary Education Review, 2* (3), 215–24.

Strong, M. (1985, January). The seven kinds of smart: How does your child score? *Redbook.*

Sutherland, S. (1984, April 26). Grand organization in mind. Review of *Frames of mind. Nature, 308.*

Thompson, K. Cognitive and analytical psychology. Review of *Frames of mind. San Francisco Jung Institute Library Journal, 5* (4).

Turnbull, C. M. (1984, January 1). The seven "intelligences." *Philadelphia Inquirer.*

Voices against the testing "explosion." (1985, December 16). *Education USA.*

Weinreich-Haste, H. (1985). The varieties of intelligence: An interview with Howard Gardner. *New Ideas in Psychology, 3* (1).

Williams, G., III. (1990, April). Radical class acts. *Omni, 12* (7).

Winn, M. (1990, April 29). New views of human intelligence. Good Health Magazine, *New York Times.*

Wohlwill, J. (1985). The Gardner-Winner view of children's visual-artistic development: Overview, assessment, and critique. *Visual Arts Research, 11.*

Magazines and Newsletters

Intelligence Connections—newsletter of the ASCD network on the teaching for multiple intelligences.

David Lazear
New Dimensions of Learning
4880 Marine Drive
Suite 515
Chicago, IL 60640
(312) 907-9588

New City News—Multiple Intelligences Edition.

Thomas Hoerr, Director
New City School
5209 Waterman Avenue
St. Louis, MO 63108

On the Beam—newsletter.

Dee Dickinson
New Horizons for Learning
4649 Sunnyside North
Seattle, WA 98103

Provoking Thoughts—bimonthly magazine dedicated to the exploration of the seven intelligences via articles and activities for the adult, child, or classroom.

Knowles Dougherty
Publisher and Editor
Institute for the Development of Educational Alternatives (I.D.E.A.)
404 NW 1st Street
P.O. Box 1004
Austin, MN 55912

Miscellaneous

Lift Off—A program for three- to eight-year-olds produced by the Australian Children's Television Foundation. Multiple intelligences provide the organizing theme.

Provoking Thoughts Game—A card game of critical thinking exercises in each of the seven intelligences.

Institute for the Development of Educational Alternatives (I.D.E.A.)
404 NW 1st Street
P.O. Box 1004
Austin, MN 55912

Teele Inventory for Multiple Intelligences—with a Teacher's Manual.

Sue Teele
P.O. Box 7302
Redlands, CA 92373

Appendix D
Workshop Presentations

The following individuals give workshops on MI theory or projects based on MI theory:

Thomas Armstrong
Mindstyles Consulting Services
P.O. Box 5435
Santa Rosa, CA 98402

Bruce Campbell
19614 Sound View Drive
Stanwood, WA 98292

Linda Campbell
Director, Teacher Certification
Antioch University Graduate Education Programs
2607 2nd Avenue
Seattle, WA 98121

Lyle Davidson
Harvard Project Zero
Harvard Graduate School of Education
Longfellow Hall
Appian Way
Cambridge, MA 02138
Workshop on Assessment and Arts PROPEL

Dee Dickinson
New Horizons for Learning
4649 Sunnyside North
Seattle, WA 98103

Leslie Fanelli
Executive Artistic Director
Theatre in Motion
121–25 6th Avenue
Queens, NY 11356
(718) 961-5481
Workshops on MI in theater using curriculum-based creative drama and music exercises

Kathleen Gaffrey
Founder & Artistic Director
Artsgenesis Inc.
310 E. 46th Street
Suite 26J
New York, NY 10017
Workshop on Staff Development and MI theory

Mara Krechevsky
Harvard Project Zero
Harvard Graduate School of Education
Longfellow Hall
Appian Way
Cambridge, MA 02138
Workshop on MI theory and Spectrum tasks

James D. Kriley
Dean, School of Fine Arts
Summer Arts/Education Institute and Graduate Program
University of Montana
Missoula, MT 59812

David Lazear
New Dimensions of Learning
4880 Marine Drive—Apt 515
Chicago, IL 60640

Linda MacRae-Campbell
19614 Sound View Drive
Stanwood, WA 98292

Lynda Miller
Smart Alternatives, Inc.

P.O. Box 5849
Austin, TX 78763

Judy Pace
Harvard Project Zero
Harvard Graduate School of Education
Longfellow Hall
Appian Way
Cambridge, MA 02138
Workshop on MI projects and portfolio assessment; teaching for understanding

Joyce Rubin
Director, Gifted Programs
Javits 7 + Gifted and Talented Program
Community School District 18
755 E. 100th Street
Brooklyn, NY 11236

Larry Scripp
Harvard Project Zero
Harvard Graduate School of Education
Longfellow Hall
Appian Way
Cambridge, MA 02138
Workshop on alternative assessment in the arts using the Arts PROPEL models.

Sue Teele
Institute for the Study of Multiple Intelligences
Education Extension
University of California
Riverside, CA 92521-0112

David Thornburg
The Thornburg Center
1561 Laurel, Suite A
San Carlos, CA 94070

Bruce Torff
Harvard Project Zero
Harvard Graduate School of Education
Longfellow Hall
Appian Way
Cambridge, MA 02138
Workshops on Arts PROPEL.

David and Jan Ulrey
Developmental Primary Consultants

377 13th Street
Del Mar, CA 92014

Julie Viens
Harvard Project Zero
Harvard Graduate School of Education
Longfellow Hall
Appian Way
Cambridge, MA 02138
Workshop on all phases of MI theory

Harvard Project Zero maintains an up-to-date list of schools and teachers that are involved in experiments with multiple intelligences. Researchers at Harvard Project Zero have compiled handbooks on Arts PROPEL and on Project Spectrum. For further information, write to Harvard Project Zero Development Group, Longfellow Hall, Appian Way, Cambridge, MA 02138.

Name Index

Adler, Mortimer, 69
Alexander, Lamar, 82
Anderson, Michael, 165

Bennett, William, 69
Bernstein, Leonard, 9
Binet, Alfred, 5, 7, 52, 163, 165, 216, 237
Bloom, Allan, 68, 69
Bloom, Benjamin, 48
Blythe, Tina, 75, 132
Bolanos, Patricia, 112
Boole, George, 133
Bruner, Jerome, 122

Carnegie, Andrew, 240
Carter, Jimmy, 215
Cassirer, Ernst, 135
Churchill, Winston, 205
Cole, Michael, 122
Comer, James, 201, 244
Confucius, 59, 190
Coolidge, Calvin, 215
Csikszentmihalyi, Mihaly, 37, 50, 242

Darwin, Charles, 52, 59, 240

Edison, Thomas, 205
Einstein, Albert, 205
Eliot, T. S., 21
Eysenck, Hans, 6, 165, 213, 218

Feldman, David, 37, 66, 89, 222
Fischer, Bobby, 221
Fodor, Jerry, 43
Freud, Sigmund, 59

Gallwey, Tim, 19
Gauss, Carl, 51
Goddard, Henry, 216
Goethe, Johann, 50, 52
Goodman, Nelson, 135–137
Gould, Stephen Jay, 218, 241
Graham, Martha, 59
Granott, Nira, 211
Guilford, J. P., 7

Hammerstein, Oscar, 43
Hatch, Thomas, 211
Heath, Shirley Brice, 221
Hirsch, E. D., 68, 69
Hoover, Herbert, 215
Humphreys, Lloyd, 218

Subject Index